100 GREATEST Rangers

By Iain King

Rangers
The 100 Greatest

Published by First Press Publishing Limited, 7th Floor,
Daily Record and Sunday Mail Ltd, 40 Anderston Quay,
Glasgow G3 8DA

ISBN 1 - 901603 - 09 - 1

Printed and bound in Scotland

Dick ADVOCAAT

RANGERS. What does the club mean to me? Nine months into my job that would have been a difficult question to answer.

Difficult, that is, until I saw our fans in Parma's Ennio Tardini Stadium after our 3-1 defeat in the last 16 of the UEFA Cup ended our European run.

All I could see was a sea of red, white and blue. All I could hear was "Advocaat's Blue and White Army".

Believe me, that defeat was hard to stomach for me because we came so close but then we had Sergio Porrini sent off and we lost it in the second-half.

Yet still those fans stayed behind cheering and I sat thinking that fans of other clubs would by now be booing their team.

It was hard for me to go on that pitch and salute them. I was full of emotion, biting my tongue to keep it all in and John Greig said to me: "Go. They are showing how much they appreciate what you have done".

I had a farewell like that after three and a half years at PSV Eindhoven when I was in a Mercedes going round the pitch with the players in front of me. Then the music was playing and that is a tough time to take, saying goodbye to a club at which I'd had many excellent times. In all honesty, I would prefer

to have slipped out quietly on my own. You think you will never see times like that again then came Parma. It was bittersweet after losing but a great moment.

I knew then that you just can't compare Scotland with Holland because here football brings so much to the people and they are so caught up in it all the time.

I have had friends from home come to Ibrox and be knocked out by the whole place. The tradition of Rangers and Celtic is so special, it's enormous.

I first came to Ibrox when I was in charge of the Dutch national squad. I would travel to Scotland to watch the likes of Theo Snelders and Hans Gillhaus when they were at Aberdeen and also Pieter Huistra, who was a big Rangers favourite.

The place even then made a big impression on me. I will always remember the marble hallway at the entrance and do you know what has stuck in my mind even now? Stan the Commissionaire, standing there in his uniform ready to take me up for my cup of tea and show

me where I could meet the Dutch players after the match. Class.

You just don't have that sort of thing in Holland. I love all those unique things about Rangers – they have a charm that gives the club a character of its own.

I feel at home but I don't use the manager's office too often, just for meetings that are one-to-one or with the scouts who want to tell me about players.

I am at home in the coaches' room, that is my place. But, you know, the Rangers' manager's office is a special room. Let me take you there.

All around are the portraits of the other managers that have graced Ibrox and I am very proud that there have only been ten and now I am part of it.

The history of the room states that when your time as manager is over you must have your picture hung in there so your successor can look at you.

Well, now there is a mural in the Blue Room too and I have already been painted for that by the artist Senga Murray.

I have to think of my media image as the Dutch perfectionist so I kept giving her hints and I'm happy now. She has made me a lot thinner!

That picture is of the man you see these days, the boy knew about Rangers from the day when they came to Rotterdam to play Sparta 39 years ago. As always they were big news.

I was just a teenage kid then and it was massive headlines that this big club were in

town. Rangers won the game 3-2 but Sparta beat them 1-0 at Ibrox to force a play-off by the rules as they were then. They still talk about that even now.

Sparta lost that game 3-2 at Highbury and I recall being a little sad – these days I'd be delighted!

When I graduated to playing the game for a living I played 455 games as a pro in Holland and 25 in Europe but never against Rangers.

Now I'm here I realise there is this kind of tradition that just gets inside you. Take the Greatest Ever Ranger – it amazed me that last summer, seven months before the event, there was so much debate and so much excitement about who would win.

The mass media coverage changes everything in the 90s. You all know Marco van Basten so well now, yet 20 years ago you would have known very little.

That is my story with John Greig. I didn't have that much knowledge about him but the Chairman soon told me all about John. David Murray is so caught up in Rangers and everything to do with the place but he told me one thing at the start.

He said: "There are an awful lot of big names at this club – but John Greig is the biggest."

So this man Greig intrigued me. I wanted to find out more and when I discovered he was working in another department away from the football I wanted him beside me.

TWO OF A KIND...
Dick Advocaat relies on Greatest Ever Ranger John Greig for advice on all matters concerning Rangers

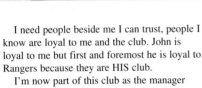

I need people beside me I can trust, people I know are loyal to me and the club. John is loyal to me but first and foremost he is loyal to Rangers because they are HIS club.

I'm now part of this club as the manager and I'm very happy I was able to bring him back to the football department. He is such a big name that if you go somewhere with him then all the doors automatically open because everybody knows him.

Yes, I didn't realise at the start how famous John was but I do now!

He is part of the fabric of this place and so is the Chairman. I've said to John a few times that I find it hard to believe how David Murray has a business empire to run yet he still has so much passion for everything that happens at Rangers.

I like the way David and I work together and I don't think that would happen at many other big clubs.

Why does he do it? He could be in the Bahamas but he isn't. Instead he is in the middle of everything here giving 110 percent. We all are, that's why so far we have been successful.

As we celebrate "Rangers: The 100 Greatest" you can be sure I will do everything in my power to make sure this club remains where it belongs. At the top.

DICK ADVOCAAT, Manager,
Rangers Football Club, March 1999

Jorg ALBERTZ

"GENTLEMEN, Jorg Albertz!", the MC's voice boomed over a capacity audience at Ian Durrant's Testimonial Dinner and the player the fans call The Hammer rose to his feet.

A smile cracked the big German's features and his trademark diamond earring glinted, he spoke yet he couldn't be heard through the tumult of applause.

Albertz had arrived at a special evening hotfoot from scoring a belter in a 2-0 Old Firm league win.

Seven days earlier he'd thundered home a classic in a Scottish Cup semi-final triumph. The goals meant the world to him, the ovation at Durrant's dinner even more.

And the midfielder signed from Hamburg for £4million by Walter Smith recalled: "Scoring twice in a row against Celtic was special, yes, but I'll always remember the ovation I got after the second one when we all rushed to Ian's testimonial dinner.

"I was introduced to the crowd and when I stood up they almost raised the roof. At a night like that, for a player I admired so much, that was very touching."

Albertz grew up with German Second Division side Fortuna Dusseldorf after he had been rejected by Borussia Möenchengladbach, the club he supported. That was to prove a costly mistake.

Jorg shrugged off ideas of going back into the family business as a car mechanic and soon earned his Bundelisga move to Hamburg.

When his form there attracted Smith he took a leap into uncharted football territory.

Albertz pointed out: "You see Old Firm games on TV in Germany and it always looked like such a fabulous spectacle to me.

"I wondered what it would be like to be a part of one of those games but that was the limit of my knowledge of Rangers.

"Yet when Walter came in for me I could see players like Paul Gascoigne and Brian Laudrup were at the club. You don't need any more invitation than that."

Jorg was soon to experience those games for himself and his first goal against Celtic, a blurring free-kick that whistled past stunned keeper Stewart Kerr in the New Year game in 1997, won its own place in football folklore.

Sky Sports' technology pegged it at 79.8mph, the hardest struck dead ball in BRITAIN that season.

Albertz has continued to relish the fixture and he said: "So many people tell you that the Celtic game will pass you by

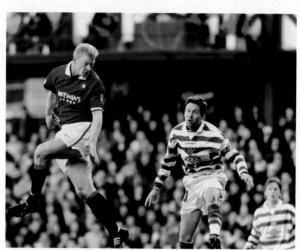

SCREEN STAR... German TV coverage of Old Firm clashes gave Jorg Albertz the upper hand on Celtic before he had even arrived in Scotland

but I didn't find that, I enjoyed them right from the start. I've found a little knack of scoring in them and I think that will always endear you to the fans.

"My relationship with them is very important to me. They have always made me feel welcome.

"They see I give 100 per cent and I think they realise I'm not pretending when I say how much the place has come to mean to me."

Speaking to Albertz can be a bizarre experience as he lapses from tutored English into sheer Glasgow slang. He's so native now he counts himself as one of the SCOTS in Dick Advocaat's dressing-room.

And Jorg, signed with Gers until 2002, is in no hurry to return home for footballing matters. He doesn't feel wanted.

Present German coach Erich Ribbeck has made it clear he feels Albertz and countryman keeper Stefan Klos have made the wrong decision moving to Scotland.

And Jorg sighed: "All they've done with me is play me at left-back. Has being at Rangers affected my international career?

"Well, I played once for the national team when I was in Germany and they played me out of position and I've played once since I came to Scotland and they played me out of position at left-back again.

"So, no, it really hasn't made much difference! Seriously, they know where I am and I don't care any more. They can pick me if they want but my main concern is Rangers."

That, of course, means the relentless pursuit of trophies under new boss Advocaat.

And Jorg is driven on by the painful memory of the dying embers of Smith's reign when he was sent off as the league slipped away despite a 2-1 win at Tannadice.

Albertz said: "That red card was very hard to take. The league is lost, you are sent off and then find you are banned from the Cup Final against Hearts the next week.

"Things really don't get much worse than that in football.

"I remember I sat in the stand at Parkhead that day and watched a lot of players who had become my friends play their last game for Rangers.

"I wanted to be out there. I wanted to help them win but I couldn't. We lost and it hurt so much."

Sammy BAIRD

SAMMY BAIRD had worked under Gers boss Scot Symon at Preston North End and the memory of his skills lingered with the Ibrox supremo.

Symon returned to Deepdale to bring Denny-born Baird back home and Sammy was at the heart of the side when Gers began their first ever European Cup adventure, losing to French side OGC Nice after a play-off match in November 1956.

Baird was to be at the core of three championship sides and thrived in a tremendous run to the last four of the European Cup in season 1959-60.

Anderlecht were hammered 5-2 in front of 80,000 at Ibrox and Baird scored twice. The Belgians were disposed of and Czechoslovakia's Red Star Bratislava followed.

That paved the way for a titanic second round clash with Dutch giants Sparta Rotterdam and Sammy netted again in a 3-2 away win.

Rotterdam won the Ibrox return 1-0, though, and with no away goals rule in place, it was on to a third game at Highbury.

Bizarrely, Sparta scored two own goals and, when Rangers needed someone to produce the vital strike, it was Baird again in a 3-2 win that took Symon's men into the last four.

The fact that they then lost by the humbling margin of 12-4 on aggregate to Germans Eintracht Frankfurt, simply emphasises the level of quality encountered in the Real Madrid team of Ferenc Puskas, Alfredo di Stefano and Gento.

That was the year the Final came to Hampden, and an awestruck crowd of 134,000 saw those all-white strips glide around stricken Eintracht in a 7-3 mauling.

Meanwhile, Baird's days at Ibrox were numbered and he became a welcome signing for clubs in need of a quick-fix expert laden with skills.

Hibs were loitering at the wrong end of the table when Sammy arrived from Gers but the Baird brilliance dragged them away from the relegation trapdoor.

And in 1962, Baird's reputation as the salvage man of Scottish football was bolstered further when his former Gers team-mate George Young – then boss of ailing Third Lanark – swooped to sign him from Hibs.

Thirds had been on a run of just one win in 17 matches then but Sammy's impact was immediate and he skippered them to Glasgow Cup victory before he was controversially freed.

He was quickly on the wanted lists and opted to take the post as player-manager of Stirling Albion.

Sammy – who would later run a pub in Bo'ness – reigned at Annfield for five years before he was sacked in 1968 with the club lurching towards Division Two.

Gers fans will salute him as a player – capped seven times for his country – who powered through his midfield work and showed that special knack for plundering goals.

He took his prowess on to the biggest stage of all when he nabbed the consolation goal for Scotland in a 2-1 defeat from France in the 1958 World Cup Finals in Sweden.

Remember that much-loved quiz question: "Who was the first Rangers player to score in the World Cup Finals?" Now you know.

Club and Country

STATS

IBROX CAREER 1955-61

GAMES

League	121
Scot Cup	16
Lg Cup	26
Europe	16
Total	179

GOALS

League	39
Scot Cup	2
Lg Cup	6
Europe	5
Total	52

MEDALS

League	2
Scot Cup	1

SCOTLAND
7 caps

Jim BAXTER

WAYWARD genius – the tag was created for Jim Baxter.

But for all the excesses that have littered his life, the battle with the bottle and the two liver transplants that saved him, one thing should always be remembered. He truly was a genius.

At the height of the Swinging Sixties, Baxter was Scotland's answer to Manchester United playboy, George Best.

Drink may have ravaged him since but the image then was one of a silky, elegant player who stood 5ft 11ins yet weighed just 9st 12lbs. He was Slim Jim, a regal footballer who could outfox entire defences with one feint or dip of his shoulder.

Baxter cost a meagre £17,500 when – at the age of just 20 – he was lured away from Raith Rovers for the bright lights of Glasgow.

His brilliance was to help Gers dominate the Scottish game in his first spell at the club before the gambling and the boozing dragged him down and led him into an ill-advised move to Sunderland.

The backbreaking graft of life down the pit has hewn so many of Scottish football's legends – from Jock Stein to Bill Shankly. Baxter was no different.

He was brought up in the Fife coal-mining community of Hill O' Beath where he laboured down the pit and starred for Raith on a Saturday.

He'd bought his mum the first washing machine in the village with his Rovers signing-on fee, and honed his skills playing in 40-a-side matches swelled by the boys from the pit after the pubs spilled out.

Baxter revelled as he eluded gangs of angry miners with the shimmies and dummies that would one day fool the world's best.

They did just that at Wembley in 1963 when he scored twice to dump the Auld Enemy and four years later he produced a performance that went down in football folklore.

Sir Alf Ramsey's heroes had won the World Cup a year earlier, yet they were outclassed and humiliated as the cocky Baxter tormented them with a bout of keepie-uppie during a thrilling 3-2 triumph.

It is hard for lesser footballing mortals to reconcile themselves with the path Baxter chose in life.

This was a player who was chosen for the Rest of the World against England at Wembley in '63 alongside Lev Yashin, Ferenc Puskas and them all. He belonged in that company.

Yet he remained chained to the Ibrox wage structure which then paid him £35-a-week while his pal Puskas was on £2,000-a-week at Real Madrid. Baxter rebelled.

He reasoned: "I only wanted a few quid more than the less gifted. We were all paid equally, which was like paying Frank Sinatra the same as the Alexander Brothers."

His standing in the game then almost saw him go to Spurs as Danny Blanchflower's replacement but the deal died at the last minute.

Then Gers refused to allow him to speak to Inter Milan and so the Italians opted for Barcelona's Luis Suarez who had been

crowned Europe's Footballer of the Year.

Jim looked back and said: "Suarez? He wasn't in the same league as me."

Yet for all the anger at the talent he squandered, it is perhaps best to simply embrace the good days Rangers and Scotland were given when Slim Jim was in his pomp and splendour.

Who else could welcome Italy to Glasgow for a World Cup tie in 1965, nutmeg the legendary Gianni Rivera and shout to Billy Bremner: "Hey wee man, one down nine to go!"

TV evidence of his brilliance is scant, which is a crying shame. But his class will still be passed from generation to generation of Gers fans who lap up the stories of his talents.

Many say he faded as a footballing force after he broke his leg in the last minute of another virtuoso performance as the club beat Rapid Vienna 2-0 in the Prater Stadium in

December 1964. Yet Slim simply shrugged: "I couldn't blame the Austrian defender for the tackle, I was taking the mickey something terrible.

"I went downhill because I left Gers and went to a bad side. I would never have left if I hadn't gambled all my money away."

The drink was to wreck his liver and the betting wrecked his life.

Jim Baxter should have quit a millionaire. Yet he now lives quietly on Glasgow's south side, close to the footballing arena where he is a legend despite an ill-fated return to the club from Nottingham Forest.

Like Paul Gascoigne in the 90s he won the hearts of the Rangers fans but could never win his battles with the demons within himself.

Yet Jim said: "I was lucky to be able to play a bit, but when all is said and done, I'm just a human being like everyone else.

"I've got no regrets. After all, I've been dead and I've been brought back."

11

Jim BETT

STAR player, dark days. Right place, wrong time. That's the story of Jim Bett's Rangers career.

It's a footballing irony that this playmaker who suffered despite his brilliance during the stormy seasons of John Greig's managership COULD have been a part of Gers' glory days.

When David Holmes kicked off the Ibrox Revolution by appointing Graeme Souness in 1986, the name at the top of the new player-manager's shopping list was Jim Bett.

Souness saw his Scotland team-mate – whose silken skills had taken him from Airdrie to Valur in Iceland, Belgium's Lokeren and Aberdeen – as the cultured influence his side needed.

And Jim, capped 25 times, confessed: "I had the option to go back TWICE and it was very hard to turn it down, because I respected Graeme as a man and a player.

"The problem was, I had travelled so much in my career. At last, we were settled somewhere. Could I ask my family to uproot from Aberdeen again?

"It was very difficult – perhaps the hardest call of my career – but I decided against the move."

Bett, now 39, lives happily in Aberdeen with Icelandic wife Audur. His sons, Baldur and Calum, are on the books at Pittodrie and youngest boy, Brynjar, also shows great promise in what must be regarded as the family business.

It was Bett's devotion to his family that kept him at Dons when Souness came calling.

And although he did go back to Iceland for a spell with Reykjavik at the end of his playing days, Aberdeen has always been considered home.

Bett's wandering career had brought him to Ibrox in 1980 when Greig splashed out £180,000 for the Lokeren player who got his big break with Valur in Iceland.

Jim had prospered in Belgium but when the call of Scotland came it proved too tempting.

Jazzer's class in midfield won him an international call-up in 1982 and he was to stay in the reckoning for eight years throughout his club travels.

When he arrived at Rangers, though, they were a team in turmoil. He maintains to this day that the pressure he saw boss Greig endure put him off management for life.

He stressed: "I had good times in midfield although they were difficult days for the club.

"But I felt sorry for John Greig because it was a team in transition.

I'M A GER... Jim Bett shows his delight about coming to Ibrox from Belgian club, Lokeren

Club and Country

IBROX CAREER 1980-83

GAMES
League	104
Scot Cup	18
Lg Cup	24
Europe	6
Total	152

GOALS
League	21
Scot Cup	2
Lg Cup	6
Europe	1
Total	30

MEDALS
Scot Cup	1
Lg Cup	1

SCOTLAND
25 caps

STATS

"The '78 treble team that had included the likes of Alex MacDonald was breaking up and his first task as a manager was to try to build a completely new side. He didn't inherit one.

"It was tough, because we'd get gates of just 15,000 or 20,000 – apart from the days when we faced Celtic or Aberdeen."

There were times to savour, though, and the 1981 Scottish Cup Final against Dundee United is top of Bett's list.

Ian Redford missed a last-minute penalty in the first game but the replay was a completely different story.

Jim recalled: "I was lucky to play alongside some class acts, guys like Bobby Russell and Davie Cooper.

"That night, they clicked and we ran out 4-1 winners. It was just nice to be able to say I won something as a Rangers player."

Bett could turn from provider to predator and he had a knack of scoring on the big stage.

He curled home a classic free-kick for Gers in the 1982-83 League Cup Final against Celtic but his team went down 2-1.

And five years later he scored AGAINST Rangers for Aberdeen in a 3-3 classic – only to see his side lose once more in a penalty shoot-out.

His nine years as a Pittodrie star far outweigh the time spent at Ibrox, yet Bett has a right to be ranked alongside the likes of Souness and Ray Wilkins in any list of great Gers creators.

When Jim assesses his career, he believes all the traumas of the Greig era may even have been GOOD for Rangers.

He was gone before the painful end, gone before the scarves flew onto the pitch and prompted the resignation of a man who'd been a legend as a player.

And Jim reasoned: "I know it brought a brief second spell for Jock Wallace but I've always believed it was those days under Greigy that kick-started the revolution that was brought about when David Holmes appointed Souness.

"Rangers began to spend the big money on players and they have never looked back.

"In some ways, I look upon the poor era I was involved in as the one that made the club wake up to itself."

John BROWN

THE PUNCH thumped into his kidneys and left him a spent force – John Brown had just learned football the Graeme Souness way. Win at all costs.

Souness was the arrogant assassin of midfield, the player with the clout and the class to trample over any team at his peak.

He was a chilling competitor and when the ruthless man who kick-started the Rangers Revolution saw a little bit of himself in Brown he had no hesitation in inking the £350,000 cheque that brought Bomber from Dundee in 1988.

Eleven years later Brown remains at the core of the club, coaching the reserve side and passing on the beliefs that made him a nine-in-a-row legend.

And he reflected tongue-in-cheek: "Maybe Graeme respected me because I had given him 'the message' a couple of times on the park but I'd taken more back from him!

"I remember one time when Dundee lost at Ibrox he punched me in tne kidneys and I couldn't do anything for 10 minutes. Now that's experience and, although as a ball-player I couldn't condone these sort of things, I learned from them!"

Brown might mock his level of skill and many came to overlook it as he showed his grit and unquenchable desire to play for the Light Blue jersey at either left-back, centre-half or midfield.

But he was an accomplished player who once scored a hat-trick against Gers at Dens Park and also bundled them out of the Scottish Cup on their own turf.

John, deprived of a move to Hearts when their owner, Wallace Mercer, said he wasn't fit enough, believed his first 'phone call from Souness about a Gers move was a WIND-UP.

Once the manager convinced Brown he was serious, the player needed no persuasion that this was the right move. After all, it was what a True Blue had wanted all his life.

John explained: "I was always desperate to do well against Gers to prove they were wrong not to sign me. Yet, even when I played with Dundee, I would come down and stand in the Enclosure for games like the 3-1 European win over Inter Milan.

"Ironically, when I played for Dundee the Bears always thought I was a CELTIC fan!"

Souness knew the truth and, while they would have their setbacks, the mutual respect remains to this day.

Brown the fan, player and coach will always rate the man who brought him to Rangers and he said: "He was a total winner and he wanted everyone to be that way.

"Often he would feud with the Press and that could turn them against us which was negative. But Graeme knew what he was

TRUE BLUE...
John Brown can't conceal his pride at being a winner with Rangers

Club and Country

STATS

IBROX CAREER 1988-96

GAMES

League	207
Scot Cup	33
Lg Cup	18
Europe	20
Total	278

GOALS

League	14
Scot Cup	4
Lg Cup	0
Europe	0
Total	18

MEDALS

League	6
Scot Cup	3
Lg Cup	3

about and although there were times when he dropped me for big names and I hated it, I thought he was great for Rangers.

"We had class acts like Terry Butcher and Ray Wilkins coming in to blend with the local lads like Ian Durrant and Ally McCoist and add the little things that would make them even better. It was perfect."

They say that when Rangers sign a fan for the team, the club gleans an extra 10 per cent from him the moment he pulls that jersey over his head. With Bomber they got that plus interest.

Two games sum up his commitment to the club best, the 1991 final day league title decider with Aberdeen and the New Year's Day clash at Celtic a year later.

In the first, he was injected to help him play and hold a makeshift team together as they won 2-0 to lift the crown. He left the pitch on a stretcher after his achilles tendon ruptured under the strain.

In the second, he finally scored the Old Firm goal of his childhood dreams when he rattled a 30-yarder in off the post to clinch a 3-1 win and jumped the advertising hoardings to celebrate.

He grinned: "Just signing for this club was one of the biggest thrills of my life but, yes, scoring at Parkhead came close.

"Most of the boys at the club could count one goal against our biggest rivals but I seemed to have to wait and wait until

that day. Ironically, when it came, I was on as a sub and got only about 10 minutes!"

Bomber was an integral part of Walter Smith's best Rangers side, the team who went 44-games unbeaten in season '92-93 to win the treble and go within a heartbeat of the European Cup Final.

But the punter inside him refuses to let him grasp the ultimate accolade for his own men. He reasoned: "That was easily the most successful team of my lifetime as a player but 'The Greatest Ever?' I'm not so sure about that.

"I can go back to the treble teams of '76 and '78 that I supported and they were MY heroes. I idolised Alex MacDonald, he was so under-rated and I can't believe he only earned one cap for Scotland."

These days the glittering eyes that once earned him the dressing-room nickname of Hannibal Lecter glint at youngsters who scurry down the Ibrox corridors away from him if they know they've been slacking.

Bomber still has a role to play and he said: "I'm trying to put a bit back now because there are so many distractions around for the kids.

"The financial side has gone through the roof now but I try to remind them what Rangers is all about.

"I tell them this – all I ever wanted was ONE DAY here. One day to call myself a Rangers player, the rest is a bonus."

Ralph BRAND

ONE of the most lethal strike partnerships Rangers has ever seen was created thanks to a thousand hours of talking football on the Edinburgh-Glasgow train.

These days, the Range Rovers, the Porsches and the Mercs are cleaned by the groundstaff boys at the carwash next to Ibrox and deposited outside the main door waiting for the stars to purr home after training.

In the 60s life was different, the players made good wages but they didn't inhabit a millionaires' world that the fans couldn't begin to comprehend.

That's why Ralph Brand took the train with his mate Jimmy Millar and that's where the M&B partnership was born.

They were to score an incredible 368 goals in 634 games for the club and were the perfect footballing marriage.

Brand's blistering acceleration set him apart and he profited throughout his career from the clever knockdowns and link-play of Millar. They were the McCoist and Hateley of their era.

Ralph – who was Bill Struth's last signing as Gers manager – recalled: "We'd come through on the train together and I would constantly involve Jimmy in tactics talks and ways we could become a better partnership.

"The boss Scot Symon knew we were friends and he'd have us rooming together, still talking football and improving.

"I even had us back working in the afternoons when that sort of thing was taboo. Extra work wasn't encouraged back then and I actually had to boot footballs behind a fence to hide them so we could use them for our extra sessions. The trainers locked them away!"

Struth left a legacy in Brand. Ralph was just 15 when he was signed as a schoolboy from Edinburgh's Carrick Vale Junior Secondary. The cost? £20!

He was to flourish into a striker who earned four league championship medals, scored in three consecutive Scottish Cup Finals and terrorised defences at home and abroad.

Brand, who earned eight caps for Scotland, was at the centre of a golden era in Europe for Rangers when the club

BRAND NEW ... Ralph's deadly partnership with Jimmy Millar saw them hammer in an incredible 368 goals in 634 games for Gers

Club and Country

STATS

IBROX CAREER 1954-65

GAMES

League	206
Scot Cup	33
Lg Cup	54
Europe	24
Total	317

GOALS

League	127
Scot Cup	29
Lg Cup	38
Europe	12
Total	206

MEDALS

League	4
Scot Cup	3
Lg Cup	4

SCOTLAND
8 caps

– too often feeding on scraps in the modern era – always dined at the top table. In 1960 Gers were in on the opening season of the new Cup Winners' Cup, a trophy they would of course win 12 years later, and Ralph helped drive them to the Final in a memorable run.

He was on the mark as Millar scored a double in the 4-2 Ibrox success over Hungarians Ferencvaros that assured their ticket into the next round and one of the most astonishing results in Rangers' four decades of European competition.

The 3-0 trouncing of Borussia Möenchengladbach on German soil was startling enough but Symon's side then followed that up with an 8-0 annihilation of the Bundesliga side at home.

Brand blasted a hat-trick.

Ralph was on target again in a 2-0 semi-final first leg win as Gers triumphed in a Battle of Britain with

English giants Wolves and earned a shootout for the trophy with Italians Fiorentina.

The Final, though, was a numbing anti-climax as Brand's side went down 2-0 in front of 80,000 at home and he recalled: "Eric Caldow missed a penalty in the first-half and we paid a heavy price for that.

"We lost 2-1 over there but, you know, it's often forgotten just the stature we had in the 60s on the continent.

"Year by year we grew in experience and we progressed because we matched the Inter Milans and the like and we learned.

"And I loved those occasions, the Ibrox European nights under the floodlights. They were so special.

"I was happy to see Rangers re-establish themselves in Europe a little with a decent run under Dick Advocaat because that is where the club belongs.

That is where we put it."

Strikers need service and Brand's came silver-plated, offered on a platter from a midfielder who still has football connoisseurs worshipping him 30 years after his heyday. Jim Baxter.

Brand believes Symon had Slim Jim's measure, knew how to get the best out of a hell-raising maverick talent.

And he said: "Scot knew how to handle him as a person and as a player too. Jim was given a licence to freewheel, allowed to roam where he wanted.

"Playing with Baxter as a striker was a real joy. You would set off on a run and you didn't even need to look back or break your stride. You knew the ball would arrive.

"He had a left foot you could open a tin with and there's one thing you will rarely notice even in what little footage there is of us in action.

"Jim could actually put BACKSPIN on the ball so it drifted perfectly into your path. Brilliant."

These days Ralph Brand drives a taxi in Edinburgh.

He's not a bitter man, indeed if you ask him about his favourite game he replies child-like that it was simply every one that saw him pull a famous Rangers jersey over his head.

But Brand IS a worried man, concerned that the code Bill Struth stood for is forgotten at the club he loves.

And he said: "I think the wages now are disgusting, the modern day footballer is too far away from what I called 'The Bears' – the men who stood in the Enclosure and cheered on Rangers.

"I don't think the players now can relate to those supporters the way the likes of Jimmy Millar and I did.

"Yes, I was Struth's last signing for Rangers and I'm proud of that because I still remember the aura of the man.

"He gave Gers a code of integrity and discipline, a set of football rules to live by.

"Sadly, I see that being eroded now but I hope all the foreign players who will play for this club in the future take just some of what he stood for on board. That's what makes Rangers special."

Bobby BROWN

BILL STRUTH strode grim-faced around the Hampden dressing-room, immaculate in his pinstripe suit yet brandishing his cane and seething at a half-time Cup Final scoreline that read Rangers 1 Morton 1.

Chastened 'keeper Bobby Brown – whose first minute blunder had handed the Greenock side the lead – stared at the floor then bent to tie his laces.

WHACK! The wooden stick thudded into the backside of the humiliated No 1. "You," growled Struth. "Pay attention to your work."

Brown will never forget the 1948 Scottish Cup Final against 'Ton in front of 131,975 frenzied fans.

Even now, at the age of 76, the memories are crystal clear and he shuddered: "I shipped a goal in the first 30 seconds, a long high cross that I lost in the wind and it went over me and bounced three times before rolling in. Imagine it, in front of all those people.

"Struth was a well-groomed man, always dressed to the nines and carrying that stick.

"I went down to tie my laces in the dressing-room and felt the cane rap my backside. Trouble."

Torry Gillick rescued his 'keeper with an equaliser that day and Gers won the replay.

But the forbidding aura of Struth still lives with the intelligent keeper who always steadfastly refused to give up his teaching job to go full-time.

Brown was a key part of a defence that was so miserly it became known as The Iron Curtain.

The names of Brown, George Young, Jock "Tiger" Shaw, Ian McColl, Willie Woodburn and Sammy Cox would go down in Ibrox legend – but that didn't help when Struth wanted a quiet word.

Bobby – a PE teacher in Denny back then – recalled: "Many times he called me up to his office and told me I must go full-time. Yet I always felt I should keep my teaching career for when I finished playing.

"It cost me my first team place in the end and those visits were always

met with trepidation because he was a fearsome man. Whether you were Willie Waddell or Willie Thornton you still climbed those marble stairs in fear."

Brown was steeped in football from his schooldays at Falkirk High where he played in a side managed by Scotland boss Craig Brown's father Hugh.

He was making the grade when the bizarre tale of the Egyptian teacher and the Army lieutenant handed him a glamourous debut in the big time against Celtic at the age of just 16.

Bobby smiled: "War was imminent in 1939 when I was called up to play for Queen's Park.

"The amateurs' first choice – an Egyptian called Mustapha Mansoor – had returned home after earning his teaching qualifications and his stand-in was a lieutenant in the Army who'd been called up!"

So the kid was in and he played his part for Queen's in a thrilling 4-4 draw at Celtic Park.

The stature of Queen's Park was very different then to the Third Division minnows we know today. Sure, this was a club full of bankers and doctors but they were also very good players. Amateurs, yes, but good enough to be a top six club in Scotland.

Brown recalled: "I was pitchforked into that game but I loved every minute.

"I knew the career might go on hold because of the War but even when I went into the Fleet Air Arm I gained valuable playing experience."

He would play for Queen's Park when he was home on leave and the War also gave Bobby the chance to guest for teams like Chelsea,

Club and Country

IBROX CAREER 1946-56

GAMES	
League	211
Scot Cup	33
Lg Cup	52
Europe	0
Total	296

GOALS	
League	0
Scot Cup	0
Lg Cup	0
Europe	0
Total	0

MEDALS	
League	3
Scot Cup	3
Lg Cup	2

SCOTLAND
3 caps

STATS

Portsmouth and Plymouth.

And one game stands out. Look up the reference books now and only three caps in a five-year spell are credited to R. Brown (Rangers).

The games played during war-time are ignored, but they will never be scratched from the memory banks of those who starred in them.

Bobby was between the sticks for the Scots against England at Villa Park when they lost 3-2.

And he said: "They had a forward line that had the likes of Stanley Matthews, Wilf Mannion, Tommy Lawton and Tom Finney.

"Matt Busby captained us that day and it was a great memory, I still look at my scrapbook cutting of that match.

"The report was by the famous Express writer Tommy Muirhead and his caption was: "The Greatest Saves I've ever seen".

"I was only 18 then but I still remember the game as if it was yesterday."

Brown emerged from the War to return to Jordanhill and complete his training as a teacher.

The call came from his Scotland skipper Busby who had recommended him at Manchester United, but Rangers were interested too and with his marriage looming he opted to stay in Scotland.

He was to be a part of three championship teams, win three Scottish Cup badges and help Gers to their first ever domestic Treble in 1949.

This is a book laced with nostalgia, and talking to Brown you feel the fervour, the rising anticipation a visit from Rangers brought to the towns he played in during those halcyon days for football.

He explained: "Towns came alive

when the Rangers came to play.

"When we were at East Fife the pits were still in full operation and they''d all work five in the morning till noon so they could be up on top for the game.

"Then you'd have 25,000 screaming at you and you were lucky to emerge with a point.

"It was always the same everywhere we went – from Queen of the South to Aberdeen."

The 2-3-5 formation that gave birth to the Iron Curtain is, of course, long since dead and buried.

Brown mourns its passing and refuses to accept that this makes him idealistic or naive.

He said: "Football is entertainment and I just don't think there's the same thrill in it now.

"I still watch games and read Dick Advocaat's comments with interest about how he has to try and break sides down. That just didn't happen back then."

Bobby's own management prowess was to be tested when he was given the Scotland job in 1967 and he stayed in charge for 27 games until Tommy Docherty took over four years later.

Brown may be 76 now but he's still active in the gift business he established, travelling from his Helensburgh home to the Orkneys and Shetland to meet contacts.

And four decades on from the days when he donned the gloves for the Gers he looks with interest at reports of a £1million-a-year basic wage packet for current keeper Stefan Klos.

Brown grinned: "When I signed for Rangers you earned £16-a-week as a first team player with a £25 win bonus.

"The great thing was that they let that mount up and you got it in lump sums at Christmas and April.

"It was a great life because you then got the guts of four months off before you started playing again.

"And you can put it all in perspective because back when I negotiated my own transfer as an amateur from Queen's Park in 1946 I had it made.

"It was enough to build me a four-bedroom bungalow in an acre of ground in Stirling. The same thing now would cost you £250,000!"

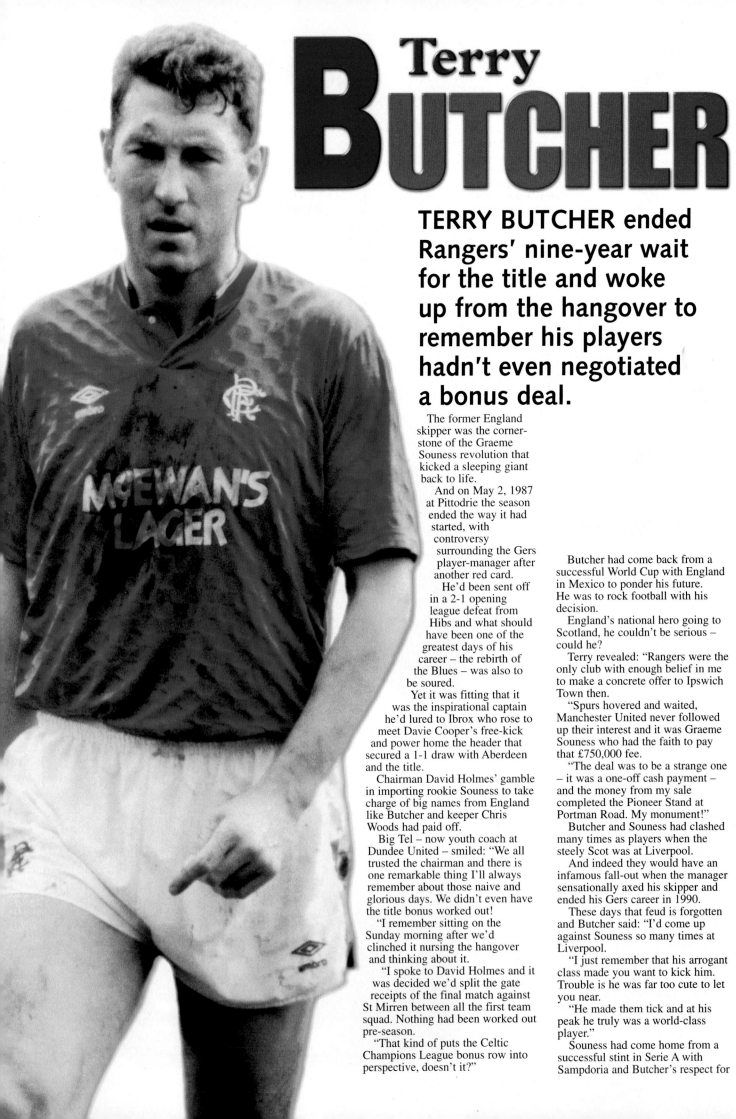

Terry BUTCHER

TERRY BUTCHER ended Rangers' nine-year wait for the title and woke up from the hangover to remember his players hadn't even negotiated a bonus deal.

The former England skipper was the cornerstone of the Graeme Souness revolution that kicked a sleeping giant back to life.

And on May 2, 1987 at Pittodrie the season ended the way it had started, with controversy surrounding the Gers player-manager after another red card.

He'd been sent off in a 2-1 opening league defeat from Hibs and what should have been one of the greatest days of his career – the rebirth of the Blues – was also to be soured.

Yet it was fitting that it was the inspirational captain he'd lured to Ibrox who rose to meet Davie Cooper's free-kick and power home the header that secured a 1-1 draw with Aberdeen and the title.

Chairman David Holmes' gamble in importing rookie Souness to take charge of big names from England like Butcher and keeper Chris Woods had paid off.

Big Tel – now youth coach at Dundee United – smiled: "We all trusted the chairman and there is one remarkable thing I'll always remember about those naive and glorious days. We didn't even have the title bonus worked out!

"I remember sitting on the Sunday morning after we'd clinched it nursing the hangover and thinking about it.

"I spoke to David Holmes and it was decided we'd split the gate receipts of the final match against St Mirren between all the first team squad. Nothing had been worked out pre-season.

"That kind of puts the Celtic Champions League bonus row into perspective, doesn't it?"

Butcher had come back from a successful World Cup with England in Mexico to ponder his future. He was to rock football with his decision.

England's national hero going to Scotland, he couldn't be serious – could he?

Terry revealed: "Rangers were the only club with enough belief in me to make a concrete offer to Ipswich Town then.

"Spurs hovered and waited, Manchester United never followed up their interest and it was Graeme Souness who had the faith to pay that £750,000 fee.

"The deal was to be a strange one – it was a one-off cash payment – and the money from my sale completed the Pioneer Stand at Portman Road. My monument!"

Butcher and Souness had clashed many times as players when the steely Scot was at Liverpool.

And indeed they would have an infamous fall-out when the manager sensationally axed his skipper and ended his Gers career in 1990.

These days that feud is forgotten and Butcher said: "I'd come up against Souness so many times at Liverpool.

"I just remember that his arrogant class made you want to kick him. Trouble is he was far too cute to let you near.

"He made them tick and at his peak he truly was a world-class player."

Souness had come home from a successful stint in Serie A with Sampdoria and Butcher's respect for

HAVING A BUTCHERS ... England skipper Terry stunned the critics down South when he moved to Scotland

him simply grew. The man who'd won the European Cup three times as a player with the Kop kings now wanted to be a manager – and he made Terry want to be a part of his adventure.

Butcher revealed: "He was so full of attitude, bursting with desire. You knew it was going to be fun to be along for the ride and I loved every second.

"Of course, there were questions in my mind about coming north but Chris Woods the England keeper was already here and that was good enough for me."

The first test of the Souness' side came in front of a friendly Ibrox crowd who accepted a 2-0 warm-up defeat from Bayern Munich because they saw signs of improvement after too many barren years.

Then came the league debut of Woods, Butcher and Souness at Easter Road and only one word summed it up. MAYHEM.

In a powderkeg match Souness was sent packing for a vicious kick at George McCluskey and 21 players were booked for their part in the melee that followed.

Only laid-back Hibees keeper Alan Rough escaped because it was too far for him to run to get involved!

Even now the memories of a dramatic day live with Butcher and he'll never forget going on the sauce with Souness in the manager's native city of Edinburgh that night. Their families hadn't moved north at the time and Terry smiled: "I remember trawling the pubs with

Graeme trying to find a place to drown our sorrows.

"We were both staying there on our own and we kept walking into hostile receptions when all we wanted to was forget everything that had happened that day.

"It was a humbling day all round. Hibs were so hyped up and the whole thing blew up in our faces."

After all the headlines Gers were in the mire yet within three months Souness had placed his first silverware in the Ibrox trophy room.

And Butcher was at the heart of it all, fouled by Celtic skipper Roy Aitken in the dying minutes of the Skol Cup Final at Hampden.

Davie Cooper scored from the spot to clinch a 2-1 triumph and the new manager was off and running.

The title was to follow but Terry's second season turned sour after a bust-up with Frank McAvennie in a 2-2 Old Firm draw was blown out of all proportion.

What was in essence a shoving match that led to red cards for Butcher, Woods and the Celtic striker somehow ended up in the 'In' tray at the Prosecutor Fiscal's office.

And Terry sighed: "Woodsy and I missed out on a League Cup Final win over Aberdeen and a medal because of the fall-out and it was a real downer.

"The court case hung over me like a black cloud and then I broke my leg in November in a challenge with Alex McLeish as we lost 1-0 to Aberdeen at Ibrox."

The club did reach the last eight of the European Cup before going

out to Steaua Bucharest but the Double went to Celtic in their centenary year.

Butcher returned to drive the club towards a Treble chase in 1989 but – faded and jaded after a punishing campaign – they lost the Scottish Cup Final to Celtic.

Terry returned from England's Italia 90 a hero after his nation went to the last four but his Gers career was to sensationally hit the skids within two months of the new season.

He scored a spectacular own goal in a 2-1 defeat at Dundee United, heading a Billy Thomson kick-out high over Chris Woods and in.

But when Souness axed his skipper for the Skol Cup semi-final with Aberdeen the impact his decision had was reflected by the fact that it made the FRONT pages of the newspapers next morning.

Richard Gough was the new captain, Trevor Steven scored the winner and it was over at Ibrox for the colossus who had become an idol with the fans.

Even now the hurt stings and Butcher admitted: "Being dropped didn't just disappoint me, it was MIND-BLOWING.

"I knew I wasn't at the top of my game but I never expected that.

"We had a major row at Ibrox when I was told and I felt I had to go away from the ground.

"I was hurt, I was embarrassed and I felt like no-one needed me to be moping around because it might distract them."

Two driven men ruled by pride, two egos but one was the manager and there was only one result.

Butcher was literally sent to Coventry – in a £400,000 deal.

He went on to boss the Sky Blues and then Sunderland but when he became a management casualty Scotland pulled him back to Bridge of Allan where he now lives with wife Rita and their family.

Butcher can still laugh at all the glory and the gaffes of his Gers career. From battering in own goals to booting in doors in fury when his team lost.

He grinned: "The ironic thing about my final game is that all my own goals were CRACKERS. I used to shout to Chris: 'Pick that bugger out!'

"As for the doors, kicking inanimate objects is my forte. I booted one at Pittodrie and another one, famously, behind Billy McNeill at Parkhead when he was doing a TV interview.

"What can I say? At least I made my mark on Scottish football."

Club and Country

STATS

IBROX CAREER 1986-90	
GAMES	
League	127
Scot Cup	11
Lg Cup	21
Europe	17
Total	176
GOALS	
League	8
Scot Cup	0
Lg Cup	1
Europe	2
Total	11
MEDALS	
League	3
Lg Cup	2
ENGLAND	
77 caps	

Eric CALDOW

JIMMY JOHNSTONE was once asked: "Did you ever pass Eric Caldow?"

Celtic legend Jinky replied: "Yes – but I was in my Jaguar at the time!"

That brilliant one-liner may sum up the impish humour of a Lisbon Lion but it also tells you a little about the qualities of a Rangers player ahead of his time.

Eric Caldow never needed to resort to clogging because he had too much class. Speed of thought and blistering pace replaced swinging the suede and booting his rivals.

Incredibly, in a top-class career that spanned 13 years with Gers and 40 caps for Scotland he was NEVER booked.

His international career was cruelly ended by a horrific late challenge from Tottenham Hotspur's Bobby Smith when Eric was the skipper of a side who beat England 2-1 at Wembley in 1963.

But Eric – now a sales rep in the building trade – reflected: "I look back and wish that it had never happened but there is no point in bitterness.

"I always remember that it could have happened when I was 18 and not 28."

Caldow's class always shone through in his playing career. There was as much chance of him being dragged in front of the SFA as there was of team-mate Jim Baxter taking the pledge and leading the quiet life.

Yet the Ayrshireman, branded the fastest defender he'd ever faced by Real Madrid superstar Gento, shrugs off compliments on that remarkable record.

He smiled: "Truth is, I couldn't tackle a fish supper! Seriously, my pace carried me through. I couldn't kick them and they couldn't catch me.

"But, yes, there is a little pride that I was never booked. Come to think of it, I was never even spoken to.

"I have to say, I look at modern players and I think they get away with murder."

From the minute he left Muirkirk Juniors for Ibrox, the slender Caldow was destined for greatness. He cost £20 – you could say Rangers got value for money.

Eric was in the line-up when Rangers began their first ever European Cup adventure in 1956 and lost out to OGC Nice of France.

And he was to be at the hub of a side who would consistently make their mark against the cream of the Continent.

They went to the semi-finals of the European Cup in 1960 only to be annihilated 12-4 on aggregate by an Eintracht Frankfurt team who were then hammered 7-3 in a famous Hampden final by the incomparable Real Madrid. The following year, Caldow & Co made the final of the newly-launched European Cup-Winners' Cup against Italian giants Fiorentina.

But Eric sighed: "That game was to be a huge disappointment because we went so close and I missed a penalty in the 2-0 first leg defeat at Ibrox.

"In all honesty, their keeper moved and was almost on the six-yard line when he saved but maybe I'd have missed the retake too.

"We lost the second-leg 2-1 and it was hard to take because we really believed that was our year.

"But those were great days for me in 1961. I remember I was voted in Europe's Best Team by a paper called the *Sunday Despatch*.

"I flew down to London one morning to get my award and flew back to Glasgow to help Gers win against Clyde at Shawfield. A great day."

The Rangers stalwart – who won five league titles, two Scottish Cup honours and three League Cup badges with his club – was at his peak.

And he did have more success from the spot at Hampden against the English in '62 when he wrapped up a 2-0 win that avenged a 9-3 Wembley humbling 12 months earlier.

This man from Rabbie Burns country was a fierce patriot and was the first-ever Rangers player to play in the World Cup Finals when he pulled the dark blue jersey over his head.

He was to move to Stirling Albion in 1966 and still relishes his career, despite that leg-break sickener at its height.

Eric said: "I have so many memories from signing for Rangers to captaining both club and country.

"I know it cost £20 to sign me and that might only get you Arthur Numan's bootlace now but this was 48 years ago.

"I think they got their money back, anyway."

Alex CLELAND

RANGERS in the 90s means transfer shopping on Millionaires Row but every so often the club plunders PoundStretchers and picks up a genuine bargain.

Alex Cleland proved to be that and much more after arriving in a £750,000 package deal with his Dundee United team-mate, Gary Bollan.

Many thought it was the tough-tackling Bollan who had the better chance of making it at Ibrox but he was to be plagued by injuries and could only watch as his friend flourished.

Cleland became the first worthy successor to Gary Stevens and, like the former Everton and England star, was an attack-minded player.

He was a model of consistency throughout his Gers days and played a key role in nine-in-a-row.

But one game will always stick in his mind. Against Celtic in September, 1995, when he drove onto Oleg Salenko's cross to head beyond Gordon Marshall and put his side on the way to a 2-0 win.

Alex recalled: "I wasn't so much out to celebrate after that one, as out for the count.

"But if the night was a blur it was a goal I'll never forget because, in the games against Celtic, I found how much that game means to so many people. Your family, your friends, everyone is affected.

"I actually stood in disbelief for a moment then went hunting for our fans before I remembered they were at the other end of Parkhead.

"To cap it all, I feel that was one of my best games for Rangers."

He experienced the highs and the lows of life with Gers yet, while he may at times have been a little naive defensively, he used every game to learn.

In the Stadio Delle Alpi against Juventus just 18 days after that Celts game his side could do little else in a 4-1 Champions League caning.

To make matters worse, Alex saw red for a frustrated kick at Alessandro Del Piero who had done him with one of the cutest turns ever seen.

Cleland sighed: "The walk to the dressing room that night will live with me forever.

"When I got there, it was just Jimmy Bell the kitman and me. He told me to forget it but the team were getting stuffed and I'd left them a man down. I couldn't.

"To make matters worse, Didier Deschamps ran up and pulled my hair to leave me even more angry as I trudged off. For days later, I felt really low but ever since I've seen that Del Piero does it to everybody. He's simply a world-class player."

Cleland's worth to Rangers was proved through manager Walter Smith's troubled final season at the club when he remained on top form despite all the toils around him. He chose to head for Everton that summer, a player who had improved on every shred of his natural ability to justify his place in the Premiership.

Club and Country

IBROX CAREER 1995-98

GAMES

League	96
Scot Cup	14
Lg Cup	10
Europe	14
Total	134

GOALS

League	4
Scot Cup	3
Lg Cup	0
Europe	0
Total	7

MEDALS

League	2
Scot Cup	1
Lg Cup	1

STATS

Davie COOPER

THE Rangers scarves were linked with Celtic colours and entwined on the famous gates of Ibrox. Davie Cooper was dead.

A HERO'S FAREWELL ... Davie Cooper is remembered by the fans at Ibrox following his untimely death

A city scarred by the bitter sectarian divide that separates its two footballing powers was united in grief. Every picture tells a story.

This was a man who had tormented Celtic, scored the goal of his life when he bewildered four markers in a ball-juggling run before netting in the 1979 Drybrough Cup Final.

Yet here, even the fans whose spiritual home belongs on the other side of the city were adding their own dignified tokens of grief as they mourned the loss of a genius.

Coop was only 39 when he was snatched away. He had a brain haemorrhage while he was training kids for a TV programme at Clyde's Broadwood Stadium.

He was still playing for Clydebank when tragedy struck and his brilliance for his other former employers, Motherwell, saw the Lanarkshire club name a stand after the maverick winger in the wake of his death.

Those clubs too saw the world through a veil of tears in the numbing wake of Davie's death, but to Rangers fans, he will always be one of them. The Moody Blue.

It was a cruel irony that the Rangers Revolution led by Graeme Souness careered into Ibrox when Coop was already past his 30th birthday. He should have been the blueprint for all that Souness wanted to achieve as he kicked a sleeping giant back to life.

Look through these pages and you will see few players from Davie's era included in this tale of 100 heroes. The truth is that for long spells in his Ibrox career, Cooper CARRIED Rangers.

Sure, he was part of a tremendous Treble team in '78, but far too often after that he was surrounded by mediocrity. For a generation of Gers fans Davie became their reason for going to the football, he was the only player the club had worth the admission money.

Coop took what used to be a traditional route to Ibrox – he starred against Gers in a Cup tie and then they bought him!

Davie's date with stardom came in September 1976 when he played for the Bankies in a two-legged League Cup quarter-final tie against Jock Wallace's big guns.

That's when he found out the essence of John Greig, the man who would later become his manager.

Davie once shuddered: "He took exactly 120 seconds before he waded in with a challenge Jack the Ripper would have been proud of.

"Just to rub salt in my wounds Greigy then growled: 'If I get another chance I'll break your leg'. He really gave you that nice-to-be-wanted feeling.

"Greigy and big Tam Forsyth played keepie-uppie with me that night but I still scored the equaliser in a 3-3 draw."

The tie became a saga. Cooper scored again as they tied the second leg and that meant a replay, yet another draw at Ibrox and then a FOURTH game.

Yet again, Davie scored at neutral Firhill and although Bankies lost 2-1, his future was assured. A £100,000 buy, Davie was an instant hit at Ibrox, his mesmerising wing skills were a throwback to a bygone era.

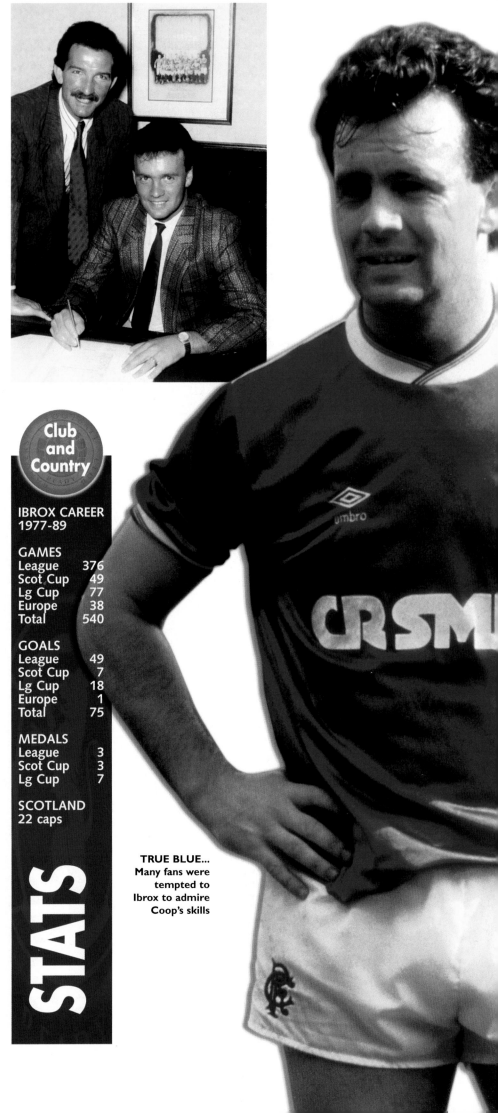

He was to give Rangers fans a sackful of memories in 12 years full of medals and mazy runs. Every supporter has his own to cherish.

That's why when he was awarded a glamour testimonial against French cracks Bordeaux, there were 5,000 fans locked outside the gates of Ibrox.

The best of Davie Cooper – where do you start?

How about Ilves Tampere? Two words that seldom feature in anyone's footballing Hall of Fame, but Coop put them there for Gers diehards.

His display in a 4-0 UEFA Cup mauling was sublime. Nutmegs, shuffles, stepovers, he did it all. Twice. One run that night when he beat four players and set up the easiest of tap-ins for Robert Fleck will live forever in the minds of those who saw it.

And goals? When he scored them himself they were always special. That Drybrough Cup epic was almost eclipsed by a thudding free-kick that flew into the top corner past Aberdeen's Jim Leighton in the classic 3-3 Skol Cup Final draw in 1987. Gers won on penalties.

Ian Durrant – the midfielder who hero-worshipped Cooper and learned from the man he called The Master -- rates that as his favourite from that priceless left foot.

And he smiled: "I was going to take that but Coop pushed me out of the way.

"He said to me: 'Leighton won't even see this'. It rocketed in and, as fate would have it, we had a Scotland get-together a week later.

"Jim came over to Coop and said: 'You know Davie, I almost got my fingertips to that free-kick'.

"Davie, deadpan as ever, replied: 'Aye, on the way back out'."

It will remain one of the greatest mysteries in Scottish football how Davie Cooper only managed to win 22 international caps, but at least he did play on the greatest stage of all in the Mexico World Cup Finals in 1986.

He'd played a key role in getting us there too, nervelessly sinking a critical penalty in the 1-1 draw with Wales in Cardiff that was so cruelly overshadowed by the death of manager Jock Stein amid the frenzy on the touchline.

That Davie too was taken from us so suddenly is still hard to take in. The Moody Blue – a tag he was given when he was too nervous to talk to the Press in his early days – had become an intelligent media pundit and had so much still to offer the game.

For players like Durrant and Ally McCoist March 23, 1995 was one of the darkest days of their lives. The country lost one of its most gifted footballers, they lost one of their closest friends.

McCoist and Ibrox pal Derek Johnstone were there at the hospital when the nightmare decision to switch off Davie's life support machine was taken.

A bereft Ally then helped carry the coffin as the searing pain of loss cut him to pieces.

He said: "The feeling in the dressing-room was that we had lost a brother.

"Although he had been away from the club for a while, Davie had never really been away. I don't think he ever will be."

Club and Country

STATS

IBROX CAREER 1977-89

GAMES
League	376
Scot Cup	49
Lg Cup	77
Europe	38
Total	540

GOALS
League	49
Scot Cup	7
Lg Cup	18
Europe	1
Total	75

MEDALS
League	3
Scot Cup	3
Lg Cup	7

SCOTLAND
22 caps

TRUE BLUE...
Many fans were tempted to Ibrox to admire Coop's skills

Alfie CONN

ALFIE CONN was in the side who won the Cup Winners' Cup and marked the 1973 SFA Centenary Scottish Cup Final with a blinding solo goal in a 3-2 Old Firm triumph.

BREAKING THE TABOO
...Alfie Conn was the first player for 50 years to move across the Old Firm divide

He was an Ibrox idol and then in the eyes of the Rangers fans he committed the cardinal sin. He signed for CELTIC.

The exciting, attacking midfielder had six often stormy years at Gers before he won a move to glamorous Tottenham Hotspur.

Then in 1977 Jock Stein swooped to bring him back north from Spurs in a £65,000 transfer.

Alfie – who would help dump his old team Gers in that season's Cup Final – at first insisted he could handle the heat of what the blue half of Glasgow saw as the ultimate betrayal.

Names like Dr Willie Kivlichan, George T. Livingstone, Alex Bennett, Tom 'Tully' Craig, and Tom Sinclair had the courage to play for both sides.

But Alfie was the first player for 50 YEARS to jump the dyke.

He bravely trumpeted then: "I'm not worried about the reaction from the Rangers fans – I just want to get on with my career.

"Nobody will be able to question my loyalty to Celtic. As a kid Rangers were my dream team but times change."

He'd left Gers at the age of 22 when he sealed a £140,000 move to England on superstar terms.

The dough? A £7,000 signing on fee and £200-a-week.

He'd gone south carrying an injury and went through a nightmare start before becoming the toast of Tottenham and earning a Scotland call-up for the 3-0 win over Northern Ireland in 1975.

His international career, though, died amidst the agony of a 5-1 hammering

for England at Wembley in the next match.

At the height of the glam-bam 70s with Spurs Alfie was a footballer with a pop-star image, guided by the same agents as Engelbert Humperdinck, Tom Jones and Frank Sinatra.

But he had a streak of arrogance in his make-up and that saw him branded a rebel as he had blazing rows with a string of bosses.

Spells at Hearts and Blackpool followed his Parkhead exit before he thrived in his 30s under Davie Hay at Motherwell.

Of course, he always lived under the extra burden of trying to live up to a famous name. Dad Alfie was part of the feared Hearts' 50s inside trio of Conn, Bauld and Wardhaugh.

His son, though, through his own skills and one explosive decision made his own mark on Scottish football history.

When he pondered the move that shocked both sides of the Old Firm Alfie reflected: "I was prepared for it and thought it would all die down after a few months – but it NEVER did."

Club and Country

IBROX CAREER 1968-74	
GAMES	
League	93
Scot Cup	13
Lg Cup	31
Europe	12
Total	149
GOALS	
League	23
Scot Cup	3
Lg Cup	11
Europe	2
Total	39
MEDALS	
League	1
Lg Cup	1
Europe	1
SCOTLAND	
2 caps	

STATS

"WHEN the time comes to make a living it will need to be with your feet," the stern schoolmistress at Darvel Higher Grade School told the eight-year-old kid. Sammy Cox nodded his head – and he did just that.

The boy who would become one of the finest Gers players at full-back or half-back actually started out as a centre-forward back then, egged on by a promise of a shilling a goal from his grandad.

Even when Sammy rattled in EIGHT against Hurlford one day the old man paid up! He was investing in the future.

Cox's grandad, whose best pal was ex-Ranger Alex Smith, was to play a key role in his development. Sammy's dad was desperate to see his kid play for Darvel and refused to let him sign for nearby junior rivals Glenafton. Another route of progress was needed.

That's when former Ibrox winger Smith – tagged the Darvel Marvel when he earned 20 caps in a Scotland career that ended in 1911 – stepped in.

Sammy recalled: "Alex stayed only a few doors away and often in the summer he took me to the public park to coach me.

"I owe so much of the success I had to those evenings."

Rangers back then had a long history of players introduced to senior soccer in the

Sammy COX

famous black and white colours of Queen's Park before they switch to the rarefied atmosphere of Ibrox.

And although Cox did eventually have a season at his dad's beloved Darvel his true talent was spotted when he played for Hurlford Juniors against Queen's and then nurtured throughout three seasons at Hampden. He learned his trade well.

He said: "As a schoolboy my hero had been Tommy Walker of Hearts and I could not believe it when I lined up against him.

"I was worried and no matter where he ran that day I followed. At the end he shook me by the hand and thanked me for my sporting behaviour and good play.

"It was one of my happiest football memories from a man I consider to have been the greatest of that period. He was everything I'd ever thought him to be."

Sammy then had a spell at Third Lanark before his stint in the RAF saw him stationed up north and called up for some duty of the footballing kind that he'd always treasure.

His first honour in the Forces saw him

turn out for the Army against the RAF at Stamford Bridge. His direct opponent? Only Stanley Matthews!

Sammy's side included Wolves legend Billy Wright and they combined to shut out Blackpool wizard Matthews in a 3-0 triumph.

But Cox later confessed: "He was the greatest, I wouldn't dare say that I knew how to stop him because he always had one more trick up his sleeve."

By now Sammy was a Dundee player but in 1946 his life turned upside down and he was demob happy when Bill Struth offered him the chance to join Rangers.

After the training sessions with Light Blues old boy Alex as a youngster he'd sat and listened to Smith's stories of his days at Rangers.

Every tale finished with the words: "Stick in son, maybe one day you'll have the honour of playing for the Gers."

Now he did and Cox said: "It was fitting that I signed my first form for Rangers in Alex's house and that he was the witness on my registration."

The Darvel Marvel had taught his pupil well and Cox was to star alongside the likes of Ian McColl and Willie Woodburn.

He was comfortable on the ball and versatile, playing in either full-back berth – though he preferred the left flank – or at half-back.

Cox's class in an era when full-backs were often technically very poor earned him 25 Scotland caps and he always cherished his part in a 1949 3-1 triumph over England at Wembley.

And Sammy, who emigrated to Canada to coach and work in 1958, never forgot the lessons Alex Smith had taught him about Ibrox life and what was expected of those who played for the club.

He sighed: "There came a time near the end of my career when I fell below the high standards of the Rangers side of that period. I was conscious of the fact and I realised that if I was to continue playing then I would have to move elsewhere.

"Nevertheless it was with a heavy heart that I signed for East Fife. Rangers, after all are the greatest club in the world."

**IBROX CAREER
1956-64**

GAMES
League	168
Scot Cup	23
Lg Cup	42
Europe	28
Total	261

GOALS
League	8
Scot Cup	0
Lg Cup	3
Europe	2
Total	13

MEDALS
League	4
Scot Cup	1
Lg Cup	2

TOUGH TALKING...
John Greig summed up
Harold Davis' iron will
by describing him as
"hard as bloody nails"

STATS

Harold DAVIS

HAROLD DAVIS heard the fearful crackle of enemy machine-gun fire then felt the searing pain as bullets tore into his back.

He slumped into the Korean mud but the brave Black Watch corporal still crawled 200 yards to safety.

The tale of this courageous Fifer is no ordinary football story. He was just 18 when he had to get accustomed to the grim world of barbed wire, fox-holes and patrols in the paddy fields.

Then he became a casualty of the conflict and lay in agony what must have seemed a million miles from home in Kure, Japan.

Doctors stitched him up, made up his lost blood and predicted that he was finished with football. He would, they said, hobble around on sticks - if he lived.

Yet Harold was to prove them wrong. His club East Fife sent his contract to the military hospital and he signed on the dotted line.

One of the most incredible fightbacks in Scottish football history was just beginning.

By the time he was home at his mother's pub in Perth he was vowing to make it back to play for Gers legend Jerry Dawson at Methil.

Davis said: "For a long time I dismissed the idea of playing football.

"When you can't walk it seems a waste of time to be thinking about that sort of thing.

"But then I felt an itch to kick a ball, I just wanted to try."

Once he had set his iron will on resuming his playing career there was only one outcome. He would be a success.

Davis soon shone again for East Fife and this ultimate team player won his move to Ibrox in just three years after the troopship brought him back from the war.

Hero Harry was the workhorse in midfield, constantly winning tackles and feeding playmaker Ian McMillan to spark Gers' moves.

He faced a battle to win over the Ibrox fans as some insisted he wasn't Ibrox class and couldn't replace Ian McColl.

But by September 1960 when he scored and inspired his championship side to a 5-1 thumping of Celtic Davis was a victor.

After all, he'd come through tougher tests than convincing football fans to like him.

When John Greig shudders and tells you someone was "hard as bloody nails" you know you are talking about a fearsome footballer.

Later in a vintage season that was to take Gers to their first Cup Winners' Cup Final and eventual defeat from Fiorentina the Euro roadshow was in Germany.

Davis & Co were three up and cruising against Borussia Moenchengladbach when the sick Germans decide to put the boot in.

All over the field there were assaults and Davis was decked – but not for long. Stealthy retribution was sought and soon the Borussia left winger was lying on the turf out cold. He was later taken to hospital minus two teeth!

Davis was a superb servant to Rangers and after a signing row in 1962 - when he eventually settled on £30-a-week and £5 appearance money - he kept turning in stalwart displays until the emergence of Greig.

Harold's right-half slot was gone and he was eventually freed to be quickly snapped up by Partick Thistle. He later had a successful stint as coach of Queen's Park.

And in 1969 he was back at Gers as a coach under the Davie White regime, ensuring players gave the 100 per cent to the Light Blue jersey that he'd always given.

Harry Davis cost Scot Symon £1,750 when he bought him for Rangers. He was one of the manager's biggest bargains, the star who fought back from the bullet.

Ally DAWSON

THE silhouettes of the two policemen could be seen through the front door of the Dawson household. Had trouble come calling?

"Right, son," one of Strathclyde's finest muttered. "You're going away... with the Rangers."

That was Ally Dawson's bizarre introduction to life as an Ibrox player when he was just a 17-year-old kid studying at Johnstone High School.

He had been called up to join the Gers party on a World Tour and Ally explained: "It's true, the first thing I knew about going on that trip with Rangers was when those two cops turned up at the door.

"In those days, once the club had the OK from your headmaster the police had to certify that they had permission to take you out of the country.

"I was busy telling my mum that I honestly hadn't been involved in any bank jobs when they explained why they were there!"

Rangers' worldwide fan club has always welcomed the visits to the massive expatriate communities in Canada and Australia and they were regular summer trips in the 70s.

Now Dawson was catapulted in alongside a host of star names who would win the Treble the following season.

Ally recalled: "I was this fresh-faced kid in alongside the likes of John Greig, Sandy Jardine and Alex Miller in the Gers defence.

"Sandy had joined us from playing for Scotland in the Home Internationals and I was in awe of him. It was amazing, you just can't buy an experience like that."

When Dawson broke through into the first team for keeps at the start of season 78-79 Greig was by then the manager.

And he faced the daunting task of trying to live up to the Treble Jock Wallace had won for the second time in three years before his shock departure from the hotseat.

Aberdeen were defeated 2-1 to bring the League Cup to Ibrox and the Scottish Cup followed after a three-game saga against Hibs.

Yet Dawson sighed: "That campaign always seems to be remembered for just one thing. Celtic winning the league – and the manner in which they did it.

"Our game against them at Parkhead was all but a title decider and we seemed on Easy Street when Johnny Doyle was sent off but they surged forward in the closing stages and won 4-2.

"The chant: 'Ten men won the league' lived with me for a long time after that.

"Ally's star was on the rise, though, and he won the first of five Scotland caps in May 1980 when he played in a 1-0 friendly defeat from Poland in Poznan.

But in another Canadian tour with Rangers, Dawson was to suffer a horrific injury that almost blacked out his career for good.

He rose to head clear in a clash with top Italian side Ascoli at Toronto's Varsity Stadium and there was a sickening cracking of heads that left the Gers defender unconscious on the turf.

The next thing he can remember of that awful day is lying stricken on a stretcher being wheeled through the hospital.

And he winced: "I still carry the legacy of that clash which put me out of football for five months.

"Not only did I fracture my skull but I had massive damage to my eardrum and I'm now two-thirds deaf in my left ear.

"So, to this day and for the rest of my life, I will have a reminder of the worst injury I suffered as a Rangers player.

"These days Ally has swapped his job as a youth coach at Ayr United to move to First Division rivals Hamilton Accies as assistant-manager to another former Ibrox defender, Colin Miller.

And, as he desperately tries to get his own message across to his players, he can afford a joke at his own expense.

Ally smiled: "The deafness is a disability to me now but it did help during my career after that when I was playing left-back. I'd be running up the wing and I couldn't hear a word the bench was saying.

FAIR COP... the police heralded the start of Ally Dawson's career

"Mind you, I didn't half take some stick in my good ear when I was trotting back."

Much of Ally's Rangers' career came through the difficult days before the Souness Revolution.

But he will always have one special memory – the day he got to grip his fingers around the Scottish Cup as skipper then turn and hoist it towards his delirious fans.

His moment came in a 4-1 1981 Final replay win against Dundee United and he admitted: "That was the biggest high of my Rangers career. The second game was one of those nights when all your class players click on one night. Davie Cooper and Bobby Russell were absolutely magnificent."

He was to be a casualty of Souness' arrival after 12 years at the club but he did play a key role in the new manager's first trophy win.

Dave McPherson was banned from the Skol Cup Final against Celtic in 1986 and Souness turned to Dawson to fill the void in central defence as Gers won 2-1.

Dawson moved south to Blackburn Rovers and had a spell with Airdrie before beginning his managerial career with a three-year stint at St Andrew's on the sunshine isle of Malta.

Although there is the lingering shadow of that injury, Dawson relished his Rangers' days and said: "It wasn't bad for a boy who thought he was getting nicked back at the start of it all."

Club and Country

IBROX CAREER 1975-87

GAMES

League	218
Scot Cup	36
Lg Cup	39
Europe	23
Total	316

GOALS

League	6
Scot Cup	0
Lg Cup	1
Europe	1
Total	8

MEDALS

Scot Cup	2
Lg Cup	4

SCOTLAND
5 caps

STATS

Jerry DAWSON

JERRY DAWSON was the only player allowed to smoke on the Rangers team bus – fearsome disciplinarian Bill Struth reckoned he was THAT special.

It wasn't that the keeper they called The Doss was a nicotine addict – indeed he was a fitness fanatic – but the manager knew it relaxed him before a game so he could light up. No-one else dared break the rule.

That ritual may have calmed him in the build-up to a big match but when the whistle blew Jerry, who won five title medals and two Scottish Cup badges during the 30s, was like a man possessed.

He terrorised his defenders, swearing at them to get out of his way when he came for crossballs.

And before all the goalkeeping gamesmanship of the modern game Jerry had his own penalty ruse, a mesmerising stare that put so many players off. Celtic, in fact, once missed THREE spot-kicks against him in a Charity Cup Final at Hampden.

They were off-target with two and Dawson held the third from George Paterson before getting up with an enormous grin on his face.

He'd signed for Rangers from Camelon Juniors and, while he wasn't the tallest keeper, he had the qualities that would also mark out his 90s' successor, Andy Goram.

Lightning reflexes, superb anticipation and bravery above and beyond the call of duty.

Dawson did have one weakness that Goram didn't possess, though – he couldn't kick a dead-ball to save his life. And boss Bill Struth told him so when he was an ambitious kid dreaming of a top team call-up.

Jerry listened intently and knew a better life than the pits beckoned if he could just solve his problem. He spent weeks practising – kicking lumps of coal!

He ruined a few pairs of boots and never did quite master the art. Dawson had a bizarre habit of falling sideways after one of his erratic kicks and gave his team-mates no end of anxiety.

But, in the end, Struth knew he could have his full-backs take goal-kicks and leave The Doss to his shot-stopping heroics.

Jerry was a showman who became a hero to the Gers fans – even making them laugh when he was SENT OFF. That came in a match with Airdrie when he'd deliberately punched a forward instead of the ball going for a cross.

Dawson stripped off his keeper's jersey and gave it to deputy keeper Scot Symon before the official ref had even decided on what action to take.

Years later Jerry would smile: "I knew I'd be ordered off and I was in two minds whether to take my shorts off and become the first Rangers' streaker."

Dawson won the Scotland No.1 slot in

A BORN SHOWMAN ...The Doss alias Jerry Dawson

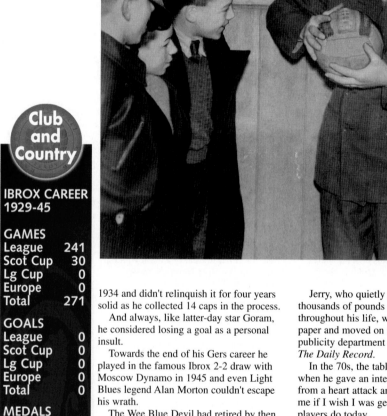

Club and Country

STATS

IBROX CAREER 1929-45

GAMES
League	241
Scot Cup	30
Lg Cup	0
Europe	0
Total	271

GOALS
League	0
Scot Cup	0
Lg Cup	0
Europe	0
Total	0

MEDALS
League	5
Scot Cup	2

SCOTLAND
14 caps

1934 and didn't relinquish it for four years solid as he collected 14 caps in the process.

And always, like latter-day star Goram, he considered losing a goal as a personal insult.

Towards the end of his Gers career he played in the famous Ibrox 2-2 draw with Moscow Dynamo in 1945 and even Light Blues legend Alan Morton couldn't escape his wrath.

The Wee Blue Devil had retired by then but had been sent to spy on the Russians. He returned to say that they tended not to shoot from long distance.

Yet George Young revealed later: "It took all of three minutes to disprove that theory when they blasted home a free-kick.

"Jerry hadn't bothered too much about organising a wall and he was caught out. He was absolutely furious!"

When he left Gers, Dawson played for his hometown side Falkirk before a successful spell managing East Fife which ended after a boardroom bust-up.

He then held a post as a journalist on the *Sunday Mail* sportsdesk where I spent so many lonely nights writing this book.

Jerry, who quietly raised hundreds of thousands of pounds for a host of charities throughout his life, was much loved at the paper and moved on to work in the publicity department of the Mail's sister title *The Daily Record*.

In the 70s, the tables were turned on him when he gave an interview after recovering from a heart attack and he said: "People ask me if I wish I was getting the money players do today.

"But, listen, I got £14-a-week and a joiner got £3 so in comparison I was well-off. And, of course, I saw a lot of the world too.

"In some ways keepers today have it a lot easier because players can't barge you. But then again, they also have to keep track of these plastic balls which bounce and blow all over the place!"

Jerry Dawson died at the age of 67 in January 1977 after battling through four heart attacks.

He will always be remembered by the other nickname that lived with him through his playing days – The Prince of Goalkeepers.

Kevin DRINKELL

KEVIN DRINKELL has a confession to make. He turned Ian Andrews into one of the biggest Old Firm scapegoats of all time – by standing on his toes.

COOL DRINKS ... Kevin Drinkell kept his head to score in one of Rangers most famous wins

Club and Country

IBROX CAREER 1988-89

GAMES

League	36
Scot Cup	8
Lg Cup	6
Europe	4
Total	54

GOALS

League	11
Scot Cup	5
Lg Cup	2
Europe	1
Total	19

MEDALS

League	1
Lg Cup	1

STATS

The grizzled Englishman was a shrewd Graeme Souness signing from Norwich City in 1988 and he was to play a vital role in one of the most famous wins in the club's history within six weeks of arriving.

Old Firm fans dream about drubbing their rivals, fantasise about scorelines like 5-1.

This season within a week of the match Celtic had even released a video of their efforts after caning 10-man Gers at Parkhead.

Yet Kevin will always remember that when his team marched 5-1 up on the Hoops at Ibrox there was still 27 minutes left on the clock!

Drinks helped carry out a footballing murder in the August sunshine in front of a stadium full of stunned witnesses.

The experience still lingers and he said: "Old Firm games had been out of my scope. I mean you don't really know anything about them in England.

"You hear about them, of course, but then you run out into all that Glasgow passion and it's something completely different. We fell behind to Frank McAvennie's goal after just two minutes – then I knew what it was all about."

Against a Celts side who'd won the Double the year before, Gers were to storm back from that setback when Ally McCoist levelled before Ray Wilkins put them in front with one of the sweetest volleys Ibrox will ever see.

Then came the goal that tore a keeper's Celtic career to ribbons when McCoist looped a speculative backward header miles into the air and ran away in delight and disbelief as Andrews fumbled it into the net.

Drinkell, though, confesses he was an accomplice in a little soccer crime and he said: "Ian Andrews was slaughtered after that game and it was unfair. I have to admit I did stand on his toes when Ally's header began to loop up into the air.

"He was hampered and hassled after that, he never got in the right position and he palmed it in.

"But that was the only goal he could be blamed for that day. Ray Wilkins screamed a volley past him and I never scored many better headers than that one."

Kevin's strike, a soaring header after some trickery from Mark Walters who himself ended the rout, summed up an influential campaign that saw him break McCoist's five-year run as the club's top league scorer.

With Super Ally toiling through hamstring trouble all that season, the part Drinkell played in bringing the title back to Ibrox cannot be underestimated.

He recalled: "When I signed, Walter Smith told me I had to watch my back because I was partner no.23 for Ally at Rangers but as it turned out he was injured for much of the campaign.

"I was the one constant that season and I had everybody up there beside me from Scott Nisbet and Ian Ferguson to Mark Walters and even an ageing Andy Gray for a few games at the end.

"I only had the one full season at Ibrox but I'm glad it meant something. That, remember, was the first of nine-in-a-row."

Drinkell had been bred on the wrong side of the football tracks in the Yorkshire fishing port of Grimsby. He remains imbued with the down-to-earth qualities that his upbringing brought him.

The season in the fierce spotlight of Glasgow is still one he treasures. It was his first chance to mix with international stars every day.

But he reasoned: "People always look upon your time at Rangers as the pinnacle but there were other good times for me.

"At Grimsby we won the old English Third Division when I was the original local boy made good and I will never forget that.

"I also played in a good Norwich team before Gers but the fact I still live in Stirling to this day – a decade after my time at Gers – shows how much Scotland came to mean to guys like myself and Terry Butcher."

The arrival of Rangers' first high-profile Catholic signing, Mo Johnston, was to spell the end of the road at Gers for Drinks.

He joined Coventry City before coming back north to finish his playing days at Falkirk and starting his managerial career at lowly Stirling Albion.

He had the club consolidated in the First Division but was left with his hands tied as no cash came in and his side broke up. They were relegated and he was cruelly cut loose from the job.

The man who had a right to be regarded as one of Scotland's most promising young bosses is now serving his apprenticeship for the second time at Montrose.

Jimmy DUNCANSON

SCORING against Celtic, the attribute always destined to make you a Rangers hero.

Jimmy Duncanson had the knack. A dyed-in-the-wool Bluenose, Jimmy's fervour never clouded his cold-eyed talent for striking in the white-hot heat of the Old Firm fixture.

He claimed 22 goals against Celtic and that was the finest tally for a Rangers player post-war until the arrival of Ally McCoist.

The fiery redhead, who could switch from inside-forward to outside-left, first joined Rangers in July 1938 from Dunoon Milton Rovers but the war robbed him of six years with the club.

He earned two wartime caps for Scotland and his pace and aggression made him a firm favourite with the fans when the conflict was over.

Duncanson and Ibrox legend Willie Thornton had an innate understanding and Jimmy rapped home 15 goals as Gers landed their first ever domestic Treble in 1949.

He was to gather eight honours with the club, three league, three Scottish Cup and two League Cup badges.

Those were the material gains of his Ibrox career but Duncanson left behind another legacy.

Sixties legend Ralph Brand recalls the core of decency Jimmy brought to being a Ranger before he ended his career with spells at St Mirren and Stranraer.

Ralph said: "He was there when I started coming through from Edinburgh to train at the club as a snotty-nosed kid.

"I was in awe of Jimmy Duncanson yet he was so down-to-earth.

"He would stop and talk to me about football and I never forgot the way he conducted himself, I used it as a lesson.

"Inside there was decency then and also a frightening determination – on and off the park.

In May 1971 Jimmy, who'd hung up his boots 16 years earlier, collapsed at his Glasgow home.

He awoke a week later in Killearn Hospital after a brain operation with his left side paralysed from head to toe.

Doctors told him it would be two years before he could walk again.

Jimmy did it in SEVEN MONTHS.

Not only that he was driving his car and back at work as the manager of a warehouse firm.

He said back then: "I wept when I woke up in hospital and found myself paralysed.

"I had lost a week out of my life when I was unconscious and I didn't even know they had operated on my head.

"All I knew was that I woke up and my left arm and my left leg were useless.

"But there and then I knew I was going to get well.

"For all my football memories one of the greatest of my life was when I was lying in hospital and found I could move two toes on my left foot.

"I shouted to a male nurse that I could move and he said: 'What do you want me to do – throw a party!' I laughed and I never looked back.

Duncanson went on to recover and live a full life, his place as a medical miracle man now established.

His place as a Rangers legend had long since been secured.

Club and Country

STATS

IBROX CAREER 1946-50

GAMES

League	93
Scot Cup	17
Lg Cup	30
Europe	0
Total	140

GOALS

League	41
Scot Cup	7
Lg Cup	11
Europe	0
Total	59

MEDALS

League	2
Scot Cup	3
Lg Cup	2

SCOTLAND
1 cap

GORDON DURIE wrote himself into the game's folklore when he became only the THIRD man to hit a hat-trick as his team clinched the Scottish Cup – then he found the match would forever be remembered as the Laudrup Final!

Such was the brilliance of Danish superstar Brian, who also scored twice in the 5-1 annihilation of Hearts at Hampden in 1996, that memories of that day will always be dominated by his 90 minutes of soccer sorcery.

Yet Durie's contribution to a clinical execution should never be forgotten. The perfect team player grabbed a gallon of glory for himself.

So often Jukebox's selfless running has set up others to grab the headlines. This time it was his turn and it was all down to a secret phone call from son Scott.

Durie – whose feat was the first for 24 years since Celtic's Dixie Deans claimed a treble in the 6-1 win over Hibs in 1972 – smiled: "Scott phoned before the game and said he wanted to see his dad score three in the Final.

"Never in my wildest dreams did I dream I would do it but the wee man was there to see it and he got my jersey too."

His 23 goals – despite a six-week break for a hernia operation – made Gordon Gers' top scorer for the only time of his Ibrox career to date and he lifted a £50 wager because he beat Paul Gascoigne!

It was the perfect domestic end to the season of his life.

And Gordon would go on to lead the line for Scotland in all three of our games in England at Euro 96.

One image of Jukebox during that tournament sums up the commitment he gives to the cause whether the jersey is of a light or dark blue hue.

Inevitably, it came in the 2-0 defeat from England at Wembley. With the Scots still only one down Durie's head was swathed in blood-soaked bandages yet he still rose to send in the effort that looked a certain equaliser until David Seaman's fingertip save broke five million hearts.

Gordon reflected: "At Euro 96 I had the best time of my Scotland career. I started all three games and the spirit of the fans was brilliant.

"The Scotland camp has a video expert called Brian Hendry and he gave all the players tapes of the fans' party at half-time.

"Our boys were giving it the lot to Status

Gordon DURIE

GOOD GORD ... Durie has been a tireless servant for both Rangers and Scotland

IBROX CAREER
1993-present

GAMES
League	117
Scot Cup	17
Lg Cup	9
Europe	24
Total	167

GOALS
League	43
Scot Cup	9
Lg Cup	2
Europe	5
Total	59

MEDALS
League	3
Scot Cup	1
Lg Cup	1

SCOTLAND
43 caps

STATS

Quo's Rockin' All Over the World and One Step Beyond by Madness.

"Those scenes were amazing. Yes, I hated the result but really who could forget Wembley?"

There have been highs for Durie ever since his footballing journey began at the humble roots of East Fife before he won his move to Hibs.

He hit the big time at Chelsea and Spurs down south before sealing the deal he wanted to come home to Gers.

And throughout his career he has always kept developing, ever the willing worker ready to learn. No-one will ever be able to accuse Durie of wasting his talent.

He has played for Scotland at a time when being handed the striker's jersey is often a precursor to accepting an extremely thankless task.

Boss Craig Brown has tailored a side without stars to work feverishly for one another and none more so than up front where the players must constantly track back to help out.

Durie's diligence fits the role perfectly and he has won deserved praise for international displays full of sweat-soaked desire.

Amidst the graft of 43 caps there have been rewards.

He broke a six-year Scotland scoring famine with the predatory header that sealed the 2-0 win over Latvia at Parkhead and took us to France 98.

And he said: "The goal capped it all off for me, especially since it was the first for

such a very long time. I feared that not playing regularly for Rangers in the run-up to the Finals would count against me but Craig Brown stuck by me."

The reason is the same that prompted Dick Advocaat into securing the veteran Durie's future as one of his first major moves in charge.

They know they have a player who will always work for the team before attempting to bask in his own personal achievements.

The only blight on Gordon's Ibrox career has been injuries, ankle ligament damage has wrecked his season under the new boss.

Still, while he's 33 and in his 18th season in the pro ranks there's few would bet against there being a few hits in the Jukebox yet.

Ian DURRANT

SEVEN OPERATIONS, 1,000 stitches yet still he remains one of THE footballers of his generation.

The flashing studs of Aberdeen's Neil Simpson may have ripped in and smashed apart Ian Durrant's right knee but they could never break his spirit.

October 8, 1988 – when the red mist enveloped model pro Simpson during a frenzied match and his horrendous tackle cost Durrant almost three years of his career – is a date etched on Ian's mind.

But he's moved on now, to life after Rangers with Kilmarnock and even a remarkable rebirth of his Scotland career when he earned caps in the wins against Estonia and the Faroe Islands as a Rugby Park player.

His rejuvenation under the shrewd Bobby Williamson at Killie has been one for football purists to savour after two wasted years withering in the shadows at Ibrox.

Truth is, Durrant couldn't bring himself to leave the place. His complex relationship with Walter Smith had left the manager so fearful of risking a talent he prized so much that he kept him wrapped in cotton wool.

Still he stayed until the 10-in-a-row dream's lingering death and the end of a glory-laden era for himself, McCoist, Gough, Goram and the rest.

Now he wears new colours but he confessed: "I don't see the point of trying to con the Killie fans, they know I'm a Rangers man.

"What they also know is that I will give them everything because this is the club who have faith in me to let me play again.

"I take my son Max to see Rangers on the District Bar Loyal bus and it's nice we can sit – as we did against St Johnstone away this season – and hear the fans singing my name.

"Even now, 'He's blue, he's white he's f***ing dynamite, Ian Durrant,' gets the hair up on the back of my neck.

"I've been back now, played against Rangers for Killie which I doubted I'd ever do and Ibrox remains the place in football that feels like home."

Ian Durrant, like Alex MacDonald before him, grew up in the shadow of the stadium in the Rangers heartland of Kinning Park.

He spent his childhood wearing his brothers' hand-me-down Gers strips, dodging through holes in the Ibrox fence to sneak in and watch his hero Derek Parlane.

Few who stood on those slopes ever graduated on to the field of their dreams but

Durrant did – and he went one better.

He recalled: "Some other players will tell you different or give you a safe answer but my fantasy as a kid was to score for Rangers against Celtic at Ibrox.

"And in November 1985 – on my Old Firm debut – I did it.

"My first attempt was blocked but when I turned the ball had sat up and Pat Bonner was lying there helpless. I toe-poked it in and to this day I still don't think it actually hit the back of the net!"

It was evidence, however, that he had arrived and from then until that awful moment at Pittodrie three years later Durrant's star was rising.

He developed a habit of scoring vital Old Firm goals. Researching this book I dug out an old video that chronicles the bitter history of this gripping fixture.

FREEZE FRAME: August 1986 and it's a sublime run from midfield that is spotted by the instinctive football brain of Davie Cooper whose pass is perfection and Durrant slots the winner low past Bonner.

Ian smiled: "It was the best reverse pass I ever saw in my life. FOUR players gone because he guided them the other way with his eyes – that was Coop. I still think about that goal and it brings back the horrible reality of Davie's death.

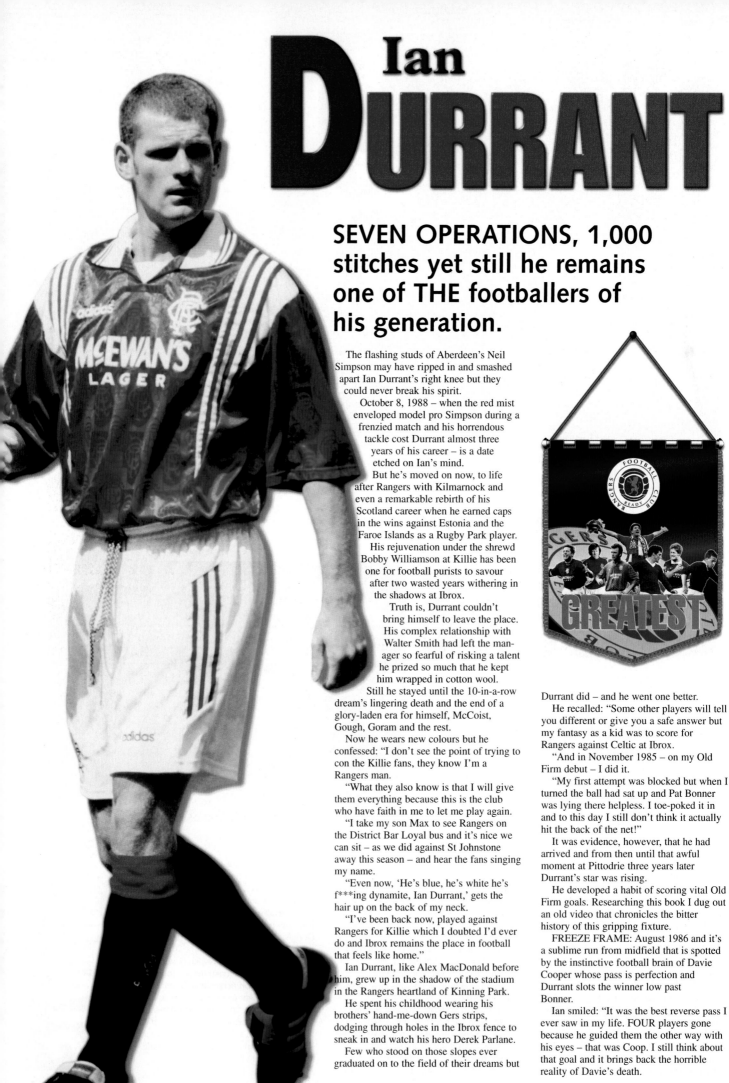

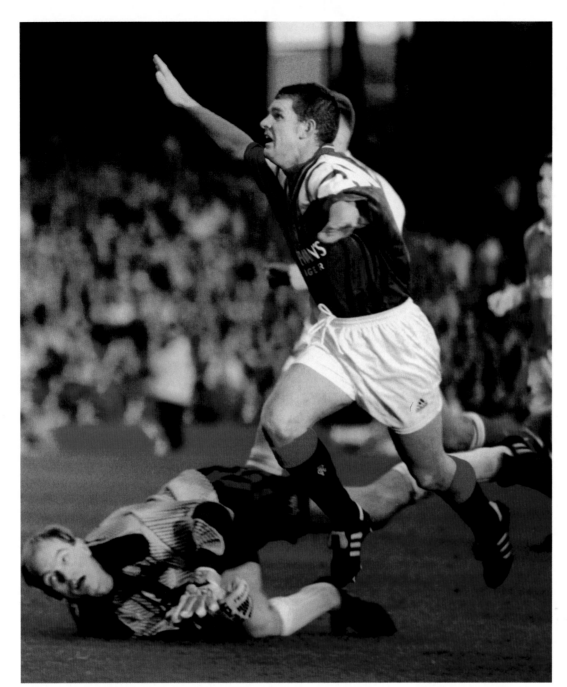

Club and Country

IBROX CAREER 1984-98	
GAMES	
League	249
Scot Cup	19
Lg Cup	40
Europe	39
Total	347
GOALS	
League	26
Scot Cup	3
Lg Cup	8
Europe	8
Total	45
MEDALS	
League	3
Scot Cup	3
Lg Cup	4
SCOTLAND 13 caps	

STATS

"Even now I find it hard to believe he's not here to moan at me any more, he was a true genius."

FAST FORWARD: Two months after that goal Durrant – the midfielder with a striker's instinct – hovered at the back post to collect Cammy Fraser's free-kick and smash home in the Skol Cup Final against the Hoops.

Cooper would score the penalty that brought Graeme Souness his first trophy as Gers boss in a 2-1 win.

Durrant said: "It was after that game that he first said to me he thought I could make it in Italy – like Graeme had at Sampdoria.

"I'd be lying to you now if I didn't say that I think about that, wonder what would have happened but for the injury.

"It's gone now and I have had a truly marvellous life out of football but, yes, I feel the Serie A would have suited me and I hope I would have made him very proud of me.

"We had our ups and downs, though. The worst mistake of my life was when I was talking about asking away and I decided to

have a go at him at training.

"I had a pop at him and when he lunged in back at me, I sprang up to my feet and sneered: 'Is that your best shot?'

"When I looked back I was haring across the training field and he was running after me with Terry Butcher and Graham Roberts on his back! Bad move."

Durrant's closest friend in football remains Ally McCoist and it seemed inevitable that when Ally weighed up his options after he left Gers that he would choose to finish his career alongside his soulmate at Killie.

Behind the endless one-liners and the mickey-taking they are like brothers and Ally confesses that after the injury he thought Ian was finished.

He says with a wry grin: "I thought he would do well to play in a pub league and he made the Champions League."

Durrant shone there too in that 1993 run with stunning goals at Ibrox in the 2-1 win over Bruges and then a classic swerving half-volley in the 1-1 draw away to Marseille.

The story of his career was

destined to be one of heartbreak after that crunching tackle but Ian Durrant chose to rewrite the script.

It was fitting that in a trophyless season filled with so many lows for Rangers the club should mark his testimonial dinner with an afternoon win over Celtic before rushing to a Glasgow hotel to honour a Rangers legend.

And behind the scenes at his benefit game there was a telling insight at the after-match banquet. A crowd of 27,000 had watched a 2-2 draw with Sheffield Wednesday and hailed Durrant's goal as if it were the World Cup winner.

Many feared he would be disappointed at the turnout but he sat in a corner quiet for once and said: "Are you kidding? I ran around there on my lap of honour and couldn't believe it was all for me.

"Remember, I used to have to sneak through the fence to get into this place. I have had my time in the middle of that pitch – now when I stop playing I'll go back to sitting with the guys who were cheering me that night."

Like they say, blue and white dynamite.

Barry FERGUSON

POTENTIAL. Just nine letters but it's a huge word in football.

That's what Rangers have in Barry Ferguson. The potential of a player who can command £15million in the transfer market, the potential to be one of the Ibrox greats. All at the age of 21.

Yet the lavishly gifted midfielder was ready to quit the club and that loss would have been the ultimate cost of the frantic and fruitless quest for 10-in-a-row.

Amid a ruinous, trophyless season that saw the end of his glory-laden era Walter Smith had blooded Barry but dumped him in favour of more experience in the run-in.

The youngster couldn't take it and a talent now tied to Gers until 2003 by shrewd Dutch coach Dick Advocaat came close to turning his back on the club.

As the plaudits rain in and the hype reaches fever-pitch level-headed Barry always remembers his darkest moments as a Rangers player.

They came when he sat in brother Derek's living-room to watch Gers – the club whose midfield they'd both adorned – go two down to Hearts in the 1998 Scottish Cup Final.

Bitterly frustrated Barry was on the outside looking in and he never saw Ally McCoist's late consolation goal. He had stormed out in fury with half an hour left.

He looked back and winced: "If ever I need to keep my feet on the ground after all the good things that have been happening I think back to that day.

"When Stephane Adam scored their second I just couldn't take it any more and I walked out.

"We were behind and I couldn't do anything. As I walked down the street away from Derek's house I felt that it summed up the season.

"I had been in the team from Christmas until February and I had played 10 games and felt good.

"Then all of a sudden I was dropped and I really didn't know why or if I had a future."

He has now. Under Advocaat Barry is flourishing into THE talent of his generation.

And while he will always feel sympathy for Smith – who had unbearable pressure heaped upon him in the chase for that tenth title – the hurt of being sidelined despite all his promise remains.

He recalled: "I thought I could do a good job no matter who else we had and I still feel that.

"I remember winning 2-1 in the Cup against Dundee at Dens and I played alongside Ian Durrant who has helped my career so much.

"Yet after that I was back in the reserves and it was very hard to take."

New Kilmarnock hero Durrant – who

Club and Country

IBROX CAREER
1994-present

GAMES
League	28
Scot Cup	6
Lg Cup	4
Europe	10
Total	48

GOALS
League	1
Scot Cup	0
Lg Cup	1
Europe	0
Total	2

MEDALS
Lg Cup	1

SCOTLAND
1 cap

STATS

LOOKING TO THE FUTURE ...
Barry Ferguson is destined for success at Ibrox

helped mould the young Fergie in the reserves as his own Gers days drew to a close – and Barry's brother Derek once left Graeme Souness pulling his hair out with their off-field antics.

Derek's Ibrox tale was to become one of unfulfilled promise.

He clashed constantly with the iron-willed Souness who had hailed him as a genius after the Skol Cup Final win over Celtic in the first year of his reign.

Yet Barry believes his brother's advice will make him at Rangers – not break him.

He explained: "Derek had bad times under Souness but he plugged away and got his move to Hearts.

"I'm glad it didn't come to that for me but my brother's advice both on and off the park has been invaluable.

"Derek went down a slippery road when he was with Gers and he simply won't allow me to do the same.

"This could all go to my head but I'm

telling you it won't happen because I know the pitfalls."

Barry has a manager who prizes him now, Advocaat and his No.2 Bert van Lingen saw something special in him right away and the contract which ties him to Gers until 2003 was hammered out.

Now the learning continues and Ferguson listens with the former Dutch national coach forever blasting on his whistle to stop training games and show his playmaker new ways to unlock defences.

For Barry his key role is what he has always wanted from the day he stood with dad Archie on the Hampden terraces and watched Derek win the Man of the Match in that 2-1 win over the Hoops.

He smiled: "Derek and Durranty were brilliant that day and it was the first Old Firm game I had been to.

"I was only eight but I remember looking out and thinking: 'That will do for me, I want a bit of that.' "

Derek FERGUSON

HE was 19, he'd slain Celtic and was Man of the Match in a Hampden Cup Final. Derek Ferguson had the world at his feet.

Boss Graeme Souness raved about him and a future as an Ibrox legend seemed assured.

Yet the Rangers career of present day idol Barry's older brother will always remain one of unfulfilled promise.

Derek is philosophical when he reflects on his Gers days and admits he'll never forget October 26, 1986 when he orchestrated a 2-1 Skol Cup Final win to earn manager Souness the first trophy of his Ibrox reign.

Ferguson and Ian Durrant – who scored the opener that day – arrived as Gers stars with commanding midfield displays and Derek said: "That game will live with me forever because my hero Davie Cooper scored the winner and I won that Man of the Match.

"I'd grown up idolising Coop and other Gers stars like Bobby Russell and Jim Bett and now I knew the feeling they'd had of being a winner with the Rangers.

"I remember I had so much belief in Davie that when Roy Aitken fouled Terry Butcher from my free-kick six minutes from full-time I was already walking back for the kick-off! I KNEW he would score the penalty."

Ferguson was flavour of the month with his manager yet bust-ups and bitterness were to scar their working relationship.

Derek hit the headlines in the wake of that Final and he said: "At first Souness rated me so highly. He said I was a better player than he had been at that age.

"But I don't think the comparison with him helped me any. We just weren't the same sort of players. I was never as hard as he was."

When the honeymoon period was over Fergie was painted as a bad boy hitting the town and Souness – just back from playing in the strict regime of Serie A with Sampdoria – cracked down.

They clashed continually and Derek was to leave for Hearts in a £750,000 move.

And he revealed: "Souness told me that if I stayed I wouldn't even be playing in the RESERVES. He made up my mind for me.

"He had come back from Italy and he wanted to instill every Sampdoria habit in us in a crash course.

"But I was a young lad and he should have remembered that he was immature as a kid too. He ran away from Spurs as a teenager.

"We had a mentality that we trained together, played together and drank together and he didn't like that.

"Yet, listen, I was young and I liked going out but when it came towards games I prepared as well as anyone else."

Ferguson was to move on from Tynecastle to Sunderland and Falkirk before switching to current employers Dunfermline.

He knows that most will look upon him as a talent lost and is grimly determined that

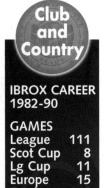

Club and Country

STATS

IBROX CAREER 1982-90	
GAMES	
League	111
Scot Cup	8
Lg Cup	11
Europe	15
Total	145
GOALS	
League	7
Scot Cup	0
Lg Cup	1
Europe	1
Total	9
MEDALS	
League	2
Lg Cup	2
SCOTLAND	
2 caps	

Barry will use up every shred of his massive potential.

Derek said: "I hope I help Barry with things both on and off the park. I don't advise him to live like a monk but he knows now when to have a drink and enjoy himself and when not to.

"Also I'd shoot my mouth off at Souness and I couldn't have cared less about his hard-man reputation.

"I'm sure with Mr Advocaat, Barry has learned to bite the bullet and keep his opinions to himself!"

Ibrox idol. Derek has been there, seen it and worn the RFC T-shirt.

He admits that he worries constantly about his kid brother but playing AGAINST him for the Pars in a 2-0 win for Gers helped quell all of that.

Fergie smiled: "It was an experience because even when it's your own brother you wonder if the hype is building the reputation. It isn't.

"I whacked him a couple of times and he just came back harder. Then I'm looking round and he's moaning and greetin' at all these World Cup stars!

"He was demanding better from them even though he's 21 and I love that.

"I know I'm biased but I have played with Ian Durrant and Paul McStay at the same age and I firmly believe Barry is BETTER."

When we spoke Derek had just been a sub for Dunfermline in a match with St Johnstone. You couldn't help but ask if he thought he'd wasted the skills that brought a paltry haul of just two caps for Scotland.

Yet of all football players Derek Ferguson is able to put the game into perspective.

He came through hell alongside wife Carole when seven-week-old daughter Lauren died after a heart operation.

And he reflected: "Yes, I could have made a few bob more out of the game if I'd stayed at Rangers.

"But I went to a big club in Hearts and I've made so many friends in my days at Sunderland and Falkirk that I just can't be negative about those days.

"Money is not my God and after what happened with my little girl I know there are more important things in life than football."

Ian FERGUSON

IAN FERGUSON is a working-class boy made good, still true to his roots in the East End of Glasgow – but he is also a member of a very elite club which has only three members.

Fergie – alongside Richard Gough and Ally McCoist – is part of a celebrated trio of Rangers players who have every title medal from the nine-in-a-row season.

In the modern Bosman era of player power and big bucks moves, Ian's thoroughly deserved testimonial at the start of next season seems destined to be the last the club awards.

It has been given to a combative midfielder who has worn his heart on his sleeve as a Gers player since Graeme Souness shelled out £1million to St Mirren to bring him to the club he'd supported all his life.

Ironically, Ferguson grew up in the shadow of Celtic Park where the Cross Bar was a Rangers stronghold and a place where punters gathered to take the supporters' bus to follow their heroes.

His footballing heritage site is covered by the sprawling Forge shopping centre these days but Ian smiled: "When I pass it, I remember the days when I was like any other Rangers fan.

"I went on the Cross Bar bus as soon as I was old enough to go to games and two guys called Neilly McLean and Joe Hobbs would lift me over the turnstiles.

"I still sit and think some days that I have come a long way for a wee boy from the East End."

Fergie grew up watching the treble teams of 1976 and 78, little knowing that 15 years later he would be part of a side who emulated their feats.

He would sing the praises of Sandy Jardine and Bobby Russell but one man's passion and commitment to the club always struck a chord.

Ian insisted: "For me, there was only one Mr Rangers. John Greig epitomises everything this club is about.

"I watched those players and that's why it is amazing for me to be able to sit and look at my nine-in-a-row medals and think I'm part of history.

"I don't think there will be another team like ours. Players won't stay as long because of the Bosman ruling and ours was a very special group.

"I don't think that you will ever see that run of success repeated."

"Don't get me wrong. I pray I live to see a 10-in-a-row but it would be very difficult to repeat that kind of dominance with Celtic rebuilt now.

"Ferguson's Ibrox arrival was a soccer saga as he trailed into Buddies boss Alex Smith's office demanding to know if the Rangers rumours were true.

When Smith finally confessed the Souness interest, Ian stepped up his pestering campaign.

He sighed: "When I knew that, I had to leave – but it took three months for the move finally to happen and it felt more like three years.

"I had declared myself and the St Mirren fans gave me a hard time but I've learned to live with that sort of thing.

"All I knew was that if Rangers wanted me, that's where I was going."

Illness and injury have blighted spells of a footballing life at Rangers and Ferguson's strength and tigerish tackling have often overshadowed the fact that he can play a bit of skilful football.

Now Rangers' longest-serving player, he has matured into a shrewd anchor man in the midfield holding role, with the marauding runs forward now curbed.

His rifling shots have brought memorable Gers goals, none more so than a stunning scissors kick that helped win the 1989 Skol Cup Final in a 3-2 classic victory over Aberdeen.

No-one on the current staff is in a better position to reminisce over the Nine – and two games stick out for Fergie.

In 1991 Gers needed to win on the last day against title rivals Aberdeen to clinch it and Ian recalled: "I was sitting in the dressing room watching John Brown take an injection, knowing that his achilles injury could flare up at any minute.

"He realised that would put him out for FOUR MONTHS but he took the needle and he went out to play a brilliant game for us –

until he went down in a heap, as if he had been shot by a sniper from the stand. That summed up the man and how much it meant to him. I think I was the only player who didn't shift position that day.

"I had Mo Johnston beside me in midfield at the end and Mark Hateley was at left-back but we won 2-0 and we did it."

Then, as the ninth crown beckoned, Walter Smith's men won a critical clash 1-0 at Celtic in March 1997.

Ferguson believes that was the killer blow to the Hoops and he said: "Once more we had a patched-up team but I've always felt that bringing back Hateley was a stroke of genius by Walter.

"Listen, I know he was sent off about an hour into the game but by then he had scared

Club and Country

IBROX CAREER
1988-present

GAMES

League	233
Scot Cup	26
Lg Cup	30
Europe	39
Total	328

GOALS

League	23
Scot Cup	6
Lg Cup	8
Europe	4
Total	41

MEDALS

League	9
Scot Cup	2
Lg Cup	5

SCOTLAND
9 caps

STATS

Robert FLECK

ALLY McCOIST has always raved about his perfect striking partners, Mo Johnston and Mark Hateley, but if Robert Fleck had hung around they might never have been needed.

Chunky little hitman Fleck – all bustling bravery and scoring stealth – played a massive part in bringing the title back to Gers after a nine-year absence in Graeme Souness's triumphal first season in charge.

Alongside McCoist, the local boy made good was lethal and he once scored two hat-tricks in the space of four days against Clydebank and then Finns Ilves Tampere in the UEFA Cup.

But just when he was scaling the heights on the park, his personal life was at his lowest ebb as his marriage hit the rocks and he fled Glasgow.

Fleck had a string of bust-ups with the hard-line Souness at Ibrox. He was fined for sneaking out to a disco on the eve of a match with Celtic, then docked another £1,000 for his part in a pub brawl in Airdrie.

And there was one occasion when he could never insist he'd had a bum rap. That was when he bared his backside to the Celtic fans in a Reserve League Cup semi-final defeat at Parkhead on Boxing Day, 1985. He was found guilty of breach of the peace and fined £150. There were, after all, 20,000 witnesses. In one of football's great ironies, Hoops boss Lou Macari would later try to sign the cheeky striker.

For all the difficulties Souness had with Fleck, he never once had a problem with his footballing ability. Robert remains one of the few players the iron-willed boss desperately tried to persuade to stay with the club. It was a disgruntled Souness who said when he left: "Robert Fleck is leaving the city of Glasgow rather than leaving Glasgow Rangers. We had to let him go because of personal problems although we didn't want him to leave."

Typically, though, the deal was a blue chip seller as Fleck went for £580,000. In 1986, the club had accepted a £25,000 offer from Dundee. His goalscoring exploits had seen Robert's value rocket over 20 TIMES in a year.

The peak of Fleck's career came in 1990 when he was phoned on a family holiday in Yugoslavia to be told to pack his bags for Scotland's World Cup Finals warm-up camp in Malta.

And, as boss Andy Roxburgh stunned the Tartan Army by refusing to play the Rangers pairing of Ally McCoist and Mo Johnston up front, former Ibrox idol Fleckie was the main man to benefit.

After Alan McInally and Mo flopped in the humiliating opening defeat by Costa Rica, Robert played a key role in the 2-1 defeat of Sweden then was reunited with McCoist in the heartbreaking 1-0 loss to Brazil.

He had thrived at Norwich, showing the class of a true goalscorer and won a £2.1m switch to Chelsea that sadly turned sour. Last year he joined up with ex-Celtic boss Tommy Burns at Reading last year but was forced to quit the game with a back injury.

He knows he failed to cope with life in the goldfish bowl existence of an Old Firm star and reflected: "The aggro I seemed to attract in Glasgow was unbelievable but in Norwich I was allowed to get on with my life in peace.

"I was sick at leaving Rangers, the club I'd always supported – but away from football, I seemed to get in all sorts of scrapes."

them to death and we had scored the goal that would prove to be the match-winner for Rangers.

"His very PRESENCE there that day struck sheer fear into them because big Mark had haunted them from the first moment he pulled on a Rangers jersey. Of course, that was the day I had my infamous bust-up with Paolo di Canio and he made a snapping gesture as if he was going to break me in two.

"Funnily enough, I waited in the Players' Lounge afterwards and, to their credit, every Celtic player came in to shake hands and talk about the game.

"Every one except Paolo, that is!"

Club and Country

STATS

IBROX CAREER 1983-87

GAMES
League	85
Scot Cup	3
Lg Cup	8
Europe	8
Total	104

GOALS
League	29
Scot Cup	0
Lg Cup	2
Europe	3
Total	34

MEDALS
League	1
Lg Cup	2

SCOTLAND
4 caps

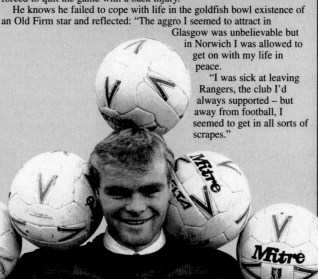

ONE THAT GOT AWAY... Robert Fleck was a class player who had to leave

FALL GUY ... Jim Forrest took the rap for a shaming defeat by the Wee Rangers

IN the wake of humiliation football clubs seek scapegoats and Jim Forrest paid a punishing price for the shame of Berwick.

Scot Symon's Ibrox giants were cut down to size in a 1-0 defeat at the hands of the Wee Rangers at Shielfield in January 1967.

It remains the biggest shock in Scottish Cup history.

Someone had to be blamed for that humbling experience and, as Symon sifted through the wreckage of a miserable display from his stars, he decided Forrest would be the man.

It was a hurtful, harsh verdict.

Jim, a natural-born goalscorer, was jettisoned and left for Preston North End bereft.

If any player in this book of 100 heroes had cause to be bitter about his Ibrox fate it was Forrest.

Yet he said: "I didn't say anything against the club then and even now, 32 years, on I prefer not to go into that.

"Yes, what happened hurt but I'm a Rangers man and you don't start hitting out at them. It's not my style."

Forrest took over from a legend in Jimmy Millar but his bravery, his pace and his aerial ability soon marked him out as a worthy successor.

And he was a hit from the start when he bagged a double in his Old Firm debut, the game that makes or breaks Rangers players.

Yet there was no week-long preparation for Jim, no secret talk telling him he'd been promoted from the reserves to wear Millar's jersey.

Instead he was given 40 MINUTES to prepare for the biggest match of his life in a League Cup tie at Parkhead.

Forrest explained: "Scot Symon would never actually tell you that you were playing.

"It was simply a case of glancing round the dressing-room to see if your boots had been laid out.

"So at 2.20pm I looked about and saw my boots lying there.

"Then I had those 40 minutes to get used to the idea of playing against Celtic.

STATS

IBROX CAREER 1962-67

GAMES

League	105
Scot Cup	10
Lg Cup	37
Europe	11
Total	163

GOALS

League	83
Scot Cup	6
Lg Cup	50
Europe	6
Total	145

MEDALS

League	1
Lg Cup	2

SCOTLAND
5 caps

Jim FORREST

"But that ploy must have worked. I scored twice in a 3-1 win and even now I find it hard to put into words what that day meant.

"The phrase 'dream come true' springs to mind because if there hadn't been a Rangers I really wouldn't have been interested in football."

Forrest played his part in the Treble team of 1964 and the following season he had a campaign that even now makes the likes of Ally McCoist envious.

The Rangers record of 39 goals in a campaign had been held by Willie Thornton but it was smashed to bits as Forrest went on the rampage at home and abroad.

Remarkably, Gers only honour was the League Cup thanks to a 2-1 Final triumph over Celtic as the Hoops won the Scottish Cup and Kilmarnock took the title.

All the while, though, Jim was terrorising defences and he recalled: "It all went right that season and I scored 57 in all competitions.

"I'm proud of that because it's the one record Ally McCoist never managed to steal off anyone!

"He had 14 seasons of trying but he could never reach that one and I'd love to see it stand for a while yet."

That Treble team always looked suited for success on the continent and Forrest proved he could score against the best in that vintage season.

He notched in the first leg in a 3-1 win against Red Star Belgrade and when the clash was tied on aggregate and went to a third game play-off he struck twice to send Gers through at Highbury.

That won a ticket to play Austrians Rapid Vienna and again Gers triumphed thanks to a 2-0 away win with Forrest scoring in a match that saw a virtuoso Jim Baxter performance marred by a broken leg in the dying minutes.

That meant a dream clash with Inter Milan and Gers were surviving in the SanSiro until a sickening fusillade of three goals in as many minutes sent the fireworks

flaring into the Milanese sky. Forrest's strike then seemed little more than a consolation.

But after six minutes of the Ibrox return Jim had breached the Inter defence once more only for the Italians and their infamous Cattenachio defence to shut up shop and survive a torrid tie.

They went on to retain the trophy with a 1-0 Final win over Benfica.

Jim still cherishes the memories but then there was 1967, then there was Berwick.

Then he was shown the door.

And he sighed: "Going to Preston was a nightmare. I was on a downer after what had happened at Rangers and, in all honesty, it reflected in my game."

He came back north after a miserable stay at Deepdale and shone once more in five happy years at Aberdeen that included a 1970 Scottish Cup Final success over his old foes Celtic.

Then Jim began globetrotting with a spell playing for Capetown City in South Africa and a short stint in Hong Kong.

The passports earned another stamp when the Forrests moved on to America and 13 happy years in San Antonio where Jim became involved in the liquor business.

A family illness brought them back in 1988 and placed Jim once more within the shadow of the club he still loves despite the bitter end of his Rangers days.

And he said: "I now live five minutes from Ibrox and I like what I see under Dick Advocaat so far.

"I have been round the world thanks to football but that's the one thing that will never change.

"I still watch the Gers every chance I get."

Torry GILLICK

EVERTON gave their fans a costly Christmas present in 1935, the signing of the gifted Torry Gillick from Rangers.

The price tag was a princely £8,000 which was then the record fee paid out by the Goodison club.

They bust the bank to secure the services of a player who was cast as an inside-forward in those days.

The modern game would prize him as an attacking midfielder with pace to burn who could spring forward and become predator or provider in the front line.

Wing king Willie Waddell lapped up the service that Gillick provided and he was a huge favourite with the Light Blues legions.

He provided managers with a wealth of options as he operated on both flanks and in all three inside-forward berths.

The stocky Gillick had been raised in schoolboy football in Airdrie and joined Gers from Glasgow junior side Petershill.

He made the transition to the big time from life with The Peasie look easy and was a key part of the Ibrox side that won the Scottish Cup in 1935.

Everton smuggled him away, though, and he was to help them to the championship in '39 before the outbreak of World War Two banished most thoughts of football.

Capped five times officially for Scotland after making his debut in a 1-1 draw with Austria in Vienna in 1937, he made three further wartime appearances for his country.

And when the conflict ended Gillick's heart dragged him back to the place where it all began – Ibrox.

The title in 1947 was followed by his second Scottish Cup badge and two League Cup wins before Torry closed out his career at Partick Thistle.

Torrance Gillick earned his place in the Rangers Hall of Fame in trying times.

He ran a Lanarkshire scrap metal business before his death in December 1971 at the age of 56.

Club and Country

STATS

IBROX CAREER
1933-35,45-50

GAMES
League	104
Scot Cup	16
Lg Cup	20
Europe	0
Total	140

GOALS
League	49
Scot Cup	5
Lg Cup	8
Europe	0
Total	62

MEDALS
League	2
Scot Cup	2
Lg Cup	2

SCOTLAND
5 caps

EASY PEASIE ...Torry Gillick joined Gers from Petershill

Tom FORSYTH

DEREK JOHNSTONE'S header hits one post then trickles along the line to glance off the other and roll out, Celtic players can only look on in horror as it is prodded home via the studs of an astonished scorer.

The year was 1973, the game the Centenary Scottish Cup Final at Hampden and Tom Forsyth had just written himself into Ibrox folklore.

That goal used to crackle in front of your eyes on the cinema screen, advertising sports shops. The message was the joy of football and it was all etched into big Tam's face as he ran away.

The finish may not have been a classic but the instinct it took to take Forsyth in there to seal a dramatic 3-2 win had actually been honed as a midfielder at Motherwell.

Jock Wallace saw something in his biting tackles and decided to make a defender out of Tom. He did more than that, he created 'Jaws'.

Forsyth's recollections of the day he won the Cup for Gers are clear to this day and he said: "All the time in the seconds before that goal you can see me willing the ball in.

"All through it, I thought Derek's header was a scorer but then it dribbled out and if you're a Rangers fan it's what you dream of.

"Inches out with an open goal to win the Cup Final against Celtic. My old Motherwell team-mate, Dixie Deans, had stood and ball-watched and I was left all alone.

"All I had to do was knock the ball over the line and I just about managed it!

"I've often thought that it would have been nice to score a screamer but then I look at the record book and it just says Forsyth scored the winner. It doesn't tell you how it went in."

It's one of the images of the last 25 years in Scottish football that sticks with you but there was so much more to Forsyth as a player.

Alongside his trusty side-kick, Colin Jackson, he was a cornerstone of the teams who won the treble twice and the Tartan Army adored him in his 22 appearances for Scotland.

The essence of big Tam was encapsulated in one heart-stopping moment at Hampden in 1976 against England, a game often remembered for Kenny Dalglish's shot that trundled through the legs of the Auld Enemy's distraught keeper, Ray Clemence.

In the last minute of that match, with the Scots 2-1 up, Southampton striker Mick

Channon was haring through and was pulling back the trigger to fire a sickening equaliser.

From nowhere, Forsyth appeared with a heroic tackle to save the day and secure a famous win. The legend of Jaws was now assured.

Tom said: "I suppose that was one of my biggest strengths once I'd settled in defence – timing of the tackle.

"I never really analysed it that much but I do remember at that time it was great to have my club partner, Bomber, alongside me for Scotland.

"He was a terrific player and a great guy, although every time I go into Ibrox these days and see him I walk all hunched up and tell him my back still hurts from carrying him all those years."

In Wallace, Forsyth found a manager who could have been computer-designed to bring out the best in him – Mr Motivator and the heart-on-his-sleeve player who wanted only to do his best for Rangers.

Tom would later go into management as No2 to his treble team-mate, Tommy McLean, at Morton before they spent a decade together at Motherwell and an ill-fated season at Hearts.

They brought the Scottish Cup to Well, of course, after the thrilling 4-3 Family Final win over Jim McLean's Dundee United in 1991.

And Forsyth never lost his admiration for Wallace's feat in moulding two teams to

win every domestic honour within three glory-laden years.

Tom pointed out: "I was a part of both those sides and noticed the very subtle changes Jock made to keep the success going.

"We were all getting older in '78 – the core of the team – and they called us The Over the Hill Mob in some quarters.

"But still he kept faith and at the right time he introduced Gordon Smith, Bobby Russell and Davie Cooper to keep us on track.

"Until you have been striving for a treble, you can't really appreciate the demands that are there.

"As you head towards the Scottish Cup Final and the title run-in, every team seems to try harder, every game gets tougher. To make it is so difficult and Jock did that twice in three seasons."

After Forsyth bowed out of Rangers, the switch into coaching with McLean at Cappielow was almost instant but he also found time to indulge his love of gardening and opened a nursery.

After the Tynecastle episode ended he has concentrated on that and a florist shop his wife runs. But always there is football.

He revealed: "Three days a week I still go the school to coach the kids and it's worth it to keep involved.

"Life has a nice pace right now and my family see more of me but I miss it. Football's like that."

Paul GASCOIGNE

"C'MON GAZZA, we need you – do it for us," the call came from Alan McLaren as an exhausted Paul Gascoigne picked up the ball in a title showdown with Aberdeen.

THE THREE GAZZAS...
Gascoigne at his best, in full flight above, after scoring (above left), and saluting the fans (above right)

With the match poised at 1-1 the wayward genius, who had already adorned the match with one glittering solo goal, glanced up and started running from 20 yards inside his own half. His strength and skills began to shrug the tackles aside.

He surged on, red shirts in his wake as the expectant cheers rose to a tumult until he muscled into the penalty box to sweep a left foot shot beyond the flailing arms of Dons' keeper Michael Watt.

It was one of the finest goals Ibrox has ever seen and Gascoigne completed the fairytale end to his first Gers season with a penalty to seal his hat-trick. Gazza had handed the club eight-in-a-row.

Three years on, McLaren's career has been cruelly cut short by injury and Gascoigne and I sit in the foyer of Glasgow's Moat House Hotel the morning after his close friend's Ibrox testimonial against Paul's new club, Middlesbrough.

Hovering at the doors are the paparazzi and the news reporters despatched by editors hungry for the latest "Gazza Shame" story.

He's been caught on film making a flute-playing gesture to the Gers fans in the 4-4 Ibrox draw – an act that once cost him a £20,000 Ibrox fine when he indulged in more Orange Walk mimicry in an Old Firm game.

That, though, is the package. With the magic comes the madness and a media that created the whole Gazza phenomenon is always ready to clatter him from the pedestal it created when he became the Next Big Thing at Italia '90.

In days gone by this would have been a bleary-eyed Gazza after another night on the sauce but he's on the wagon now.

And he reflects: "There were so many special days for me at Rangers but I don't think that game with Aberdeen could be topped.

"The other players knew how much it meant to me that day.

Club and Country

**IBROX CAREER
1995-98**

GAMES
League	73
Scot Cup	8
Lg Cup	7
Europe	15
Total	103

GOALS
League	30
Scot Cup	3
Lg Cup	4
Europe	2
Total	39

MEDALS
League	2
Scot Cup	1
Lg Cup	1

**ENGLAND
57 caps**

STATS

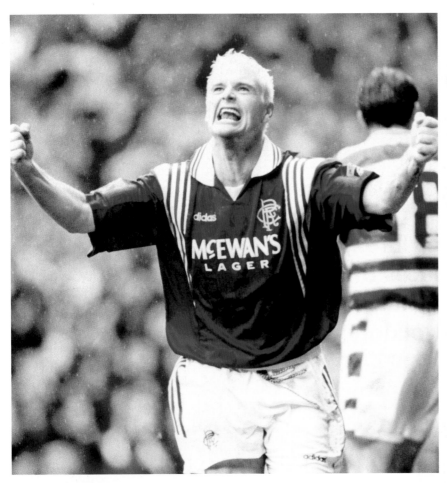

I'll always remember Ian Durrant lifting me on his shoulders and parading me around as I clung on to my match ball.

"I haven't had too many days in the game when everything just clicks the way it did then."

Walter Smith knew what was coming when he brought Gascoigne from Lazio and made him Scotland's record signing in a £4.3million deal.

They arrived at Glasgow Airport with Paul's now ex-wife Sheryl pushing trolley-loads of designer luggage. With Gazza there would always be excess baggage.

Chronicling his Ibrox career is a journey from trauma to triumph, tears to titles.

From his Ibrox debut in a 4-0 pre-season win over Steaua Bucharest when he was stitched up by Ian Ferguson and first aped playing the flute in front of the Gers fans, he was never far from controversy.

There would be red cards in Europe against Borussia Dortmund and then in a shambolic 4-1 defeat from Ajax before an Old Firm early bath in a 1-1 draw two years ago.

Yet for the fans the dark side could be tolerated because of the skills which can still light up any footballing stage.

And Gazza recalled: "I'll always remember when Walter signed me he told he wanted eight, nine then 10-in-a-row. He told me that was why I was coming and that season was special because I was able to

cap it all by winning the Player of the Year awards from both my fellow professionals and the football writers.

"My best memory would have to be that goal against Aberdeen. What makes me laugh even today is the sight of Davie Robertson going mental behind me.

"He's screaming with his mouth wide open and he was just this quiet lad who hardly celebrated anything. That showed how much it meant."

Typically, Gascoigne's Old Firm debut was marked with a goal. A classic as he ran the length of the field to get on the end of Ally McCoist's pass to clip over Gordon Marshall and seal a 2-0 Parkhead win.

The fixture was to take him through the entire gamut of emotions and for all that Celtic fans hated him, there was a grudging respect there too.

He smiled: "In Italy players at every other club talk about Lazio-Roma and how incredible the game is – it's the same in Britain with Rangers-Celtic.

"At Lazio the fans don't care if they lose the UEFA Cup or the league, but if you lose against Roma you'll come out and find your car kicked in. That's how bad it is.

"Well, I've played in both and I can tell you that the Glasgow game is pure HATRED. They despise each other for 90 minutes.

"In my experience, though, that is where it ends. It would

surprise people to know that, when I have been low, I have had letters from CELTIC fans as well as Rangers supporters."

Gazza played a major role in ensuring Rangers' domestic domination and for me, the casting of the England playmaker as the source of all the club's European ills was harsh in the extreme.

He blew it with those red cards but his brilliance illuminated a 2-2 draw with Dortmund at Ibrox and he scored a solo goal against Steaua that is unforgettable.

Gascoigne shrugged: "The stick I took about Europe? Well, the one thing I was always sure of was the headlines whether I played well or had a stinker.

"Listen, I'm human. I'm allowed to have bad games but I also know that, at Rangers, I would be the one singled out if we did well."

Managing Gazza. It's like juggling gelignite. This emotional character was so often wallowing in one crisis or another of his own making off the field.

Smith would haul him out of it. From the pep talks to dragging him round to his own house for Christmas dinner when the troubles with Sheryl started.

The manager went above and beyond the call of duty and Paul said: "I will look back on my Ibrox days as those when people knew how to get the best out of me.

"Walter and Archie Knox were fantastic and their man-

management was magnificent.

"The Gaffer helped me through bad times. He invited me round for Christmas dinner and I said no, but the next thing I knew he was there chapping on my door to bring me round.

"He has a magic family and from the first night out when I argued with his wife Ethel about what love meant, I knew I'd fit in."

The only love affair that ever worked out for Gazza in his three years at Rangers was with the Light Blues fans. It shows no sign of abating.

As he prepared to face the Press to explain himself once more, he told me of plans to do his own autobiography. Where would he start?

Feeling immediate sympathy for the poor bugger who gets that ghost-writing assignment, I asked how it had felt to be back at Ibrox at last.

He said: "The reception I had at Alan McLaren's testimonial was phenomenal and I will be back a lot more now.

"I've broken the duck at last. I said 'Goodbye' on the pitch and now I can come back to be a Rangers fan. This club is part of my family.

"Walter gave me my life back and put a smile back on my face. I enjoyed my football again at Rangers and I hope I repaid him."

On purely footballing terms Paul Gascoigne did that alright – with interest.

Andy GORAM

DEEP inside the heart of Ibrox, tears rolled down the faces of a group of hard men who had written their names into Ibrox folklore.

May 16, 1998 wasn't just the end of a season – it was the end of an era. The team who had achieved nine-in-a-row had been asked to go a bridge too far and they'd crumbled.

Boss Walter Smith had already announced his intention to quit and a trophyless season also meant the departure of a host of Gers legends. Andy Goram was at the core of it all.

For all the lurid headlines about his private life there can be no disputing the right of the man they simply called 'The Goalie' to walk into the Ibrox Hall of Fame.

And he will never forget his last night in the company of the team he believes won't be bettered in Gers' history.

They were all there inside Ibrox after the Scottish Cup Final defeat to Hearts – the men he knew so well.

His gaffer, the No 2 Archie Knox, Richard Gough, Stuart McCall, Ian Durrant, Ally McCoist and Brian Laudrup. All there and all very emotional.

Andy revealed: "The night after we lost the Cup Final we came back to Ibrox and it was very sombre.

"Players were leaving – myself, Ally McCoist, Ian Durrant and the rest – and the management team of Walter Smith and Archie Knox were going too.

"There were people crying whose WIVES hadn't even seen them in tears.

"After seven years it was bound to hurt not playing for the club I love. But I just have to get on with life without Rangers. That's the reality.

"Everyone felt it was the end of something special. Once Walter had said he was going we knew the writing was on the wall for the rest of us."

In seven trophy-laden years at Rangers Goram became the greatest goalkeeper the club has ever had.

Yet it's often forgotten that he was heavily criticised at the start of his Gers career, losing a fluke goal to Hearts' Scott Crabbe and playing a part in a miserable Euro exit at the hands of Sparta Prague in 1991.

The sheer strength of character inside this £1million bargain signing

STATS

Club and Country

IBROX CAREER 1991-98

GAMES

League	182
Scot Cup	26
Lg Cup	19
Europe	31
Total	258

GOALS

League	0
Scot Cup	0
Lg Cup	0
Europe	0
Total	0

MEDALS

League	5
Scot Cup	3
Lg Cup	2

SCOTLAND 43 caps

from Hibs would never allow him to be painted as an Ibrox flop, though.

He became the man Celtic fans loved to hate because he seemed to save the heights of his brilliance especially for them.

At the peak of his powers Gers built a nine-game unbeaten run in Old Firm games and much of it was down to Goram.

His bloody-minded defiance of his bitterest rivals led Celts' boss Tommy Burns to famously say: "When I die they will put on my tombstone: 'Andy Goram broke his heart'."

It's not stretching it to say the influence Goram had on those matches actually contributed a significant part in the downfall of the popular Burns at Parkhead.

And The Goalie said: "All those Celtic victories, I treasured every one.

"There's no doubt in my mind that is the most important thing for the fans – and it was the most important thing for the players of my era.

"They stick a mile out for me and it made me laugh when the guy presenting my video went down to Tommy's new club Reading to interview him.

"He said: 'Goram? Goram? That b*****d is the reason I'm here in the first place'.

"I loved it because I had a lot to do in those games, I never had a quiet one. In

other games for Rangers as a keeper it can become a question of concentration – of making that one save when you're called into action – but not against Celtic.

"And everything you do in those games gets exaggerated."

Perhaps, but there can be no hiding from the fact that some of the saves Goram produced in Old Firm games were almost beyond belief.

The evidence came in a magnificent 3-3 draw between the arch rivals at Ibrox in November 1995 when predator supreme Pierre van Hooijdonk smashed in a volley from point-blank range.

Goram flew across and somehow readjusted his body to paw the ball away. Breathtaking.

Andy smiled: "That game was ridiculous, people still hold up the famous 4-4 match but I thought when they tied it up in that one both teams settled for it.

"Our game was tilting either way right to the finish and there's no question for me that the save from Pierre was the greatest of my life."

Season '92-93 will always evoke precious images for Rangers fans. The team went 44 games unbeaten, they won the Treble and were within a heartbeat of the European Cup Final.

Goram had 25 clean sheets in that campaign and the levels he hit redefined what could be considered a good season for a

keeper. He was immense.

There was a chemistry with that team Andy insists will never be repeated and he said: "There will never be a feeling amongst players at Rangers like the camaraderie we had then. At the time we didn't realise it, we just went with the flow.

"But if we had Paul Gascoigne or Brian Laudrup then we would have won the European Cup. That's a certainty.

"We were a great team who fought so hard in every game – all we needed to go that one step further was the little bit of magic Gazza or Brian would have given us.

"But the friendships made between those players will last forever. When I was at Sheffield United on loan Stuart McCall and Stephen Wright played against us with Bradford and we spoke afterwards about how the bonds between us would never be broken."

So now Goram must get on with his life and someone must take over his mantle. He begs for a fair deal for those who must try.

Andy rates German Stefan Klos highly and believes Lionel Charbonnier was on his way to being his long-term successor before that cruel cruciate ligament injury in the UEFA Cup triumph over Bayer Leverkusen.

Goram stressed: "Charbonnier had a great game against Celtic and then kept the club in Europe against Leverkusen before he was injured.

"I know it is difficult for him to come after me because after a month here I was compared to Chris Woods.

"People should wait until the end of a keeper's stay at Gers and then compare.

"As for me, life goes on but the one thing I will always feel about my connection with Rangers is pride.

"I made the greatest team in the fans' votes and I was a very proud man but I'm proud of everything I achieved at the club. Proud of nine-in-a-row and proud of the people I worked with."

BLUE PRIDE...
Goram is convinced there will never be a closer, more successful team to upstage the proud Gers who equalled Celtic's nine-in-a-row league record

GOUGH TO A FLYER ... Nine skipper Richard was a rock in the heart of defence

Richard GOUGH

THE craggy face of one of football's hardmen crumbled, he bit his lip yet the tears of joy flowed. Richard Gough lifted the league trophy and Rangers had won nine-in-a-row.

No-one played a bigger role in equalling Celtic's fabled championship record than the club's inspirational captain.

And that raw outpouring of emotion at Tannadice on a dramatic night in May 1997 was the sign of the end of an era.

True, Gough would return from America and Kansas City Wizard the following season to try to bail out boss Walter Smith as he was stricken by injury to Richard's £4million replacement Lorenzo Amoruso.

But the skipper sees that season as a vain rescue mission, his real task had been achieved the night he hailed the Nine.

Richard's last campaign ended without a trophy as boss Smith's nagging fears were realised.

Walter had wanted to leave when his team reached Scottish football's Holy Grail but chairman David Murray, for once letting his heart rule his head, persuaded him they could win Ten together.

Amidst the frenzy Gough would be brought back but he reflected: "We tried but perhaps Walter should have followed his instincts and gone after Nine. The next season was a bridge too far."

It all ended in tears of woe this time as even the hope of a silver send-off to the departing heroes was denied them.

As boss Smith, Gough, McCoist, Durrant, Goram, McCall and Cleland bade farewell to the club Hearts rocked them 2-1 in the Scottish Cup Final. It was over.

Richard, bound for America's Major League Soccer again but this time with San Jose Clash, waved goodbye to the Gers faithful at Parkhead.

But he was all cried out and he said: "Leaving the second time around couldn't mean as much as it did after nine-in-a-row. My tears had been shed.

"I'd broken down three times when I left. Once when I lifted the trophy, once when I said goodbye to everyone at the club the next morning and then again when I turned round to look at the stadium for the last time as a Rangers player.

"This time I knew I'd done my best. I came back to help because Walter asked me and Rangers needed me."

Club and Country

IBROX CAREER 1987-97, 97-98

GAMES
League	317
Scot Cup	37
Lg Cup	37
Europe	36
Total	427

GOALS
League	25
Scot Cup	2
Lg Cup	3
Europe	4
Total	34

MEDALS
League	9
Scot Cup	3
Lg Cup	6

SCOTLAND
61 caps

STATS

Gough, born in the Swedish capital of Stockholm and raised in South Africa, had been a long-time target for Gers after he arrived in his dad's native land to earn a contract at Dundee United.

But with Jim McLean reluctant to let him go to a rival it took a successful spell at Spurs before he finally returned north to Ibrox to become the club's first ever £1million signing in 1987.

He was to be a massive influence on Rangers, not only in defence but also on his raids forward. And that was shown in only his second match.

Richard was pitched into an Old Firm match and if these games are usually powderkeg fixtures this one had the whole fireworks factory thrown in!

Referee Jim Duncan toiled from the off and after a skirmish between Gers keeper Chris Woods and Frank McAvennie all Hell broke loose.

Gough recalled: "The actual incident was handbags at dawn, it's hard to believe looking back now all that sprang from it. I felt the referee lost the place."

Woods and McAvennie were sent off, Terry Butcher soon joined them, Graham Roberts went in goal and conducted the Gers fans' singing. And they all ended up in COURT.

Reports were sent to the Procurator Fiscal. Football was in the dock and three players paid with a criminal record.

Richard sighed: "Graham Roberts, who

was probably the guiltiest of the lot got off Scot-free.

"As for the game I remember going two down when big Terry scored an own goal and then he got a red card too, it was like a nightmare.

"It was 10 v 9 when Billy Stark lobbed Robbo but hit the bar and I thought we were looking at a 6-0 hammering.

"But somehow from somewhere we found the reserves for an incredible comeback. I set up Ally McCoist to pull one back and what happened next was a dream.

"Durranty set off on a lung-bursting run down the right and when his cross was blocked he got another over and it broke to me four yards out to poke in an equaliser. What a debut.

"I just remember how distraught their players were and a true Celtic man like Peter Grant slumping to his knees in the penalty box, just the way the Gers fans liked to see him!"

These days the most successful captain in Rangers' history can be found in San Jose's Britannia Arms when he's with him family. You'll catch him there early morning enjoying his fry-up and watching the Gers games come in on satellite.

He pays his $20 with the rest of the punters then smiles when they remind him of games like his first as Gers captain after Graeme Souness' sensational decision to axe Terry Butcher.

That came before a Skol Cup semi-final

with Aberdeen in 1990 and Gough said: "Terry had come back from the World Cup Finals where he had been outstanding for England but he wasn't right. His knee was giving him Hell and Graeme was so angry.

"Terry scored an own goal at Tannadice that was the final straw between them and it all blew up.

"He was dropped and never played for the club again. I have so much time for Terry both as a person and a player and it was a crying shame his Rangers days ended the way they did.

"He has a right to be regarded as a legend at Ibrox. Now here I was, his replacement as skipper."

Gough got off to a flyer in his captaincy when Trevor Steven burst out from his playmaker's role in midfield to seal a 1-0 semi-final win over the Dons.

The Final was against Celtic and Gough wrote a fairytale script to lift his first ever silverware as Ibrox leader.

He smiled: "Who can forget going into extra-time then getting on to the end of a free-kick to poke home the winner.

"I jumped the hoardings and looked into the Rangers End and thought I quite liked being skipper!"

Gough's relationship with the Gers fans has always been a puzzle. They recognised his class but he was never quite allowed the same acclaim as Butcher or Roberts.

They were clenched-fists figures who courted and received adulation. Richard, the ultimate pro and magnificent defensive organiser, simply got the job done.

He was Scotland's Player of the Year in 1989 yet in the last three seasons of nine-in-a-row he refused to be shackled by a veteran tag and played the best football of his life.

Gough was the core of a side who achieved so much and went to within a heartbeat of the European Cup Final in 1993.

While he always was the consummate professional Gough knew the value of bonding and team spirit with that squad.

After all, his most famous quote still remains: "The team that drinks together, wins together!"

When he's reminded of that the smile lingers then dies as he says: "That Champions League season will always live with us all when we look back on our careers because we were so close.

"Marseille edged us out and beat AC Milan in the Final then became embroiled in the bribes scandal and I have to say that throughout that campaign we felt there were things not quite right about their games.

"So much has been uncovered already about the skullduggery involved but I believe that to be the tip of the iceberg.

"It hurts that was going on because they were a great team to face and perhaps didn't need it but the fact remains they cheated to get past us."

That was the one prize that eluded a player who won 61 caps in a stormy Scotland career before he quit after a bust-up with boss Andy Roxburgh.

Somewhere in a secret bank vault in Glasgow lie nine title medals, three Scottish Cup and six League Cup badges. They are the deposit of glory in the account of a legend.

John GREIG

"LEDGE, haw Ledge!," the cry echoes down the marble staircase from the players' lounge as the instantly recognisable figure makes his way through Ibrox.

TRUE GRIT ... John Greig who earned the nickname Ledge

John Greig MBE is heading towards the PR chief's cramped office in the inner sanctum of the stadium.

On other days during 40 years at Rangers his studs have clattered off the dressing-room floor and his brow has furrowed over problems at the imposing desk in the manager's lair.

That's why he has the nickname. Ledge, you see, is simply short for LEGEND.

He began to earn that tag on September 2, 1961 when Ian McMillan was rested and a nerve-ridden teenager was given his debut against Airdrie.

Freed for now from fending off newspaper hacks and finding players for TV stations to interview, Greig perches forward in his seat and smiles: "Remember my first game for Rangers, how could I bloody forget it?

"When I ran out at Ibrox that day I suddenly realised my dreams were coming true.

"It all seemed a million miles away from dribbling a tennis ball round someone in the street and trying to flick it between the fence and a lamp-post to score.

"Now here I was playing head tennis with Jim Baxter over a broom stuck between two chairs as he tried to calm me down before I went out.

"Yet when we got there I scored the opener, we won 4-1 and I was off and running."

As a kid at Ibrox, Greig was surrounded by greatness. Bob McPhail took him aside for fatherly advice and Jock "Tiger" Shaw – then third team boss – used to give him a run to Queen Street in his beat-up old Vauxhall to get the train home to Edinburgh.

When he graduated through the ranks the train journey from the capital saw him fighting over who paid for the toasted rolls with Jimmy Millar, Ralph Brand and Billy Stevenson.

Millar and Brand, the lethal M&B Partnership, constantly talked tactics while Stevenson pondered the daunting task of finding a way into the team past Jim Baxter.

Greig, then an inside-right who dreamed of making the No.8 jersey his own, pointed out: "Billy joined the great Liverpool side instead, that was the quality we had.

"I was very lucky as a kid to experience those journeys. Those guys helped me overcome any nerves when I got into the first team."

Greig's grit and guile was to become the perfect balance for Baxter's flair and flamboyance on the left.

Boss Scot Symon knew what he had, a natural born leader. It was only a matter of time before he handed him the armband.

And John said: "That was one of my proudest moments – the day he asked me to be captain of Rangers.

"I'd looked at men like Bobby Shearer, Eric Caldow, Ian McColl, Willie Woodburn and Davie Meiklejohn and thought they were legends.

"Now if I was spoken about in the same breath as them I knew I was getting somewhere."

Greig's steel and skill helped his side to the Treble in 1964 but in the East End of Glasgow Jock Stein was about to begin fashioning a footballing dynasty. Celtic's Lisbon Lions were coming.

Their incredible European Cup triumph over Italian giants Inter Milan was to spark nine championships on the

WATER
MOMENT ...
John Greig
with the Cup
Winners' Cup
in 1972

trot. When Rangers threatened to shatter under the pressure, John was the glue that held them together. English champions Everton came calling, Bill Nicholson's Spurs wanted his signature.

When Rangers needed him, Greig stayed put. He confessed: "Yes, during the days of adversity when Celtic had the Lisbon Lions I could have left this place.

"I think the fans knew that but they also knew I would always give it 90 minutes and they also knew I'd chase every lost cause.

"And I believe those were the days that cemented the relationship I have with the hard-core Rangers support to this day."

Those fans prize the enduring image of Greig, a toothy grin glinting through the goatee beard as he parades the Cup Winners' Cup around Ibrox on the team's return from the 3-2 Final win over Moscow Dynamo in Barcelona in 1972.

Eleven years earlier he had been a disgruntled young player gutted at failing to make the travelling squad for the Final with Fiorentina.

Defeat then hurt but a repeat in 1967 against Bayern Munich in Nuremberg, a week after Celtic became the toast of Europe, cut to the quick.

And John stressed: "By the time Barcelona came I had witnessed two Finals and we had lost both. I was a mature player by then and I felt a huge responsibility.

"It has been proved since how hard it is to reach that stage of a European tournament and I felt like I had this massive weight on my shoulders."

Incredibly, he faced the biggest game

of his life with a broken bone in his foot.

He hid the extent of the injury from the club and paid secret visits to a specialist in Edinburgh three times a week as the Final loomed.

Greig has always suspected boss Willie Waddell knew how badly his most influential player was struggling.

And he reasoned: "I think Willie realised if I was taken to a hospital and X-rayed my foot would have been put in plaster and I'd have no chance."

Waddell gambled. John, as always, played through the pain barrier and the rest is history.

When his mind drifts back to that sultry Spanish night and the reverie begins, his face is a mask of contrasting emotions.

The JOY of making history, the PAIN of seeing it soured as the fans spilled onto the pitch to celebrate and pumped-up policemen waded in with their batons thumping into their targets.

John sighed: "It's one of the biggest highs of my career yet one of the biggest disappointments too.

"The Spanish police completely mishandled the whole situation. I could have understood their actions if there were 30,000 Russians there as well and there was a chance of friction.

"But there were NONE, all this was Gers fans celebrating. Who were they going to fight with – themselves?

"That deprived my team the chance of celebrating and denied the fans the party they deserved. We were eventually banned from Europe for a year and that team broke up without a chance of us defending the trophy."

Club and Country

STATS

IBROX CAREER 1960-78

GAMES
League	498
Scot Cup	72
Lg Cup	121
Europe	64
Total	755

GOALS
League	87
Scot Cup	9
Lg Cup	17
Europe	7
Total	120

MEDALS
League	5
Scot Cup	6
Lg Cup	4
Europe	1

SCOTLAND
44 caps

Greig, though, would inspire the rebirth of the blues under Jock Wallace.

He was the beating heart of the Treble sides of 1976 and '78 and when Wallace announced his bombshell decision to quit in the wake of that second clean sweep there was only one man Waddell would turn to.

When the news broke, the Ibrox skipper was watching his nephew playing in a junior match. He went straight home to bed. He knew a taxing day was ahead.

After 496 league matches and a record 857 games in total for the club, the veteran footballer became a rookie manager.

The emotional scars of what eventually became a torrid reign in the hotseat remain and Greig reflected: "The most disappointing aspect of that whole episode was that I had signed to PLAY for another year.

"We'd just won the Treble and we had another shot at the European Cup and although I was 36 I still felt I could do a job. In the last six years of my career I devoted myself to playing.

"When the players had days off I'd train but I didn't grudge it because it was buying me extra years. Management took all that away from me."

An American Dream of two years playing and coaching in the States was gone. Instead Greig strode from the dressing-room to the manager's office.

Yet he insisted: "With hindsight people ask why I took the job. How could I turn it down?"

CONTINUED ON
NEXT PAGE ...

John GREIG

...CONTINUED

"Whether I was ready or not didn't matter because, if I hadn't taken it, for the rest of my life I would have wondered what it would have been like."

Against the unreal backdrop of a stadium with just three sides as the rebuilding of Ibrox began, Greig knew the time was coming to reconstruct Rangers on the field.

It would ultimately mean the demolition of a side that meant so much to him – the team who had twice swept all before them in Scottish football.

Yet in his first season as boss the club won two cups and marched into the last eight of the European Cup.

It is a measure of the frenzy of football in the bitterly-divided city of Glasgow that this campaign is often only remembered by Gers fans as the season Celtic won the league after winning the decisive Old Firm match with 10 men.

That still rankles and John pointed out: "In Europe we beat Juventus – with seven of Italy's 1978 World Cup team – and PSV Eindhoven, who hadn't lost at home in 25 years of European games until we defeated them.

"We lost to Cologne in the last eight and that game proved one thing to me.

"I looked at the faces and I knew for some of them they had accepted it was the end for them at this level.

"The problem has always been lurking, I had to manage a team I'd played with and seven of them were over 30.

"Now I could see that I HAD to change it because you must always have ambition at this club.

"I had seen Rangers move on Jim Baxter, Alex Scott, Ralph Brand and Jimmy Millar. I knew it had to be done with these guys too but it was very hard."

Seasons of transition – they are allowed at Rangers and Celtic but only if you keep winning trophies. That's an Old Firm reality check.

As Greig battled to recreate former glories in the eerie setting of the Ibrox building site the pressure mounted.

The New Firm of Aberdeen and Dundee United emerged and as Gers toiled the worry lines etched into that famous face.

It all ended as scarves rained down on the track in disgust after a string of home defeats and John quit a broken man.

He admitted: "Yes, I was hurt when the scarves came on although deep down I felt the real Rangers fans knew the difficulties.

"But it hurt all the more that my wife and son suffered terrible problems because of my job.

"They bottled it up, never told me about it at the time. I wish I had known then because I would have gone earlier. Nothing means more to me than my family.

"Yet, out of the thousands of Rangers fans, the ones throwing scarves were in a minority. Even when I left the respect I got from supporters was unbelievable.

"In an odd sense it enhanced my reputation because a lot of fans thought I was hard done to.

"When I left, though, I knew I NEVER wanted to be a manager again."

John didn't want to work for any other club and everyone knew it. For seven years he put himself

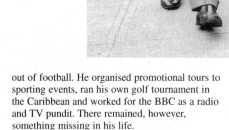

DRESSING-ROOM TO MANAGER'S OFFICE ... John Greig with Willie Waddell

out of football. He organised promotional tours to sporting events, ran his own golf tournament in the Caribbean and worked for the BBC as a radio and TV pundit. There remained, however, something missing in his life.

The gap was filled by Graeme Souness who encouraged chairman David Murray to bring Greig back to Rangers.

It was Souness, too, who first gave John the nickname Legend in a training ground bust-up with Ally McCoist and Ian Durrant.

Graeme encouraged Greigy to don the boots again for a game but Durrant and McCoist kept shouting to John: "Here, Gaffer."

Souness' anger boiled until he screamed: "Look, I'M The Gaffer – he's a LEGEND!" The name stuck.

John had known Souness from their Edinburgh days and often travelled south to watch the Scotland skipper and Kenny Dalglish in action for Bob Paisley's Liverpool.

And he revealed: "You know, I told him to his face when he left here for Anfield he was doing the wrong thing.

"But I was delighted Walter got the job. He deserved it and I knew he could do it.

"The days of a manager staying with a club for a long time have gone but his was a great era."

Now Greig is at the heart of a new era alongside Dick Advocaat. Don't be fooled by the PR chief name tag, he means much more than that to the Dutchman they call The Little General.

As the hush-hush moves to lure the former Holland coach to Scotland continued, Greig was given the task of showing Advocaat around.

And John recalled: "One day we were out at the training ground at Stepps blethering.

"Dick said: 'John, you are a football person. I want you on MY team.'"

"That meant a lot. And it has been a tremendous experience so far."

As Advocaat and No.2 Bert van Lingen plot their Rangers' Revolution, Greig's role is vital.

He gives advice on the grounds they'll play on, warns them of unforeseen dangers in the teams they will face.

Greig confesses now that despite his vow never to get back in the hotseat he always kept thinking like a manager throughout the Souness and Smith years.

Now the meticulous Advocaat asks his advice and taps into John's vast knowledge. The respect is mutual.

Greig stressed: "I'm involved again and it's very exciting. I feel like a kid in a candy store once more.

"He has done a marvellous job.

"Remember, he has come to a new culture against new opposition.

"This is a man who has been in charge of the Dutch international team. I shared a pitch with Cruyff and Neeskens and I know how good that nation is.

"For the last 30 years that's the one country I've watched develop and admired.

"Now we have their manager and our chairman deserves a medal the size of a frying pan for getting him."

January 1999 saw Advocaat and Greig, two football men thrown together in the one cause, strolling in Florida near the Orange Bowl in Miami.

Dick had led his country there at the World Cup Finals five years earlier.

And Greig said: "He pointed over to it and I could see the pride in his face.

"Dick said to me: 'John, they say football is about today and tomorrow but sometimes the past matters too.'"

Greig is desperate to help shape Advocaat's bright future now but it's his own history that has earned him the nickname he deserves – Legend.

ALL those old guys you've stood beside in pubs who chunter: "Ach, there's no entertainment, where's the characters in the game, eh?" Blame Willie Henderson.

Chances are they once watched a short-sighted 5ft 4ins winger whose ball control and speed made him unstoppable when he was in full flow.

Henderson was to Rangers what his great friend Jinky Johnstone was to Celtic. Yep, it's like the old guy said – he was an entertainer.

He was the jewel in the crown of a glittering array of talent up front during a golden era in the early part of the Swinging 60s.

Willie forced the excellent Alex Scott out of the side one season and inspired his side to the Treble the next.

He was a sparkling part of a team who consistently challenged the best in Europe.

Henderson's side were hammered 6-0 in Spain by Real Madrid in 1963 but they never forgot the lesson.

Four years later they dumped the likes of Borussia Dortmund and Real Zaragoza – the latter on the toss of a coin – out of the European Cup Winners' Cup.

Willie scored the clincher to see off Slavia Sofia in the semi but there was to be Final agony with defeat from Bayern Munich in Nuremberg.

Then there was the run to the last four of the Fairs Cup before it all collapsed in disgrace on a shameful night when Gers fans rioted against Newcastle in 1969.

Some lows then but highs too and the eyes surrounded by laughter lines twinkled behind the trademark tinted glasses as Henderson recalled: "Rangers were well to the fore and we had a forward line that everyone could rhyme off the tip of their tongue – sadly they did it BACKWARDS. Wilson, Brand, Millar and Henderson!

"It was a marvellous time in Europe for this club and that defeat was in the days of the great Real Madrid team of Puskas and Di Stefano. Truth is we were known throughout the continent and not many wanted to draw us.

"These days those players are a misty memory for many but I'm telling you there were teams around then who were phenomenal yet we competed very well in the European arena."

Domestically, there was a time when Henderson helped fashion complete dominance as that Treble in '64 suggests.

Willie HENDERSON

The star who made his debut as a 17-year-old kid in a 2-1 win over Clyde revelled in it all.

And he smiled: "I'll always remember one day when we played against Celtic in the Scottish Cup at Ibrox and I picked the ball up ten yards inside my own half.

"I went on a mazy run and beat two or three players, beat the linesman and dodged the referee before unleashing a left foot shot into the net.

"I waved to the Celtic fans and got back to the halfway line to look up at one of their players.

"His face was all twisted with hatred and he insisted I was a piece of fruit then insinuated that I had no mother or father! I rather liked that."

Willie was to leave Ibrox for Sheffield Wednesday and eventually Hong Kong Rangers. He left the fans with a thousand memories.

When you go back in time with Willie Henderson, though, it is no journey into the past with a sad ex-player hankering for former glories. He devours life now just as he did then.

The big cigars have never been far from his lips since he quit. He lived for eight years in the sunshine of Fuengirola, owned a pub on the Costa del Sol and another one in Belfast.

He shrugged: "That's the norm for football players because when you retire it's a bit late to start studying to be a lawyer.

"I loved my game as much as I love life. I mean once you're in that pine box you don't have a lot of time to enjoy yourself."

Henderson's outlook on life is admirable, his motto No Regrets. But when you scratch the surface, he reveals the reason behind the only sadness that tinged his time with the club.

This little genius – who left Gers with the honours from four Scottish Cup, two league and two league cup victories – sighed: "My favourite manager was Scot Symon who was a proper gentleman. It was a great shame when he left.

"If Symon had always been the manager then Willie Henderson would have been a one-club man.

"Any player who had been here for 12 years would have a lump in his throat going out the door and I was no different."

Yet he couldn't let the interview end there – not on a downer.

One more stroll down Memory Lane takes you into the heart of Glasgow during Henderson's heyday.

And he recalls: "I was walking down Sauchiehall Street and two young ladies were walking down with Gers scarves on.

"One was whispering to the other: 'That's Willie Henderson.' When they reached one asked: 'Excuse me, are you Willie Henderson?' I was in a bad mood and gruffly said: 'Naw, Ah'm no.'

"She said: 'Excuse me.' I turned back boiling and said: 'What now?' She replied: 'Well, you're just as ugly then!'"

Club and Country

IBROX CAREER 1960-72

GAMES
League	276
Scot Cup	44
Lg Cup	60
Europe	46
Total	426

GOALS
League	36
Scot Cup	5
Lg Cup	11
Europe	10
Total	62

MEDALS
League	2
Scot Cup	4
Lg Cup	2

SCOTLAND
29 caps

STATS

51

LOVE AND HATE ...
Mark had to win over the
Gers faithful after push-
ing fans' favourite Ally
McCoist onto the bench

Mark HATELEY

HE scored for England against Brazil in the Maracana and starred for AC Milan in the San Siro but Mark Hateley insists there's NOTHING bigger than Rangers.

The man they called Attila the Hun in Italy became a Light Blues legend as he marauded through defences in a deadly partnership with Ally McCoist.

Yet the striker who would be at the centre of many Gers triumphs endured six months of hell when he came to the club at first.

He had been out injured for the best part of 18 months with Monaco before Graeme Souness paid £1million to lure him back to Britain.

And to make matters worse when he checked in at Gers he committed the cardinal sin in the eyes of the punters – he kicked Ally McCoist onto the bench.

Hateley recalled: "It was very difficult, it was always going to be that way because I had come in off an injury and I hadn't played for a long time.

"And, yes, there was stick to take too because Ally McCoist was the King here and people thought I was taking his place.

"It took the fans a while to realise that I was always going to be playing as the targetman with Ally or Mo Johnston."

McCoist, of course, was quickly labelled The Judge as his feuds with Souness kept him on the bench.

Yet Hateley thinks being there HELPED an idol cast into the shadows.

Walter Smith was to quickly jettison Johnston to Everton when he took over and the double act that sparked Gers to the Treble in 1993 was born.

Mark reasoned: "The time that Ally had on the bench let him see the way I played. That's why when we did become a partnership we were very successful very quickly.

"You will NEVER get another striking partnership that will emulate that in the modern game because players move around so much. To score the goals we did in that space of time won't happen again."

If that was a champagne season the following campaign was flat beer – despite the team dredging up the reserves to go within an ace of the domestic clean sweep.

The sparkle had gone with McCoist on the sidelines after a broken leg he suffered as Scotland's World Cup dream ended with a 5-0 humiliation in Portugal.

Hateley carried a massive burden and he shouldered it to win every personal plaudit available.

The former Coventry and Portsmouth hitman said: "The double of Player of the Year from my fellow pros and the football writers in one season meant the world to me.

"But I honestly loved every minute of my time at Ibrox. I feel I was well-loved here because I was so committed. This place makes you like that. Rangers are the biggest club I ever played for – BIGGER than AC Milan.

"There's a great support, great facilities and everything that surrounds it is big time."

Teams that go 44 games unbeaten, win the Treble and go within one goal of the European Cup Final aren't born every day. They are special.

Skipper Richard Gough once famously said: 'The team that drinks together wins together.' A maxim that might not quite survive in the Dick Advocaat era!

Yet Hateley believes the bonds forged between the group that Walter Smith honed will never be broken.

And he stressed: "We became friends off the park too, togetherness was such a huge part of that squad.

"We didn't have great individuals but we had a great team spirit, a never-say-die attitude. When I come back to Ibrox now I feel as if I have never been away and that's so important to me."

With winning came the wind-ups, with losing the antidote of laughter.

And Mark's favourite left him in stitches in the Amber Regent Chinese restaurant in the heart of Glasgow.

He recalled: "The players were there one night with all the wives and Coisty had been at the toilet and got the disinfectant blocks that they put in the urinals. They look just like after-dinner mints and he swapped them on the plate.

"John Brown gobbled one up, spat it out and chased Ally all over the restaurant!"

Toilet humour. Yet it was the sort of nonsense Hateley missed when he quit Gers for Queen's Park Rangers. The yearning was always there to come back.

He scored 3 goals in 27 league games at Loftus Road and even had a surprise six-game loan spell back in the Premiership at Leeds United.

But at the age of 35 in the midst of the frenzy of the nine-in-a-row run-in came the call he'd least expected. On the other end of the phone was Walter Smith.

March 16, 1997 at Parkhead was one of the biggest days in Gers' history and the manager – his team ravaged by injuries – was in his hour of need. He turned to a man whose qualities he knew he could count on.

Hateley was back in the Old Firm fray and he will never forget the chance Smith gave him to be in on history in the making.

Mark said: "Walter played such a massive role in my career and he was a very strong character. His face to the media is very different to what you see behind the scenes. In fact, though they are often portrayed as opposites there were actually many similarities to Graeme Souness."

Hateley's return to the frenzy of Britain's bitterest derby was to be a tale of contrast.

He was at the peak of ecstasy when he knocked on a long ball and Ian Durrant sped on to loft the ball over Stewart Kerr for Brian Laudrup to tangle with Malky Mackay and bundle it home.

Yet he was then in the depths of despair when he was involved in a brawl with Hoops keeper Kerr and sent off.

Hateley had been on the park for just over an hour yet he had made a massive impact and he said: "Coming back was what I wanted to do, I had always wanted to finish playing here. That was my dream. I will always appreciate what Walter did for me, it was inspired! And it paid off.

"Sure, I was sent off against Celtic but the time I was on was vital because I was involved in the goal. I felt the red card was a bad decision but I'd done my bit.

"I scored against Dunfermline too and I feel that the move served its purpose."

That goal in the 4-0 win over the Pars was to prove Hateley's last for the club.

He relished being part of the nine-in-a-row party at Tannadice then management beckoned.

Mark started at Hull City but when tennis millionaire David Lloyd, the club's big-bucks backer, threatened to pull the plug it all turned sour.

Hateley had learned the sickening taste of defeat as a boss and he would soon know the feeling of losing his job.

Yet he remains upbeat about his future and confident that he will be the better for a job he even offered to do for nothing.

Mark said: "Yes, Hull has been a difficult time but if I pondered on things that were in the past I'd have given up years ago. I live in the present. That's why I've lasted so long in this game.

"The Hull experience hasn't bruised me. It has just made me more determined to be a success as a boss.

"I offered to work without wages and the whole situation couldn't have been more different than my Ibrox days.

"But I'll mark it down to experience and my ambition remains the same – to one day manage Rangers."

Club and Country

STATS

IBROX CAREER
1990-95, 97

GAMES
League	169
Scot Cup	17
Lg Cup	19
Europe	17
Total	222

GOALS
League	88
Scot Cup	10
Lg Cup	11
Europe	6
Total	115

MEDALS
League	5
Scot Cup	2
Lg Cup	3

ENGLAND
32 caps

JOHNNY HAMILTON reckons his emergence at Rangers saved the bruised and battered shins of Scotland's midfielders – because it meant John Greig moved back to defence.

Johnny HAMILTON

Jock Wallace shrewdly combined the craft of Hamilton with the passing ability of Tommy McLean and the all-action style of Alex MacDonald to fashion a midfield that won the Treble in 1976.

Hamilton had an inspirational season in Gers' clean sweep and he smiled: "In that year everything just clicked in midfield. There's no doubt the secret was that we got Greigy out of there.

"There was a great blend with myself, Tommy McLean and Alex MacDonald and that left Greig at left-back to do the business there.

"What an inspiration that man was. He never knew the meaning of defeat.

"I used to call him Johnny Hauf-A-Team."

Few players have arrived at Ibrox on a free transfer but Hamilton became part of that select band when Eddie Turnbull surprisingly let him go in 1973 after his Hibs side had won the League Cup.

There's mischief in Johnny's voice when he recalls those days and you feel he might just have engineered his bust-up with Turnbull to achieve his

goal. He confessed: "In all honesty, Eddie Turnbull and I fell out and I have to say I may have caused a lot of the trouble between us – I was just desperate to sign for Rangers."

Wallace landed his man and it paid off. Hamilton would drop deep to spark moves off and he became an integral part of the team that won the Grand Slam.

He fell out of the first team picture at Gers when, ironically, Bobby Russell – a kid Johnny had coached at Possil YM – arrived from Shettleston Juniors to take his place.

After spells at Millwall and St Johnstone Johnny worked on the oil rigs for a time after he hung up his boots. These days you'll find him in

the Safeway distribution depot near his Uddingston home, checking out the lorries before they travel around Britain.

It's bizarre when you work in the modern day football to think of Ralph Brand the taxi-driver or Johnny Hamilton the rigger. Men plucked from the working class to be worshipped by full houses at Ibrox simply returned there a little better off when they finished playing.

These days if you pull on a Rangers jersey you're made for life.

Johnny Hamilton doesn't carry one ounce of bitterness, but the £4000 that his Treble team earned as a bonus certainly puts today's wages into perspective.

MISCHIEF
...Hamilton pulled more than a few punches to get that dream move from Hibs to Ibrox

---

Pieter HUISTRA

PIETER HUISTRA said a dazzling farewell to Rangers as the Land of the Rising Sun beckoned.

When the Dutch international bowed out to earn his fortune in the Japanese League with Hiroshima San Frecce in January 1995 he went the right way. He did it in style.

Huistra cracked two superb goals in his farewell match to mastermind a vital 3-2 win at Falkirk that kept his team on course for seven-in-a-row.

Now with Belgian side Lierse, Pieter recalled: "That was a very emotional day. I had so much to look back on at Ibrox like being part of the Treble team that went on that great European run."

Graeme Souness made many more lavish splashes in the transfer market, but Huistra represented £300,000 of the shrewdest cash he ever invested.

The pencil-slim left winger followed in the studmarks of the great Davie Cooper and the mesmeric Mark Walters and – whilst not as flamboyantly gifted – did the jersey justice.

Huistra promptly won his move and a thousand "Blue Pieter" headlines were born! In a rich vein of form he was an arch provider of chances and, when Walter

Smith took over, Pieter often duelled with the enigmatic Alexei Mikhailitchenko for the role wide on the left of midfield.

Ironically, one of Huistra's most memorable Gers goals came with his RIGHT foot when he buried a critical equaliser in a 1-1 away draw with Belgians FC Bruges during that Champions League run in 1993.

The now-axed rule that restricted Gers to three foreigners in Europe, though, often made Huistra a big game casualty. He could be a luxury player when the chips were down and boss Smith signalled he believed that when he left Huistra out of the side to face Aberdeen in the dramatic last-day title decider in 1991.

Pieter reflected: "I had played almost every game and people thought I was injured but I had to tell them I had been dropped. I can't even describe how hard it is to take when you're told you are not involved. I would ask Walter Smith why and he would tell me it was tactical.

"I came to look at it this way. At least I had helped Rangers get to these big games."

Johnny HUBBARD

SCENE: PHOTOGRAPHER Alex Prior looks out onto a dusty football pitch and spots the figure of a little wizard dazzling defenders with his direct wing play.

KING JOHNNY ... penalty specialist Hubbard endeared himself to fans for his style of play

When the action is finished he trots towards a player called Johnny Hubbard and utters the words every boy from the blue half of Glasgow back home prays to hear.

"Son, I can get you a trial with the Rangers. Will you come?"

The breathless reply arrives: "Rangers? Never heard of them. What about Motherwell or Clyde?"

And that is how the legend of Johnny Hubbard Penalty King almost died before he kicked it into life.

These days the little South African, who won three titles and a Scottish Cup badge with the club, is a sprightly 68-year-old who still coaches kids from the ages of seven to 10 for Rangers.

But back then he nearly blew his big chance and he recalled: "Alex was working out in South Africa in 1948 and he told me he would get me a trial with the greatest team in Great Britain – Glasgow Rangers.

"I'd never heard of them, only Motherwell, Clyde and Aberdeen because they had toured our country.

"But there was only mum and me left in the house in Pretoria and I decided to come – that was 50 years ago!"

His determination to make it abroad made Hubbard – who tipped the scales at a meagre nine stones – an instant hit with the Gers legions.

Crucially, though, he also had excellent control and a direct crowd-pleasing style to help him towards his goals. And then, of course, came the penalties. Hubbard's record from the spot during his decade at Ibrox was startling. He took 68 – he scored 65.

And even now this little Springbok, who was capped four times for the Scottish League, can remember the three keepers who defied him.

He insisted: "I didn't really practise penalties, I just knew how to take them and it worked at Gers. I can still remember the men who saved those three that got away. Walker of Airdrie, Jimmy Brown of Killie and Bert Slater of Falkirk – they were the lucky ones!"

From those contrasting roots in South Africa, Hubbard became an integral part of the Ibrox set-up and learned the tartan customs on and off the park.

For this adopted Scot there was haggis

IBROX CAREER 1949-59

GAMES
League	127
Scot Cup	19
Lg Cup	41
Europe	6
Total	238

GOALS
League	77
Scot Cup	5
Lg Cup	23
Europe	1
Total	106

MEDALS
League	3
Scot Cup	1

SOUTH AFRICA
1 cap

STATS

and Hogmanay – then beating Celtic on New Year's Day. And in 1955 he was to write his name all over the most famous footballing fixture of the Scottish League's calendar.

Even now, the man who still scouts stars in Ayrshire for Rangers can smile: "That game will always live with me because we beat Celtic 4-1 and we didn't just win.

"I scored a hat-trick in the last 14 minutes! And one of them, of course, was a penalty.

"You couldn't get through to someone nowadays how that felt back then. There were 95,000 all-ticket inside Ibrox and my popularity with the Rangers fans was assured from that day on."

Johnny – deservedly awarded an honorary MBE for his services to football on his retirement – was to become one of a select band of players who have played for their countries against Scotland at Ibrox, starring for South Africa alongside Gers team-mate Don Kichenbrand in 1956 as his country lost 2-1.

Their scorer? Hubbard with a penalty!

Denmark's Brian Laudrup was to mimic his achievement with the winner against Craig Brown's side in another friendly on his club's home turf.

Yet for all the highs Hubbard experienced, none conjures up Rangers' darkest day than the result which, for any fan of that era, remains in the depths of their footballing psyche. The song, still belted out joyously by their bitterest rivals, will always remind them of the scoreline in the 1957 League Cup Final.

"Oh, Hampden in the sun – Celtic 7 Rangers 1."

A nightmare for Hubbard, who was then pushed out in front of the television cameras with delirious Celt Charlie Tully for the post-match interviews.

Jolted Johnny refused to cave in as Tully savoured history and he grinned: "I looked the interviewer straight in the eye and said "What's Charlie talking about? We were the best team because we had EIGHT chances. We just couldn't put them away."

FIELD OF
DREAMS...Jackson
missed Gers' 3-2
triumph over
Moscow Dynamo,
but still scored 40
goals for his club

Colin JACKSON

COLIN JACKSON hobbled on to the Nou Camp turf and tried to come to terms with it all – 24 hours earlier he'd been dreaming of the biggest game of his life. Now he was out.

Misty-eyed recollections of Rangers' greatest day in 1972 often overlook the fact that the towering centre-half was cheated out of his place in history by a freak training ground accident the day before the match.

Jackson will never forget the disappointment of missing his side's 3-2 European Cup Winners' Cup Final triumph over Moscow Dynamo.

And Colin, the original Ibrox Bomber before John Brown inherited the nickname in the 90s, recalled: "The day before training we were going through an exercise and I stood in a hole in the ground and turned my ankle.

"I knew straight away I was in trouble and within two minutes it had swollen up like a balloon.

"It dawned on me right away that I was out of the biggest game of my life.

"That swelling was never going to go down in 24 hours. It was over."

Stricken boss Willie Waddell shuttled his heartbroken defender back to the team hotel and a hurried meeting put Derek Johnstone back into the heart of defence.

Alfie Conn was off the bench and into the starting 11 and Jackson was left desolate.

Ironically, he had been drafted into the side the year before to replace Ronnie McKinnon who had suffered the agony of a leg-break.

Now the two crocks would share a room on the day the club wrote their name into European legend.

And Jackson sighed: "I remember Ronnie and I tanned a few beers on the day of the game to try and drown our sorrows.

"But when we went out to walk on the park you realised what you were missing and it hurt very badly. There was a lump in my throat. I got a medal but it's small consolation for missing out on an occasion like that."

Club and Country

STATS

IBROX CAREER 1963-82	
GAMES	
League	341
Scot Cup	53
Lg Cup	75
Europe	36
Total	505
GOALS	
League	23
Scot Cup	8
Lg Cup	8
Europe	1
Total	40
MEDALS	
League	3
Scot Cup	3
Lg Cup	5
SCOTLAND	
8 caps	

It was a hurtful low but in 19 years at Gers Jackson savoured many highs.

He was an integral part of the Treble teams in '76 and '78, but walking down Memory Lane for this book dragged him back to those European nights once more.

He explained: "Sure, the two Trebles were high points for me but I'll also always remember the Euro run when we beat the likes of PSV Eindhoven and Juventus.

"We lost in the last eight to Cologne but I'd admit now that we really thought we were going all the way."

Nottingham Forest were to lift the 1979 European Cup with a Final win over Swedes Malmo.

And Bomber wanted a Battle of Britain with them before the Germans scuppered his plans.

He said: "We fancied Forest in the semis and I remember talking to Gordon Smith and saying we could do them because they had Larry Lloyd at the back and Gordon would have too much pace for him. But it wasn't to be.

"That side was made for Europe – with the class of the likes of Bobby Russell and Tommy McLean we could pick apart the best of defences."

Jackson plundered 40 goals in his Gers career and many of them came from McLean's ammunition, it was a potent threat.

Wallace's side would be toiling and then came the Bomber mission. Witness the 1979 League Cup Final against

Aberdeen with the game tied at 1-1.

One deft chip from McLean and Jackson was marauding away from his markers to power a header beyond Bobby Clark.

Colin smiled as he recalled the partnership which led to many Gers goals: "Tommy was magnificent at pinpointing crosses and so many of my goals came from his service.

"Mind you, he fought a battle with the fans because he was the height of nothing and couldn't tackle.

"The punters back then liked nothing more than someone getting stuck right in and playing for the jersey, skill often came second!"

Jackson, now a finance broker in Glasgow, remains an Ibrox fixture as he hosts hospitality suites on matchdays and plays a key role in forming an Ex-Players' Association for one-time Gers stars.

And when he looks back on his Light Blues days he recognises the part played by the club's very own Mr Motivator, Jock Wallace.

Colin said: "You look at those Treble teams and he had a special little something as a manager.

"He wasn't the best tactician in the world and I recognise that, but he made up for those frailties by developing a brilliant team spirit.

"We had a tremendous togetherness. That carried us through."

Sandy JARDINE

FROM the wreckage of a Gers catastrophe emerged one of the classiest defenders Ibrox has ever seen.

In the wake of the humiliating Scottish Cup defeat at Berwick Rangers, February 4, 1967 was seen as the dawn of a new era for the club.

It began with a 5-1 win at home to Hearts and it heralded the first appearance in the Light Blues top team of Sandy Jardine.

A footballing lifetime later he would play his 1,000th game in a Jambos jersey AGAINST Rangers – and still be on the winning side!

Jardine was a player ahead of his time, the Thinking Man's Defender, and the plaudits rained down on him throughout 17 years at the club he still serves.

These days he is Rangers' Sales and Marketing Manager and he turns his shrewd brain to selling the club brand throughout the world.

Yet one commodity he cannot buy in bulk is the class and dignity that characterised everything he did in a Light Blue jersey. He simply had that bred into him.

Edinburgh-born William Jardine – he earned the Sandy tag because of his hair colour – only has John Greig and the legendary Dougie Gray ahead of him in appearances for Gers.

And as we spoke at the launch of the search for the Greatest Ranger he looked around the splendour of the luxurious Ibrox Suite that overlooks the pitch he once graced and reflected: "You know, losing 1-0 at Berwick was bad for this club but it was good for me.

"I am constantly asked to pick out my best memory of being a Rangers player but there isn't one. My best memory lasted for the 17 YEARS I played here.

"And my best recollections are about the laughs we had and the friends I made. That was what it was about – that and winning."

There was to be plenty of that. Sandy scooped three league medals, five Scottish Cup and five League Cup badges in domestic football. And he was made for Europe.

Jardine had been a top team regular for just three months when the club reached the Cup Winners' Cup Final only for a surprisingly negative side to perish 1-0 against Bayern Munich in Nuremberg.

Five years later, though, he was at the pinnacle. He scored a classic left-foot shot past Sepp Maier to gain revenge over Bayern in a 2-0 semi-final second leg win in front of 80,000 frenzied fans at Ibrox.

And Jardine was a key part of the side who clutched the same trophy after that memorable triumph over Moscow Dynamo in Barcelona.

When the embers of that night were reignited into bright flames with victories over Juventus and PSV Eindhoven six years later he was there once more at the heart of it all.

By then the skipper on that Euro glory night was manager of the club and Sandy has no doubt where John Greig belongs in this Haul of Fame.

As the quest for 250,000 Rangers fans worldwide to decide their top man began in front of a packed media conference he said: "The Greatest Ranger? It has to be Greigy because he was such a magnificent Ibrox servant.

"He typified for me what a Rangers player should be. So many people tagged him as some sort of hammer-thrower but he had a lot of skill and he never got credit for that.

"It irks me that they just regard him as this whole-hearted figure and nothing else. For consistency and what it means to be a Ranger there is only one man."

Jardine thrived at Rangers under five different bosses – Scot Symon, Davie White, Willie Waddell, Jock Wallace and of course Greig.

He had earned the loyalty he was shown in 1982 when the chance to move to Hearts and take a step up as assistant-boss to old Ibrox pal Alex MacDonald arrived.

Rangers let him go and the learning process as a manager began – he continued teaching the rest how to play just as he always had.

Four years after he walked out the Ibrox exit door with a huge lump in his throat Sandy Jardine was named Scotland's Footballer of the Year at the age of 38.

He took Hearts to the brink of the Double only to see his dreams die yet his personal achievement remains undiminished. What was the secret, how did he keep going? His answer is simple.

"My Indian summer just refused to end," he smiled.

"It was fitting that just as my debut had been for Rangers against Hearts my 1,000th game was to be the opposite fixture with the Jambos winning 3-0.

"I was the first player in Scotland to reach that 1,000 game milestone. How did I do it? Sheer class and ability!"

The laugh is raucous and ready and then Jardine the consummate pro is desperate to point out he was only joking.

When the serious examination of a remarkable career gets underway he points to a task-master who drove him to the limits – and beyond.

Wallace's punishing sessions on the Gullane Sands when a string of players were left throwing up – or feeding the seagulls as it was known – have become a fashionable target for football derision. Jardine LOVED them.

As big Jock drove his players on another strength-sapping trip to Murder Hill Sandy gritted his teeth and thought of the benefits.

And he reasoned: "If you look into your records you'll see that the vast bulk of players raised at Rangers under the Jock Wallace regime played well into their 30s.

"We put our fitness in the bank and Gullane Sands did us the power of good. I was to take Hearts back there when I went into management myself.

"One of the reasons the teams that won Trebles in '76 and '78 were so strong is that we were fitter than anyone else. Just look at the number of games we won in the dying minutes.

"Football is not just about ability, sometimes you get there by sheer physical effort and we had that in abundance."

He's 50 now yet Jardine retains the image of the man who earned 38 caps for Scotland, the player who alongside Celtic's Danny McGrain gave us a justifiable claim for the best full-back pairing in the world.

Tynecastle came to mean a lot to him but in deep conversation you will always find where his heart really lies.

He treasures the medals he won with Rangers and he sighed: "What brought it home to me was when I was at Hearts and I was alongside people like John Robertson who is a legend at that club.

"He played there all his life – apart from a little spell at Newcastle – yet he didn't win a medal until he was on the bench in the 1998 Scottish Cup Final against Rangers.

"When you are a player you dream of the triumphs I had. Then you come towards the end of your career and all you think about is finding a way to stay in the game.

"Yes, there was a huge lump in my throat when I came to leave Gers. I always hoped I could come back."

Club and Country

STATS

IBROX CAREER 1965-82

GAMES
League	451
Scot Cup	64
Lg Cup	107
Europe	52
Total	674

GOALS
League	42
Scot Cup	8
Lg Cup	25
Europe	2
Total	77

MEDALS
League	3
Scot Cup	5
Lg Cup	5
Europe	1

SCOTLAND
38 caps

BATTLING FIGURE ... Sandy Jardine shows his will to win against Cutty Young

DEATH THREATS, a phalanx of bodyguards surrounding him, distraught Rangers fans burning season tickets in the streets. Mo Johnston had arrived at Ibrox.

The fury fuelled by religious intolerance and the seething hatred that greeted Graeme Souness' daring swoop to snatch Mo from under the noses of Celtic starkly illustrated the courage behind the manager's decision.

Souness didn't just clear the obstacles of bigotry that were hampering Rangers, he smashed them down with the signing of the highest-profile Catholic player in Scottish football.

International frontman Johnston had bettered himself beyond recognition in France with Nantes, he was THE striker of the moment. But his football ability was the last thing on the agenda.

The Gers boss had scrapped 116 years of tradition in one fell swoop and he had bulldozed the club into a new era by landing a player who had once been an idol of the Celtic legions.

A decade on from one of the biggest stories our game has ever seen Souness' bravery has been rewarded with the vision of a new cosmopolitan club captained by Italian defender Lorenzo Amoruso.

A club where what school you went to is no longer the preamble to any football conversation. They owe Souness – and Johnston – a massive debt.

Mo, now 35 and starring in midfield for Major League Soccer side Kansas City Wizard, said: "It was a tense time then, a strange world.

"I had bodyguards because the club decided I needed protection and for a month I felt like a rock star.

"Rangers never passed on any mail to me but I was always aware of the death threats. It was something I was used to because I had them at Celtic too.

"It disturbs you that it even goes through someone's mind to kill you over football but I couldn't let that sort of thing rule my life.

"Even though I had been warned that I should never go out in Glasgow again within 10 days I was down from my home in Edinburgh seeing my mum and my pals."

Johnston – reared as a kid with Partick Thistle before making his name at Watford then becoming a Hoops hero – has never forgotten his Glasgow roots.

Yet as he relishes his American dream he admits he could never return to live in a city that remains tainted by the sectarian divide despite his mould-breaking move on the football field.

In the States Mo is just a player for a soccer team trying to establish a foothold in a vastly different sporting market.

Here to some twisted minds he is still the Anti-Christ.

Life has moved on for Johnston but it still rankles both the player and his agent Bill McMurdo that they were cast as the villains in that Gers move, accused of

MO MONEY ...
It was Rangers' willingness to splash the cash that saw Johnston sign at Ibrox under the noses of Celtic

Mo JOHNSTON

reneging on a switch from his French club Nantes back to Parkhead.

Mo was actually paraded in a Celtic shirt before he chose Rangers but he rapped: "The truth is that Celtic lost out on that deal because they wouldn't pay the money.

"They struck a deal with Nantes but the club had no right to do any sort of contract.

"A company owned the rights to my transfer and they were trying to put me into the likes of Torino in Italy and Montpellier in France.

"I didn't want that because I wanted to come home and Celtic looked an option before all the troubles started.

"Rangers showed the desire to get it done and I decided I had to do it.

"Looking back it was a momentous decision but I never really saw it like that.

"I knew the implications but I'm not a nervous person.

"And there's no hiding from it, there was a little Devil inside me saying: 'Do it, prove them all wrong.'"

Johnston was desperate for a flyer but it didn't happen as opening league defeats from St Mirren and Hibs piled on the pressure.

His third league game took him into the lion's den at Parkhead and the derision rained down on him as he squandered a series of chances in a 1-1 draw.

He confessed: "I felt I'd let myself down in the first game against Celtic. I missed a few sitters and the cynics said I couldn't bring myself to score against the Tic.

"But I went away from that match knowing I just had to work harder and it would come. I was playing well enough but I just couldn't score."

That work ethic was now ingrained in Johnston. With Nantes he was coached by Croatian Miroslav Blazevic who would lead his nation third place at France 98.

Mo relished that and he reckons there's

no question playing with the likes of Belgian superstar Frankie Vercauteren improved him vastly.

He had left these shores the arch predator and returned still a potent striker but also a master at linking the play.

Five months before his Gers debut he had come back to Hampden as rain battered down and dismantled France with both goals in a World Cup qualifying win that took us a huge step nearer Italia 90. It was only a matter of time before he clicked at Gers.

And he recalled: "The feeling when I got the first goal with the winner against Aberdeen went beyond relief."

He was off and running, it was the first of 15 league goals that made the ever-present Johnston the club's top Premier scorer that season.

And there was never going to be any doubt about the one that mattered most. His first strike against Celtic.

It came on November 4, 1989, with the clock ticking down on a frantic Ibrox clash and the game tied at 0-0. Gary Stevens' cross was weakly cleared by Chris Morris.

For a split-second the ball stuck under Mo's boot then he had it gathered and from 20 yards he smacked the ball low past Packie Bonner. Ibrox erupted.

And Johnston – who was to volley home another classic in a 3-0 Ibrox Old Firm win as the title neared – smiled: "I had done it, the goal they said I'd never score. I looked around at the fans after my winner and thought now I could be accepted."

Mo Johnston will finish his football career accused of many things. But no-one will ever say he was a bad player and no-one will ever say he lacked bottle.

I remember shuddering when I spoke to a Gers fan who said he considered that Dons game when Johnston scored his first goal as a DRAW.

He wouldn't count Mo's header

because a Catholic scored it – that's the poisonous atmosphere Johnston was operating in.

There will always be those who decry him but the vast majority of decent Rangers fans accepted Mo because he worked his tail off for the team.

And Mo insisted: "I knew I'd been truly welcomed when the Moodiesburn Rangers Supporters' Club invited me to their dance as their Player of the Year. That was the Gers kitman Doddie Soutar's club and it was my first award from the fans.

"Then Larkhall RSC invited me and the club were very nervous about it.

"There was advice for me to snub it but I couldn't do that.

"That was the Rangers heartland and, yes, I was scared when I walked in but they were superb to me. I sang a few songs and they taught me some new ones."

For Johnston much of the appeal in the return home had been the chance to link up with Scotland pal Ally McCoist.

They formed a deadly partnership but just when it was beginning to click Souness changed the script and brought in Mark Hateley.

And Mo argued: "I enjoyed my season with Ally and I have always looked back and thought there was simply no need to break us up.

"It's true Mark proved a magnificent player for Rangers but I have always felt it was change for change's sake."

Johnston went on to win the title once more in 1991, playing a pivotal role in the final day win over rivals Aberdeen that clinched it.

But with mentor Souness gone he was soon on the move once more, south to Everton before returning home to Hearts and Falkirk.

These days the Player of the Year trophies keep coming for a super-fit veteran Johnston who is now 10lbs LIGHTER than he was in his Gers heyday.

He relishes the lifestyle in Kansas and he confessed: "There are times when you yearn for Glasgow but this is home now.

"I'm proud of what I achieved. I played for Celtic and Rangers and I scored in the World Cup Finals for Scotland against Sweden in 1990.

"Those are memories I will always have and one day I'll be able to tell my kids all about the day I broke down a religious barrier in Scotland. I just wonder if they'll understand."

Club and Country

IBROX CAREER 1989-91

GAMES

League	76
Scot Cup	5
Lg Cup	13
Europe	6
Total	100

GOALS

League	31
Scot Cup	1
Lg Cup	9
Europe	5
Total	46

MEDALS

League	2

SCOTLAND
38 caps

STATS

TOP MAN... Johnston was Gers top scorer in his first season at Ibrox hitting the net 15 times

Willie JOHNSTON

WILLIE JOHNSTON buried five years of heartache when his two goals in the 3-2 win over Moscow Dynamo clinched the 1972 Cup Winners' Cup for Rangers.

Club and Country

IBROX CAREER 1964-72, 80-82

GAMES
League	246
Scot Cup	42
Lg Cup	65
Europe	40
Total	393

GOALS
League	91
Scot Cup	10
Lg Cup	16
Europe	8
Total	125

MEDALS
Scot Cup	1
Lg Cup	2
Europe	1

SCOTLAND 22 caps

STATS

Bud was one of only four survivors from the side who had lost the Final to Bayern Munich in the year that Celtic's Lisbon Lions overcame the mighty Inter Milan to be crowned Kings of Europe.

Sandy Jardine, John Greig and Dave Smith had also suffered through the misery of defeat in front of a partisan German crowd in Nuremberg in 1967.

And Willie recalled: "All I remember was the simple feeling that we couldn't lose again in Spain.

"I'll never forget what it felt like after we lost to Bayern, defeat was made ten times worse by the fact that Celtic had won the European Cup the week before.

"They got a heroes' welcome when they returned to Scotland and we got one man and a dog."

The madness of the Old Firm meant that Gers' glory run to that '67 Final – a sequence that saw Glentoran, Borussia Dortmund, Real Zaragossa and Slavia Sofia dumped out – was forgotten.

All that mattered was that Rangers had failed where Celtic had triumphed.

And Johnston said: "I feel that defeat – and not the Scottish Cup loss at Berwick Rangers earlier that season – was what cost Scot Symon his job and that wasn't right.

"I always remember the look on his face the night we lost in Germany. We were having a drink in the hotel bar and he said: "Enjoy your pint lads and just forget about it."

"Yet you knew he couldn't. He walked up the stairs to his bed a very sad man."

That's why when the chance came to earn the club's first European silverware once more the four survivors vowed to leave the Nou Camp as winners.

They inspired the team around them and even volunteered for a stint on Jock Wallace's infamous Murder Hill to get in peak condition after an enforced month-long lay-off when the Scottish season ended before the Final.

Bud laughed: "That's without doubt the first time any Rangers squad ever ASKED Jock to go Gullane Sands.

"We'd played bounce games but we felt we would toil in Spain unless we worked on our fitness.

"And we were right because after Colin Stein and I had put us 3-0 up we died in the closing stages and almost let them back in."

Gers held on and Johnston's place in

the club's history books was sealed yet he was to leave Ibrox at the end of that season in turmoil.

The firebrand Fifer had always walked a line between magic and mayhem on the park.

His short fuse often landed him bother with refs and after eight years at Rangers he felt like a marked man. So when the out-of-contract star sat down with Willie Waddell at the end of that season the Gers supremo was in for a shock.

Bud explained: "Waddell put a massive six-year deal in front of me and said: 'Sign that, Bud.'

"But I couldn't, everything was closing in on me at Rangers and I had to get away.

"I had to go, there was no way forward for me in Scotland any more.

"I'd had a fall-out with Alex Forsyth of Partick Thistle, been sent off and been slapped with a 10-week ban by the SFA.

"I really feared that if I stayed at Rangers then the next red card would see me suspended for SIX MONTHS."

He chose the option of moving to West Bromwich Albion and like his fellow scorer in that '72 Final Stein, who had a good stint at Coventry, Johnston found he relished the change in English football.

The challenge of meeting new teams on different grounds sparked him back to life and it was never dull under managerial maverick Ron Atkinson.

Willie stressed: "That was a great team because we had the likes of Cyrille Regis, Laurie Cunningham, Len Cantello and Ally Brown.

"Yet although we did get into Europe we really should have won silverware.

"We got to the FA Cup semi-final in 1978 and lost to Ipswich who went on to win it against Arsenal and I've always felt that should have been our year."

It was a year, of course, that was to have darker undertones for Bud when he went with the Scotland squad to the World Cup Finals in Argentina.

He took a pill called Reactivan, which he insisted was for hayfever, and found it was on the list of FIFA's banned substances.

A distraught Johnston was sent home in disgrace after failing the drug test as Ally McLeod's Army lost to Peru and drew with Iran before a defiant closing win over Holland.

Willie needed a place to escape to in the furore that followed and he found it in the fledgling North American Soccer League with Canadian side Vancouver Whitecaps.

Johnston said: "I was in a team of rascals over there and I had a magic time. We had other Brits like Alan Ball, Kevin Hector and Trevor Whymark and we were the feared side then."

In fact, Willie's Whitecaps won the Soccer Bowl after turfing out the all-star New York Cosmos – Johan Neeskens, Carlos Alberto and Franz Beckenbauer and all – in the semi-final.

Rodney Marsh's Tampa Bay Rowdies, a team that also included former Aberdeen forward Davie Robb, were the victims in the big showdown.

But while he lapped it all up Ibrox was soon calling again for Johnston as his former team-mate Greig – now the boss – needed help with a very special mission.

Willie explained: "I got this call from Greigy and he said: 'I want you to come back for two years and kick Davie Cooper's arse!'"

Greig planned some psychological warfare on the enigmatic winger who he felt would react to the threat of Johnston taking his jersey if he didn't turn it on.

And Johnston, who now runs the Port Brae pub in his native Kirkcaldy, smiled: "Those were his exact instructions and that's what I did. Coop was a great player but he was The Moody Blue after all.

"I went to Hearts for a spell after that and then into the pub business when I finished.

"Management was never for me, I always remembered the look on Scot Symon's face when he climbed those stairs in the hotel after that Bayern game – that put me off for life."

DOUBLE TROUBLE...
Willie Johnston's two goals against Moscow Dynamo helped Gers win the Cup Winners' Cup

Derek JOHNSTONE

THE bus that transported 40 family and friends from Dundee to Hampden carried a home-made plaque that read "The DJ Special"

And the 16-year-old superkid they were travelling to see play in his first showpiece game for Rangers scored the League Cup Final winner against Celtic.

If I were a staff writer for Roy of the Rovers it's likely that recounting this tale would win me nothing more than my P45 from a comic book editor fed up with my fanciful tales.

Yet he'd need a reality check.

This is the story of Derek Johnstone and it really DID happen that way in front of 106,263 fans at Scotland's home of football on October 24, 1970.

Everyone will tell you that it is the tale of a dream debut but DJ actually arrived on the scene for Gers a month BEFORE that Celtic match – yet he still wrote the headlines all the same.

The teenage striker scored twice in a 5-0 Ibrox hammering of Cowdenbeath and he was in good company as John Greig also grabbed a double and Alex MacDonald completed the rout.

Those three players would become the hub of two Trebles later but rookie Johnstone was soon placed back in the reserves with Colin Stein reinstated as the the first choice striker.

As the feverish preparations continued at Ibrox on the Friday before the match boss Willie Waddell and his coach Jock Wallace were plotting a masterstroke.

The team didn't travel to luxury bases to prepare for Finals in those days and Derek recalled: "I remember I was just about to jump in the bath after training.

"Willie Waddell poked his head round the door and told me to come to the bootroom.

"He sat me down in there with big Jock Wallace and said: "There's six tickets for tomorrow's game.""

DREAM START ...
Derek Johnstone
was a fresh-faced
kid of 16 when he
scored the winner
against Celtic in
the League Cup
Final showdown

"I just said: 'Thanks very much because a few of my family are coming through.'

"Then Waddell said: 'Well, you'll need those tickets because you're PLAYING. Get a good night's sleep.'

"Here I was at the age of 16 facing a crowd of 106,000 and they wanted me to get a good kip!"

The kid from Dundee was in the big time. He raced back to get on the train home and tell his family.

Reaction in the Johnstone household was swift and Derek – now a top radio broadcaster with Radio Clyde – said: "Within an hour a massive 40-seater bus had been hired and everyone in my street was going.

"The amazing thing is we only had SIX TICKETS but they just wanted to be there. And that plaque on the front that said: 'The DJ Special' is one of the nicest memories you can have from football."

Derek tried to obey Waddell's orders to the letter but a 16-year-old kid just out of school could never be expected to blank out the meaning of this game.

Sure, he'd had that memorable day against Cowdenbeath and, yes, he was the hot property in the reserves with a prolific strike rate. But this was different.

Yet class footballers can forget the frenzy around them and live on the skills and instincts they have honed.

Johnstone was to quell his nerves to steal ahead of the Celtic defence and glance home an unforgettable winner.

It was the start of something big for a player now only topped by Ally McCoist in the post-war league scoring stakes.

Yet he confessed: "I tossed and turned all night and dreamed of scoring the winning goal.

"I had been scoring regularly for the reserves yet my selection was still a huge gamble.

"Celtic must have been thinking: 'Who the Hell is this they have brought in? They soon paid for that! Seriously,

scoring the goal just made the day sensational.

"It's a cliche but it really was Roy of the Rovers stuff."

No-one can deny a player the precious commodity of winning over the Rangers fans early on.

There are players in this book – like Ally McCoist and Mark Hateley – who had to dredge deep down into their reserves of character to become idols at Ibrox.

McCoist was once left in tears when the entire ground bawled: "Ally, Ally – Get to ****" after a shock Scottish Cup exit at the hands of Dundee during the dark years before the Souness Revolution.

Hateley, ironically, was the target for abuse when he arrived in 1990 to dump the by then lionised McCoist off his pedestal and onto the bench.

Johnstone had no such trials and tribulations, he was an instant hero.

And he reasoned: "I've always felt that's the reason why I've had such an affinity with the Gers fans – because I got off to an amazing start.

"I scored on my debut and then came THAT Final, I was in their hearts right away.

"I look at people like McCoist and Hateley who have come here and gone through a lot of stick before becoming heroes.

"I don't know if I could have survived that because I was so young."

Johnstone's Gers career, though, was always going to be more than a survival mission.

His versatility as he shuttled between the key roles of centre-half and striker made him a priceless asset.

And it was in defence that he shone in that famous European Cup Winners' Cup Final win over Moscow Dynamo in 1972.

DJ was the man to benefit from the training ground accident that left Colin Jackson nursing an ankle injury.

And to this day he remembers the cold professionalism and honesty that typified Bomber.

Johnstone stressed: "I would have been a sub in the Final if it wasn't for Colin's integrity.

"I watched his fitness test and he could have got away with saying he was OK. But he knew his ankle wasn't 100 per cent and he called off.

"The great bonus for me is that I was alongside Dave Smith who is the finest defender I have EVER played with.

"He said: 'Don't be nervous, go for everything because if you miss it I will be behind you. Those are the words any defender wants to hear."

Smith's calm assurance helped Gers build a three-goal lead before the heartstopping finale when the Russians dragged them kicking and screaming back to 3-2.

Johnstone, though, helped the team cling on to their place in history and his medal became the one he treasures most alongside three league, five Scottish Cup and five League Cup badges.

It's as a striker that he will be remembered best, a penalty box player who thrived on the ammunition served up by wingers like Tommy McLean and Davie Cooper.

He scored 38 goals and made a towering contribution to the Treble in 1978 in a potent partnership with Gordon Smith.

Yet when the World Cup Finals came in Argentina that summer form striker Johnstone was there on the bench as stricken Ally McLeod pulled at his hair and wore the features of a condemned man.

We lost 3-1 to a Peru side McLeod had called Dad's Army and Johnstone stayed in the shadows.

It was a fatal mistake.

He was only to win 14 caps for Scotland which seems a paltry reward but Derek – who also had a spell at Chelsea and an ill-fated stint as boss of Partick Thistle – is rich in memories.

And he remains a man who lives for the goals and the gags.

These days he is still the self-styled punters' pal, arguing the toss every Saturday night on the infamous Radio Clyde Open Line that has become football's answer to The Samaritans.

And he grinned: "The Greatest Goal? For me that would be a 20-yard volley into the corner against Celtic because efforts from outside the box were a rarity for me.

"To cap it all we were 1-0 down when I levelled and Quinton Young scored the winner.

"The Greatest Gag? In the 70s at training Derek Parlane and I always had a classic at a corner when we would pull the other's shorts down when he wasn't looking.

"It just had to be done in a game and I got away with it one day when I got on his blind side and his drawers went right down. It was, of course, the day he forgot to put his underpants on.

"It wasn't a pretty sight. Half an inch less and they would have been calling him Denise. That's when they realised it was wee Derek Parlane and big Derek Johnstone!"

Club and Country

STATS

IBROX CAREER 1970-83, 85-86	
GAMES	
League	369
Scot Cup	57
Lg Cup	85
Europe	35
Total	546
GOALS	
League	132
Scot Cup	30
Lg Cup	39
Europe	9
Total	210
MEDALS	
League	3
Scot Cup	5
Lg Cup	5
Europe	1
SCOTLAND	
14 caps	

Kai JOHANSEN

"I WAS lying under this pile of players celebrating my goal when Willie Henderson grabbed a fistful of the front of my jersey and said: "Now you're a Ranger."

Kai Johansen remembers the moment as if it was yesterday, the 25-yard screamer that ripped into the Celtic net and brought the 1966 Scottish Cup to Ibrox.

The Danish defender's thunderous strike edged the Hampden replay 1-0 and brought his club some rare respite during an era of Celtic domination.

He awoke the next morning to the headlines of King Kai.

These days, the larger-than-life Johansen is still in Glasgow, the boss of a thriving business that includes beauty shops, tanning salons and launderettes.

He remains part of the Old Firm fabric and he smiled: "I didn't really know what Willie meant at the time but I did the next morning.

"The first year at Gers had been a disaster but from that moment forward I was really accepted by the fans and I loved that.

"It made it even better that the goal was an absolute beauty, one of the strikes of my life and that I got the better of John Hughes to score it.

"Yogi and I always had a grudge going, there was a vendetta between us.

And after that game he was dropped for three games, which delighted me!"

Johansen was part of the Danish invasion at Morton dreamed up by the Cappielow supremo, Hal Stewart.

His form in Greenock was to earn him a £20,000 Ibrox switch and he developed into a truly modern right-back, always bombing on to help the attack.

Kai was an integral part of the team that reached the 1967 Cup-Winners' Cup Final and he scored a critical Ibrox goal in a 2-1 second round win over German giants Borussia Dortmund.

Losing the trophy to Bayern Munich hurts to this day and he sighed: "There was so much pressure on us then, all you read about was Celtic so it was a terrible blow.

"The fact that it happened a week after they'd won the European Cup simply made matters worse.

"We had the chances to beat Bayern but Scot Symon had chosen to play without a recognised striker and we lost 1-0.

"It was heartbreaking."

Johansen's days at Gers came during a lean era and when he left in 1970 the only winner's medal he clutched was the

Club and Country

STATS

IBROX CAREER 1965-70	
GAMES	
League	158
Scot Cup	21
Lg Cup	32
Europe	27
Total	238
GOALS	
League	4
Scot Cup	2
Lg Cup	2
Europe	1
Total	9
MEDALS	
Scot Cup	1
DENMARK	
20 caps	

GREAT DANE... that's Kai Johansen who hit a Cup Final winner against Celtic

Scottish Cup badge his goal had earned four years earlier. He had 11 happy years in South Africa, playing then coaching with Arcadia Shepherds, before looking out his passport again.

Kai grinned: "I went to live in the south of Spain and then France and for seven years I just enjoyed myself until my family told me I had to stop being a playboy!

"I think I had a feeling a lot of professional athletes have.

"For years, everything is strict and your life is controlled by training. When's it over, you need to cut loose and I did just that. When he decided to put his life on a new course, there was only one place for the globe-trotting Johansen to settle – Scotland.

His company, Consol, now has 34 outlets and employs 72 people and the affable Dane is happy in the country he regards as home.

Kai reasoned: "There is something about this country that makes you love it, mostly the people I think.

"I'm sure Rangers players like Jorg Albertz would tell you the same these days.

It's a special country and a special club."

And Johansen has never lost the feeling for Gers that was hammered home to him the day Henderson clutched his jersey.

Kai pays for his tickets at every home game and stands in among his friends, bawling on Dick Advocaat's side.

He said: "I like what I see with Dick in charge and I feel if he stays for, say four years, then the club will once more be in a European Final – just as my team were.

"He has a system and a discipline instilled in them and I'm sure even now he is starting to feel that unique passion that goes with Rangers.

"I felt it every time I pulled on the jersey."

FOOTNOTE: Kai has now won himself a lasting place in Glasgow rhyming slang and become a barometer for girls to judge what sort of guy is chatting them up.

If he asks: "Fancy going up the Kai Johansen? (Dancin')" he is a Rangers fan. If he asks: "Are you coming to the Wim Jansen?" he probably wears a Celtic scarf on Saturdays!

THE RHINO... Kichenbrand's massive physique gave opponents nightmares

Don KICHENBRAND

DON KICHENBRAND broke the mould to become Rangers' first high-profile Catholic signing 34 YEARS before Mo Johnston – only problem was he never told a soul.

When the rugged striker they tagged "The Rhino" was stampeding through defences, Gers still clung to the ethic of a purely Protestant club – and he wasn't about to rock the boat.

Kichenbrand, one a family of 11, had starred for a club called Delfos in Johannesburg to attract the attention of agent Charlie Watkins.

The Mr Fixit persuaded boss Scot Symon into the deal then stood with his prize asset as they waited for the flight to Scotland and stardom.

Don recalled: "Charlie suddenly turned to me and said: "You're not Catholic are you?"

"When I said 'yes' he almost collapsed and told me never to mention it again.

"I was born a Catholic and still was when I played for Rangers but no-one knew."

Ironically, boss Symon had felt he was breaking down another Ibrox barrier with the Kichenbrand deal. He thought Don was BLACK.

His background was never mentioned throughout his Gers days and Kichenbrand became a huge favourite with the Light Blues fans, winning a title medal in 1956.

He had a superb campaign that year and scored a vital winner at Parkhead in the Ne'erday game, latching on to Billy Simpson's lob to outpace Jock Stein and lob the ball home.

And Don – who later moved to Sunderland before returning to South Africa – recalled: "In every game I played against Celtic, I scored. It gave me a great thrill and I remember those games with pride.

"It was really strange to be called an Orange bastard by Celtic fans during Old Firm games, though!

"I would have loved to have shouted at The Jungle: "I'm one of your lot!" But I never did."

Whatever your beliefs on Kichenbrand's decision to hide his roots, there's no disguising that he, too, suffered from prejudice of a different kind at Ibrox.

A grudge grew between Gers and Queen of the South during his days at Ibrox and the Dumfries fans sent the bustling front man hate mail, taunting: "Get back to the jungle and eat your antelope meat."

Kichenbrand responded the only way he knew how – he scored goals in a hate game against stunned Queens. Five of them.

Despite the complex background of his Rangers days, Don loved the club and was distraught when he recommended one of the best kids he'd ever played against to the club and saw him snubbed. The youngster's name was Richard Gough.

Kichenbrand had played against a teenage Gough when he was in an Old Crocks' side against a University Select.

And he revealed: "John Greig was manager then and I got on to him straight away.

"Rangers tried him out but he didn't sign, he joined Dundee United instead. He would later, of course, cost the club £1.5m from Spurs.

"It would have saved Rangers a fortune if they had signed him first."

The story of Don Kichenbrand, the secret Catholic, remains one of the most remarkable of the club's recent history.

In these enlightened Dick Advocaat days there will be smiles over his cloak and dagger lifestyle.

But it should be remembered that, only a decade ago, some fans were burning their season tickets in the street when Maurice Johnston signed.

Don – who worked with Gough's dad in a stationery firm before retiring – knew what he had to do to be accepted and he confessed: "I even joined a Masonic Lodge in Lanarkshire to help hide my secret. I couldn't admit it to anyone, it would have ruined a wonderful life for me.

"Listen, I may be a Catholic but I became a True Blue, I didn't have to work at it. It was the best time of my life and the biggest thrill was to pull on that jersey."

Brian LAUDRUP

MIDNIGHT, Ibrox: May 7, 1997. Brian Laudrup looked out of the window of the Rangers team bus and marvelled at the joy one flashing header had brought.

His solitary goal had downed Dundee United at Tannadice and a fabled footballing record set by fiercest foes Celtic had been equalled. Nine-in-a-Row.

Denmark's finest export was to bring so many magical moments to Gers when he arrived for £2.2million from Italian side Fiorentina.

From the Laudrup Final when he tortured Hearts in the 5-1 Scottish Cup caning of 1996 to the unbelievable goal he scooped in from the byeline against Aberdeen.

A bargain? Walter Smith pulled off one of the transfer heists of the century.

Brian's own Rangers memories, though, are dominated by one milestone night in the club's history.

He reflected: "There were so many great moments but there is no question scoring the goal that won Nine-in-a-Row ranks highest.

"The reason? Well, it just meant so much to so many people.

"I'll never forget that it was midnight when we arrived back at Ibrox yet still there were 3,000 people there to greet us.

"So to get the goal was marvellous enough – never mind with the only header of my Rangers career!

"I remember the team going for a meal and a drink that night and there was just this intense feeling of relief around the table. We had done it."

Laudrup savoured the taste of success and thought of the debt he owed the man who had ended his miserable stay in Florence and put the joy back in his football.

He had been shackled in Serie A, his skills strangled by coaches who constantly wanted him to stick to the system. Smith bucked that trend and set him free.

The result was two Scottish Football Writers' Association Player of the Year awards and the unleashing of the best player I have EVER seen in a Light Blue jersey.

Brian dedicated one of those trophies to his manager and he stressed: "It meant the world because it meant so much to Walter Smith. I think I had a special relationship with Walter and he is not only a special coach but a special man too.

"He would never get as much publicly but I know that when he took over from Graeme Souness he saw the Nine as his mission despite the fact that only two of those championships had been won when he got the job. For him to go out and realise that ambition was incredible. I don't care what anyone says about Scottish football, to win nine on the trot anywhere is unbelievable.

GREAT DANE ... Brian wowed Scotland with his silky skills and became an instant Ibrox idol

Club and Country

STATS

IBROX CAREER 1995-98	
GAMES	
League	116
Scot Cup	13
Lg Cup	4
Europe	17
Total	150
GOALS	
League	33
Scot Cup	5
Lg Cup	3
Europe	3
Total	44
MEDALS	
League	3
Scot Cup	1
Lg Cup	1
DENMARK	
82 caps	

"We survived through two very strong Celtic seasons to do it and I think through every one of us there was a feeling that this was for Walter as much as ourselves."

Brian's finest game for his manager was without doubt the game that will always be known now as The Laudrup Final.

Gordon Durie grabbed a hat-trick in the thrashing of Hearts as Laudrup the soccer sorcerer scored twice as he weaved his spells in the Hampden sunshine.

It was his perfect day and it ended in bizarre fashion as he allowed his halo to slip for once!

Brian smiled: "There are very few games in your life where it will all click together as it did that day. I can remember one other in the Danish Cup Final for Brondby against Ikast when we won 6-3 and I scored a couple as a kid.

"But it didn't compare to that day at Hampden.

"It's ironic that it came after a season when I had been troubled a lot by injury, it was such a sweet way to forget all those problems.

"The Goalie and Gazza even got me on top of the bus drunk which I have to say was a rare slip on my part!"

Laudrup's career had been at a crossroads when he arrived at Ibrox. Let's face it, Scottish football got him because he was damaged goods at the time.

His confidence was evaporating at Fiorentina and then he was left cooling his heels in the stand as Silvio Berlusconi stockpiled foreign stars at AC Milan. Rangers rebuilt him.

From the first moment he set foot in the club he felt at home.

And he said: "The camaraderie is so

68

unique. I came into a side that had been together for four or five years and once they've taken you out for the first dinner you feel like a part of a FAMILY.

"I had a difficult and at times lonely spell in Italy and that feeling of belonging at Rangers meant so much to me.

"Don't get me wrong this was a team of hardened professionals and at times too much was made of Richard Gough's famous 'The team that drinks together, wins together' quote.

"But those so-called bonding sessions really worked.

"Goughie will tell you I was a useless drinker, though, because on one break in Monaco I was his partner in a game where you have to have doubles of every spirit on the gantry.

"Let's just say I will always remember going on the trip to Monaco but I don't remember coming back!"

Brian's skills had taken him from his homeland at an early age to Bayer Uerdingen and Bayern Munich in Germany before the Italian sojourn.

After nine-in-a-row he could have added Dutch giants Ajax to his list but a last-gasp plea for chairman David Murray kept him in Glasgow.

The decision was to backfire as time caught up on Gers and Smith's side buckled under the strain of another title bid to end the season without a trophy.

Yet Laudrup insisted: "I don't look back on staying for another season as a bad idea. I had four years at Rangers and if you'd told me at the start I would have just one bad one then I'd have taken that.

"What I had was three years that hit the peaks for myself and the team and that's exceptional in football.

"That last one was difficult because Walter had announced he was leaving and we knew that for so many of us it was the end at Rangers too.

"Celtic really got it together again under Wim Jansen, Gazza left before the end of the season and in the end it was just too much for us.

"But I have no regrets. What happened simply showed that team was human and had a breaking point.

"No, I prefer to look back on my time as a Ranger with nothing but positive thoughts. I had the time of my life."

Laudrup was to leave for Chelsea and after shining on the biggest stage of all for Denmark at France 98 and scoring a classic in a thrilling last eight defeat from Brazil he rocked the football world.

Just three months into his hugely lucrative Stamford Bridge deal he quit the club to go home to FC Copenhagen and then announced his retirement from international football.

Now 30, this family man is at ease back where he started with wife Mette and kids Nikolai and Rasmine settled.

The travelling is over.

And Brian explained: "The last couple of years, that feeling had been gnawing away at me. I wanted to come home and it really is as simple as that.

"For most of my adult life I have been on my travels in Germany, Italy or Scotland and it is a strain on both ' yourself and your family. Perhaps people don't realise that.

"I've been well-rewarded and I was at Chelsea too but in the end there's more to life than money and my heart brought me home."

As you watch the Advocaat Era unfold you can't help but ponder what Laudrup would have brought to the team. Cosmopolitan, supremely gifted, the ultimate pro was made for it.

The Dutch coach yearned for him to stay but Brian's mind was made up to leave and his thoughts now throw light on his reasons.

He said: "Since I left people often say that I would have suited the new regime under Dick Advocaat.

"But you know what? They're wrong. I was part of the old era, the one built by Walter Smith. That was MY time and I made the right decision to go when Walter did.

"A lot of things have changed at Ibrox and it's New Rangers now, I was part of the old days, the old way and I was proud of that."

BACK TO HIS ROOTS... Stuart McCall is proud of his tartan ties

STUART McCALL returned to the home of his heroes and won the Battle of Britain.

One of Rangers' most famous triumphs sums up the courage, commitment and class that the Yorkshire-born midfield dynamo brought to the club through seven seasons laden with silverware.

Gers' clash with Leeds United in the European Cup in 1992 meant more to Stuart than any other Gers' player as he made an emotional trip back to the club he'd supported as a kid.

He recalled: "I had been brought up watching stars like Billy Bremner, Eddie Gray, and Joe Jordan and they were Leeds players who reminded me of my Scottish roots.

"And my heroes as a kid were guys I worshipped at Elland Road, players like Tony Currie and Frank Worthington.

"I don't know why I didn't turn out a maverick genius like them!

"Seriously, it was always the big question, could Rangers survive with England's big boys? Well, now was our chance to show them."

Leeds skipper Gary McAllister silenced Ibrox within a minute of the first leg with a clattering volley but John Lukic fisted an Ian Durrant corner into his own net before Ally McCoist gave Gers a 2-1 advantage.

The scene was set for a titanic tussle in the second leg but Scotland star Stuart, whose dad gave him his tartan background, was stunned by the arrogance of those in England as the tie loomed.

He said: "The English media were obnoxious. They belittled us and it was never a case of if Leeds were going through but a case of by how many.

"What disappointed me was that former Leeds players like Johnny Giles and Norman Hunter weren't the only ones showing us no respect, the Scottish ex-Elland Road boys – people like Eddie Gray and Peter Lorimer – were at it as well."

They were to be proved wrong. Big style.

Rangers soared in front with a blinding volley from Mark Hateley and McCoist scored a classic second on the break with a diving header.

Stuart McCALL

Eric Cantona's late goal was a crumb of comfort on a night when players like keeper Andy Goram, defensive lionheart John Brown and McCall gave the display of their lives.

Stuart said: "We scored two goals that will never be forgotten and we proved a point to the English who had so often sneered at Scottish football.

"There was no sweeter feeling than seeing those journalists and "experts" scuttle away into the night with their tails between their legs.

"Alex Ferguson even came into the dressing-room to congratulate not just Walter Smith and Archie Knox, who'd been his No.2 at Manchester

United, but also all of us. I think he was proud to be Scottish and an ex-Rangers player that night."

The party that followed that match is now Ibrox legend.

A slightly rumpled Walter Smith emerged for breakfast in the team's Manchester hotel to find McCall and Durrant still in the bar clutching Havanas.

He glowered: "Don't you think we should stop chaps, we do have a game on Saturday.

It was against Celtic and they won that too.

Stuart grinned: "We knew we were flying out from Manchester on the Thursday morning and we'd arranged an after-hours do for the players and their families at a nightclub there.

John McCLELLAND

JOHN McCLELLAND inspired Northern Ireland to weave a World Cup fairytale at Espana 82 but his dream job as Rangers skipper ended in a nightmare feud over money.

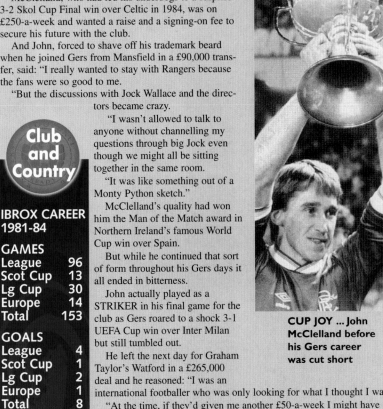

The big stopper was a class act in a weak team, a cool defender who never panicked and always tried to play himself out of danger.

He was a rock in a troubled era but his Gers career was cut short after a bitter contract dispute.

McClelland, who had led his underdogs to a surprise 3-2 Skol Cup Final win over Celtic in 1984, was on £250-a-week and wanted a raise and a signing-on fee to secure his future with the club.

And John, forced to shave off his trademark beard when he joined Gers from Mansfield in a £90,000 transfer, said: "I really wanted to stay with Rangers because the fans were so good to me.

"But the discussions with Jock Wallace and the directors became crazy.

"I wasn't allowed to talk to anyone without channelling my questions through big Jock even though we might all be sitting together in the same room.

"It was like something out of a Monty Python sketch."

McClelland's quality had won him the Man of the Match award in Northern Ireland's famous World Cup win over Spain.

But while he continued that sort of form throughout his Gers days it all ended in bitterness.

John actually played as a STRIKER in his final game for the club as Gers roared to a shock 3-1 UEFA Cup win over Inter Milan but still tumbled out.

He left the next day for Graham Taylor's Watford in a £265,000 deal and he reasoned: "I was an international footballer who was only looking for what I thought I was due.

"At the time, if they'd given me another £50-a-week I might have stayed.

"But the picture that Rangers tried to paint of me was that I was being awkward and greedy.

"The truth is the club was being petty-minded and because I wouldn't agree to exactly what they wanted they stripped me of the captaincy and threatened to sideline me forever. Things seem very different at Ibrox now."

Rangers paid the price for losing McClelland in the winter of 1984.

They'd lost just 10 goals in 20 games when he was in the line-up then shipped 21 in the 12 matches after he left culminating in a 5-1 thrashing at Aberdeen.

McClelland was to move onto Leeds United after Watford and returned north to St Johnstone where he starred at the heart of defence before an ill-fated stint as player-boss.

His Rangers story remains one of what might have been and the man from the troubled province regrets that because he knows what his captaincy meant to people back home.

John stressed: "They identified with the club and myself as skipper.

"To be honest, one of the reasons I was prepared to stay at Rangers for the rest of my football days – if the money had been right – was the captaincy. And for that I didn't get any extra pay – nor did I want any."

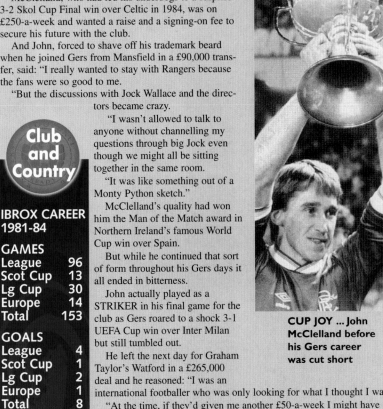

CUP JOY ... John McClelland before his Gers career was cut short

---

"We couldn't have picked a better place to go because Manchester United fans HATE Leeds and everyone there was treating us like Gods!"

Stuart McCall made his name at Bradford City and was a tower of strength to the club during the horrific aftermath of the fire that ripped through Valley Parade on a matchday and claimed 56 lives.

His own father was injured in the blaze and the emotional ties bonding him to the club saw him return there when his Ibrox days finished.

Back in that Treble season the vastly under-rated McCall – a shrewd £1.2million Smith signing from Everton – was in the form of his life.

The natural energy and tenacious tackling that were his trademarks often overshadowed a deft passing touch that was to earn him 40 caps for Scotland and his famous solitary international goal in the 2-1 win over Sweden at Italia 90.

He was the beating heart of the side that won Nine-in-a-Row and, even now as he masterminds first club Bradford's resurgence, he remains a keen Gers fan, often shuttling north to support the team.

Stuart stressed: "When Walter left it was right that the rest of us – Goram, Gough, Durrant, McCoist and myself – should go too.

"It was so sad that we couldn't leave the Gaffer with a trophy and went out losers in the Cup Final against Hearts but I can look at Rangers from a distance now.

"And I think there is a spirit we had that is special in football and they must strive to make sure it stays there.

"It was best summed up for me in the Scottish Cup semi-final against Celtic in my first season.

"We had David Robertson sent off after six minutes but we survived and Coisty scored to win it for us.

"We went through 84 minutes short-handed and beat our biggest rivals – that's what Rangers are all about."

Peter McCLOY

HE set up the goal that brought the Cup Winners' Cup to Ibrox, he hung on crossbars going for shots and he often took the goalkeeper's rocky rollercoaster ride from hero to villain.

But for 16 years Peter McCloy – the Girvan Lighthouse – held his place with the club to become Rangers' longest serving No 1 of all time.

The gangling 6ft 4ins star was brought in from Motherwell in 1970 in a player-swap deal that took Bobby Watson and Brian Heron the other way to Fir Park.

For all his occasional unconventional style, McCloy was to see off a host of challengers for his famous yellow jersey. And, of course, he had one of THE most monstrous kick-outs seen in the modern game.

Gers used it to their most telling advantage in Barcelona's Nou Camp Stadium when the Gas Meter's towering clearance found Willie Johnston to put the Scots three up in their eventual 3-2 Cup Winners' Cup Final triumph over Moscow Dynamo.

It would be criminal to write off the Gers sides the keeper played in as Route One specialists. Not when the Treble teams included the deft touches of McLean and Russell, Cooper and Smith. But equally, there's no doubt that Gers could always turn to The McCloy Ploy.

Peter explained: "It was a tactic we had in the bag if we needed it.

"It's easy to decry it and I'd hate to watch it all the time but it has its uses. Let's face it, we scored a goal off it on one of the biggest stages of all.

"In that European campaign we switched from our usual more attacking formation to 4-4-2.

"And the thing was that I could shell them so long that if Willie Johnston – who had the pace to hurt any team – or Colin Stein didn't get there, our midfield were still collecting their defence's clearances in the final third.

"Jock Wallace trained teams so they were super-fit and our midfielders could get up and down all day. We eventually ran over the top of a lot of teams.

"I never did get around to scoring from a kick-out. The closest I came was when I bounced one over the Toronto Blizzards keeper on tour but it came back off the underside of the bar."

Goalkeeper is the loneliest position on the field and that is magnified a hundred-fold at either of the Old Firm clubs where the slightest hint of an error is seized upon.

For all the physical attributes this

YELLOW JERSEY...McCloy was always easily recognisable, not least for his height

former all-round schools sports champion carried with him to Ibrox, the biggest one he had to learn was mental toughness.

Peter said: "You could lose a goal at Motherwell and then make five or six saves and the positive was accentuated.

"But then I came to Rangers and discovered it was the opposite there.

"You'd be inactive for long spells and then if there was a lapse of concentration and you lost one you were slaughtered."

One such famous McCloy incident actually came when Gers WON a trophy and sealed the Treble with a 2-1 Scottish Cup Final win over Aberdeen in 1978.

Wallace's side were cruising and then Steve Ritchie hit an outlandish miscue that spun miles in the air before looping behind the big Gers keeper.

In his desperation to get back McCloy hared towards his own goal, leapt up – and was left hanging on the crossbar as the ball dropped lazily into the net.

Peter laughs about that one now and

he smiled: "I remember afterwards I was on holiday and Aberdeen's Joe Harper came in to the same bar and asked me how I'd felt on Cup Final day.

"I said: 'I felt fine when I went up to get my winner's medal, how did you feel?'"

McCloy idolised Gordon Banks and studied the England legend's technique whilst he also listened and learned under former Berwick Rangers 'keeper Wallace when Jock was coach under Willie Waddell.

Once the former jungle-fighter took over as manager, there was less time to develop their relationship. But Peter, who coached at the club until 1988 before a fall-out with then boss Graeme Souness, said: "I often said that the only time I played against Jock was the time Motherwell put seven past him at Berwick, so he couldn't have been that good.

"But he did help me a lot and where

some people might knock his training methods, I think they were the making of that team.

"We had so much confidence in our fitness that we knew no-one would match us that way.

"Our physical shape gave us self-belief and when you have that in 11 guys with a lot of ability pulling the same way then you have something special.

"Put it this way, I don't think that after the Bosman ruling we'll ever see 11 Scots bring home a European trophy again."

Two years ago McCloy lapped up the 25th anniversary celebrations of that Barcelona triumph and insists it was only then he realised he'd kept 257 clean sheets in a goalkeeping record total of 644 games for the club.

When he quit playing Peter mixed coaching 'keepers at a host of clubs with working for an insurance firm – before promotion to sales manager put paid to his involvement in football.

He is now General Manager of Brunston Castle Golf Club near his Girvan home. However, Peter interrupted his work recently to make the trip back to Ibrox to sign 100 replicas of his famous yellow jersey from that Cup Winners' Cup Final.

They were framed for fans to buy and Peter pointed out: "That I'm asked to do that so long after we won the Cup shows the level of the achievement.

"There was a camaraderie and a togetherness about that team that was special and it overcame a lot.

"In the semi-final, for instance, Bayern Munich were a more skilful side than us but it was Rangers who wanted that trophy more – and we got it."

SIMPLY THE BEST… John Greig proudly displays his Greatest Ever Ranger trophy at the awards ceremony in the Thistle Hotel on Sunday, 21 March 1999

*SECONDS OUT... Super striker Ally McCoist collects his award for being voted the second
Greatest Ever Ranger from Chairman David Murray*

*WING KING... The late Davie Cooper was voted into the Greatest Ever Rangers Team, as well as finishing
third in the Greatest Ever Ranger award. His brother John is pictured collecting the award from Terry Butcher*

BLUE AND WHITE DYNAMITE… Ian Durrant didn't win any awards but he certainly enjoyed himself

GETTING SHIRTY… Paul Gascoigne looks delighted at being announced as a member of the Greatest Ever Ranger Team alongside greats Richard Gough, Jim Baxter and Brian Laudrup (background)

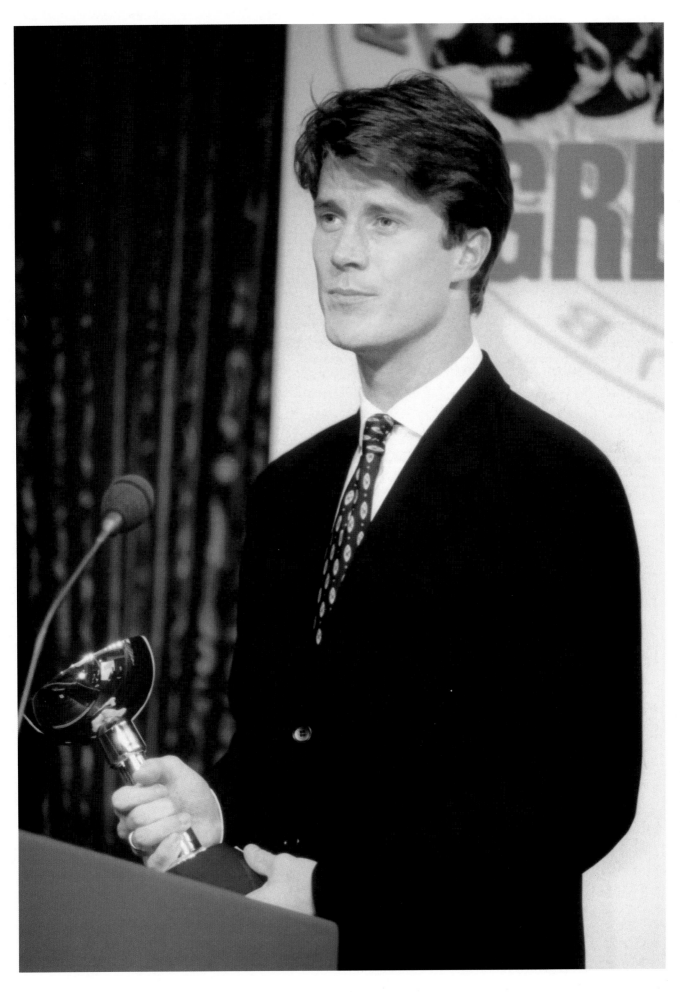

GREAT DANE… Brian Laudrup clutches his Greatest Ever Non-Scot trophy after beating off tough competition from Englishmen Paul Gascoigne, Terry Butcher and Mark Hateley

STAR STRUCK… Gazza was so overcome at his place in the Greatest Ever Rangers Team that he asked John Greig to sign his shirt so he could frame it!

PICTURE THIS… Andy Goram always seems to be the centre of attention these days, and the Greatest Ever Ranger's night was to be no different

WHAT A LINE-UP... Walter Smith stands proudly with most of the Greatest Team – Goram, Jardine, Greig, Gough, Baxter, Butcher, Cooper, McCoist and Hateley. Gascoigne and Laudrup were called up later

TALKING TACTICS... Nine-in-a-row great Richard Gough and current captain Lorenzo Amoruso are deep in discussion about the joys of leading the Light Blues

HAPPY MEMORIES… Sandy Jardine holds tightly onto his Rangers shirt in the Greatest Ever Team line-up

RAZOR SHARP… Ray Wilkins and Bobby Shearer, two great names from Rangers' past, make their way into the Greatest Ever Ranger dinner

IN GOOD TUNE… Derek Johnstone was on top form despite missing out on the Greatest Ever Rangers Team

TREBLE TALK… Brian Laudrup, Mark Hateley and Andy Goram – three of the stars of Rangers'
Nine-in-a-row campaign – meet up again after the dinner

EYE OPENER… Current Gers Giovanni van Bronckhorst and Arthur Numan seem to have shocked
former Light Blue Pieter Huistra – surely they haven't mentioned their wages!

IN SAFE HANDS… Andy Goram has a tight grip on his Greatest Ever goalkeeper trophy

PUT IT THERE… A delighted Jim Baxter is congratulated by Nine-in-a-row management team Archie Knox and Walter Smith on making the Greatest Ever line-up

HUGGY BEARS… Mark Hateley and Ally McCoist, one of the greatest striking partnerships Rangers have ever had, are re-united in the Greatest Ever Team line-up

STOP SIGN... The Girvan Lighthouse Peter McCloy signs a goalkeeper's top on his way into the dinner

JUST REWARDS... Willie Waddell, Campbell Ogilvie and David Murray were all awarded trophies for their outstanding contributions to the club. Willie Waddell's wife Hilda is pictured collecting his award

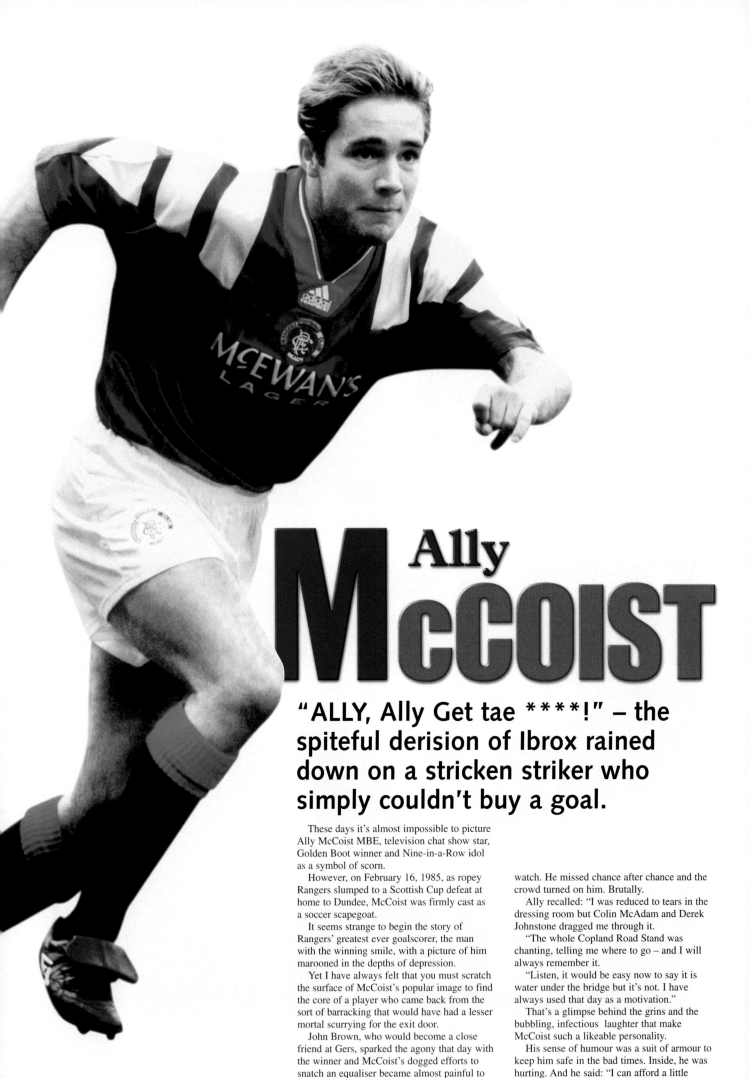

Ally McCOIST

"ALLY, Ally Get tae ****!" – the spiteful derision of Ibrox rained down on a stricken striker who simply couldn't buy a goal.

These days it's almost impossible to picture Ally McCoist MBE, television chat show star, Golden Boot winner and Nine-in-a-Row idol as a symbol of scorn.

However, on February 16, 1985, as ropey Rangers slumped to a Scottish Cup defeat at home to Dundee, McCoist was firmly cast as a soccer scapegoat.

It seems strange to begin the story of Rangers' greatest ever goalscorer, the man with the winning smile, with a picture of him marooned in the depths of depression.

Yet I have always felt that you must scratch the surface of McCoist's popular image to find the core of a player who came back from the sort of barracking that would have had a lesser mortal scurrying for the exit door.

John Brown, who would become a close friend at Gers, sparked the agony that day with the winner and McCoist's dogged efforts to snatch an equaliser became almost painful to

watch. He missed chance after chance and the crowd turned on him. Brutally.

Ally recalled: "I was reduced to tears in the dressing room but Colin McAdam and Derek Johnstone dragged me through it.

"The whole Copland Road Stand was chanting, telling me where to go – and I will always remember it.

"Listen, it would be easy now to say it is water under the bridge but it's not. I have always used that day as a motivation."

That's a glimpse behind the grins and the bubbling, infectious laughter that make McCoist such a likeable personality.

His sense of humour was a suit of armour to keep him safe in the bad times. Inside, he was hurting. And he said: "I can afford a little

COOL HEAD...
Ally McCoist
beats Celtic
keeper Gordon
Marshall for
one of his 27
Old Firm goals

smile at what I achieved after that day but the memory of that afternoon will always make me appreciate the good times.

"I never thought about leaving Rangers but it put a lot of things into perspective for me. I was genuinely trying my best and if the fans could be like that with me, then what could they be like with other people?

"I know for a fact that the same people who screamed and told me where to go were jumping up and down like lunatics later when the goals were going in.

"I have always maintained after that there are two things I hate about the average football fan – his face!

"Seriously, it was all a lesson for me. I could have gone out the back door but I came in the front and I vowed that was the way I was leaving.

"I took more abuse but, before you hail my bravery, remember I had McAdam and Johnstone with me."

Coisty was at the crossroads back then. A memorable hat-trick in the 3-2 League Cup Final win over Celtic a year earlier had been forgotten.

Now came the test of his character that was to make him as a Rangers player – and the master of the wind-up believes wily boss Jock Wallace played him for a sucker.

He smiled: "I'll always remember he called me in and told me Cardiff City were in for me. To this day, I don't know if he was setting me up or not.

"I think he was trying to see what I was made of. I said I had no interest in speaking to them and he said: "Fine".

"If I'd said I'd talk to them, then he would have produced a club – Cardiff or whoever – to take me away from Rangers.

"He was a master of kidology and psychology, though, and I'll never know the truth."

Wallace's departure from Rangers paved the way for Graeme Souness to cut a swathe through the club. His arrival would prove a double-edged sword for penalty-box predator McCoist.

Souness brought back the good days but would leave Ally a gutted figure on the bench so often that he was tagged The Judge.

The first season was memorable, though, as the new manager led the club to the title – despite being sent off on the day the crown was clinched with a 1-1 draw in Aberdeen.

And McCoist stressed: "Winning the title the first time at Pittodrie was superb, one of the best days of my life.

"We went back to my local in East Kilbride, the Calderwood Inn, and Jimmy Nicholl was dancing on the bar in his Y-fronts because we went in with our strips on and he gave everything away!"

Yet the relationship with Souness was to turn sour after the Gers boss purchased Mark

Hateley from Monaco for £1million in the summer of 1990.

Ally's dream partnership with Scotland pal Mo Johnston was broken up and he was dumped.

He insisted: "I refuse to look at those days as dark – they were just less bright than the other ones!

"It was all part of the learning process at the club and it hasn't all been a bed of roses.

"The Souness period when I wasn't in the team, I could have done without.

"I feel he honestly believed that Mo and Mark up front was right for the team, the best partnership.

"Mind you, it suited him that he could show people he was The Boss when it came to me."

Again the steel inside was tested to breaking point as Souness let the fans know in no uncertain terms that he was in charge.

They pleaded for Ally's inclusion, implored the manager to give him a start but he refused to buckle. Then came the Cheltenham Affair.

Sandwiched in between two Old Firm defeats, Ally went to the races and ran straight into a public war of words with his manager.

Even now, after all the success and the prized record of 27 goals in games against Celtic, he remains bitter about that bust-up.

And he said: "The Cheltenham situation was bollocks. We had two days off and (a) At

CONTINUED ON
NEXT PAGE ...

87

Club
and
Country

IBROX CAREER
1983-98

GAMES
League 418
Scot Cup 47
Lg Cup 62
Europe 54
Total 581

GOALS
League 251
Scot Cup 29
Lg Cup 54
Europe 21
Total 355

MEDALS
League 8
Scot Cup 1
Lg Cup 9

SCOTLAND
61 caps

STATS

Ally McCOIST

...CONTINUED

no time was I not allowed to go to the races. (b) At no time did I miss any training.

"I know for a fact that other boys were at the golf during those two days and Souness had BANNED them from playing.

"What I did was allowed, yet I was forced to make a public apology through the media.

"That's when I feel I was clever with the wording. I said: 'In the manager's opinion, there has been a breach of club discipline.' I made it clear that it wasn't MY opinion."

Cataloguing the battles Ally came through to carve his place as a Rangers legend brings you to the skills of a truly awesome finisher.

The records that fell in his 15-year reign of terror are too numerous to list, suffice to say there is only one goalscoring tag that suits. The Greatest.

He worked his way through more than 40 striking partners in his Rangers career and enjoyed comparing their qualities for this book.

Ally reflected: "Mo was brilliant and such a contrast with the style of Mark Hateley. I also loved playing with Robert Fleck.

"Johnston and I were playing with Scotland at the time we linked up with Rangers and were very successful.

"I feel Souness broke us up too soon. Mo's first season with Rangers when he came back from France was immense. He was one of the best strikers in Europe then. It was broken up too early.

"But goals-wise, the most successful had to be Hateley. We were telepathic in the end and we scored 140-odd between us in two years."

McCoist was at his peak in that unforgettable 1992-93 season when Gers won the treble, went 44 games unbeaten and to within a hair's breadth of the European Cup Final.

He scored 49 goals, only to break his leg in Scotland's 5-0 defeat in Portugal and end the season on an agonising low.

Ally, of course, went on to join Richard Gough and Ian Ferguson as the only players to

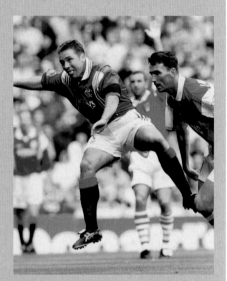

grasp all nine medals from a famous title sequence.

He was to bow out of Rangers the only way he knows how. Scoring.

His final goal for the club in the '98 Scottish Cup Final wasn't enough to save Walter Smith's side from a 2-1 defeat by Hearts.

Now 36, he has relished this season alongside best friend Ian Durrant at Kilmarnock but it looks like being his swansong. A TV future beckons for one of Ibrox's favourite sons.

And he said: "I hope Rangers succeed and go on to greater things than our team did, especially in Europe – but they have a hard act to follow.

"I was gutted that last night when I left but the blow was softened because so many of us were going at the one time.

"Everyone else in the team was in bits but, as usual, I was the only one LAUGHING. Yet it was the end of an era and I knew it. Truth is, I had no tears left."

ALLY McCOIST provided a mountain of memories for Rangers fans and an avalanche of goals. Here he chooses Coisty's Top Ten.

Leeds Utd 1 Rangers 2, European Cup, November 4, 1992
GREAT. I silenced a whole stadium with one far post diving header from big Hateley's cross. Did I mention they were English?

Rangers 2 Hibernian 1 League Cup Final, October 24, 1993
OVERHEAD kick into the far corner on my comeback from a broken leg. Fairytale, considering the size of my backside. Gordon Strachan said: "You're always taking a chance with those but look at the cushion he had to land on."

Rangers 2 Aberdeen 2, Premier League, December 22, 1990

TOOK a throw-in and turned to hitch-kick a screamer high beyond Theo Snelders with my LEFT foot! Souness didn't even clap.

Aberdeen 0 Rangers 2, Premier League, May 2, 1992
IN as a double entry because I have seldom scored two better in a match. A nutmeg on Stephen Wright in the build-up to one assured my continuing popularity up north.

Rangers 3 Celtic 2, League Cup Final, March 25, 1984
MY third against Celtic in the Cup Final. Hit a penalty, Pat Bonner saves it and the Celtic End jumps up. Pop in the rebound – Celtic End slumps down. One of life's great moments!

Celtic 0 Rangers 1, Scottish Cup semi-final, March 1992

TRUE GERS. We played for 84 minutes with 10 men when David Robertson was sent off but I rapped home the winner from 18 yards.

Rangers 2 Grasshoppers 1, Champions League, November 20, 1996
ALL I had heard from Durrant was Champions League this, Europe's elite that. All because I hadn't scored in the tournament. I got both in this one.

Scotland 1 Switzerland 0, Euro '96, June 18
SCREAMER. Not a typical McCoist goal as I melted one in from 25 yards but I'd missed two easier chances.

St Mirren 1 Rangers 2, Premier League, February 8, 1992
DEFT switch of feet, past Les Fridge and in the net. Frank Worthington phoned me and said it was a belter.

EIGHT league medals, five Scottish Cup and three League Cup badges for Rangers, 14 caps for Scotland and the job as international manager when he finished playing.

You could say Ian McColl made a success of his football career.

McColl was considered the final cog in the wheel of a dominant Gers side following his signing from Queen's Park after the Second World War.

Yet the man whose strength and distribution turned him into an Ibrox idol admits he was in awe of the place when he first arrived from the Amateurs.

Ian, now 71 and still a very keen thinker on the game, said: "You have to remember that I had come from a club with a charming attitude and a motto: "For the love of the game."

"Now I was 18 and I was in a very different world. The club motto at Rangers might well be "Ready" but it should be "For the love of winning."

"I don't mind confessing that it took me a while to adjust to that but once I did I settled well enough."

That is an understatement, of course, as he shone at wing-half and amassed a bundle of honours few players in Britain could match.

A highly intelligent man – he has a BSc in civil engineering – McColl quickly showed his new team-mates he had the brawn to go with his brains when it was needed on the field.

But it was his passing skill that made him an integral part of the flowing 2-3-5 or W formation that the team used then.

Ian studied the way Gers played a system that would bemuse fans in the defence-minded 90s.

And he said: "It actually fluctuated, because people in the Rangers' side learned to tuck in and it was nearer 4-2-4 in operation.

"I try to explain that to people today when I watch games but I have to say some of the stuff I see BORES me.

"There is too much needless interplay at the back when the name of the game should always be attack. Yet while studying the system is interesting, what made that Rangers team was the personnel.

"I had played against them a few times with Queen's as a teenager and been so impressed.

"I mean, you couldn't help but be daunted

Ian McCOLL

by men like Willie Woodburn, Sammy Cox and Jimmy Duncanson."

McColl, though, earned their respect and became a vital figure in a side that dominated from winning the game's first ever treble in 1949 and then in to the early 50s.

He enjoyed every new experience life with Rangers threw at him and, even now, ponders how that side would have fared had there been European competition in those days.

McColl smiled: "I do remember flying out to Lisbon in 1948 for a special challenge match with Benfica.

"We hadn't even heard of them then, to be honest, but they were THE club in Portugal.

"We soon realised this was a massive club full of stars but we hammered them 3-0 on their own turf, anyway."

When it came time to bow out as a Rangers player, Ian McColl did it the only way he knew how – as a winner.

He was recalled for the 1960 Scottish Cup Final against Kilmarnock after an injury to Harold Davis and he starred as two Jimmy Millar goals gave Gers a 2-0 win over Kilmarnock in front of 108,017 at Hampden.

Ian smiled: "There are things you can always look back on but I don't suppose anything will stay with me like the memory of my last Scottish Cup Final.

"I like to think I gave a good account of

myself and that was a nice way to bow out, although I did also help us win the Charity Cup after that.

"I finished on a high and that's the best way to go."

In his final season at Ibrox, McColl was the best-paid player in BRITAIN as the club recognised his service by paying him first-team bonuses whether he played or not.

He often sat with boss Scot Symon then and spoke of the way the game was developing.

And Ian recalled: "I remember Scot saying to me that the day would come when a player would stop playing for Rangers and never have to work again.

"I thought he was in Cloud Cuckoo Land but here we are. It's arrived.

"It's worth reflecting that, because of England's maximum wage rule at the time, no-one earned more than me in that final season and I pocketed £3,000 for the YEAR."

His worth as a football thinker was spotted immediately when he hung up his boots and the call came from the SFA to take over the Scotland team.

He took over in a golden era when Scotland could choose from a host of stars playing for England's top sides.

Sure, there was the 9-3 hiding from England in 1961 to recover from but that was avenged the following year and then in '63 Jim Baxter

inspired McColl's men to a 2-1 Wembley win.

Overall, Ian won more than he lost in a five-year reign and he said: "There was a frustration in being boss.

"You could pick the likes of Baxter or Denis Law and try to tell them something and then they'd go out and play as they bloody well liked!

"But in those days you had Bill Brown, Dave Mackay and John White at Spurs, Frank McLintock and Ian Ure at Arsenal and Law and Paddy Crerand at Manchester United.

"Oh, that we had that number of stars at England's top clubs now!"

When his Scotland stint ended in 1965, McColl moved to Sunderland for three years as boss.

But when that turned sour, he turned his back on the game at the age of just 41 – a move he now regrets.

He reasoned: "I'd had enough and I didn't need football. I had my education to fall back on and started my own civil engineering company.

"I just got fed-up of a game where directors of clubs could treat you like dirt. I walked away, although I often look back and think it was too early."

Like everything in his life, the business was a success and there's no question Ian McColl's decision then was football's loss.

Alex MacDONALD

ALEX MacDONALD surged through from midfield to score a trademark goal AGAINST Rangers and still received a standing ovation around Ibrox.

Now that's when you KNOW you're a legend.

Doddie's magical moment came in 1980 when he returned to his old stamping ground with new club Hearts.

And Alex, brought up in Kinning Park in the shadow of Gers' home, recalled:"I remember running through and when I scored there was this eerie moment of silence.

"Then as one the whole stadium rose and they were chanting my name. I couldn't believe it.

"I couldn't have ever imagined a tribute like that.

"I thought they would string me up!"

MacDonald was the constant inspiration of Gers' midfield in the 70s from the Cup Winners' Cup side to the Treble teams.

His left foot passes prompted and probed and his sneaking late runs into the box brought him a sackful of goals.

Yet when Davie White paid St Johnstone £50,000 for him back in 1968 Doddie was in danger of being branded a dud at first.

The Gers boss watched MacDonald star for Saints against Dunfermline in an unfamiliar wide right role and decided he could be used there at Ibrox.

Alex grimaced: "I remember one early game against Clyde at Shawfield when I was trying to take in-swinging corners with my RIGHT foot as if I was Willie Henderson.

"No wonder the punters thought I was hopeless!"

As he toiled playing out of position there were other worries crowding in on local hero MacDonald.

Suddenly, the boy who'd stared up at that famous, forbidding front entrance for years as a kid was allowed to walk through the doors as a player.

Like Ian Durrant in later years, his presence in the Gers' first team was a source of pride in the tight-knit community of Kinning Park.

And Alex stressed: "Like Durranty I knew just what Rangers meant to people in that area.

"To be honest, I had a lot of problems adjusting to the fact that I had finally got inside the doors after all those years of dreaming about it.

STATS

Club and Country

IBROX CAREER 1968-80

GAMES
League	336
Scot Cup	50
Lg Cup	79
Europe	38
Total	503

GOALS
League	51
Scot Cup	15
Lg Cup	18
Europe	10
Total	94

MEDALS
League	3
Scot Cup	4
Lg Cup	4
Europe	1

SCOTLAND
1 cap

HIGH FLYER... Alex MacDonald was a constant inspiration in the Rangers midfield in the 1970s

"I felt dwarfed by the whole place and I remember I used to feel knackered BEFORE matches.

"I wondered what was wrong with me. Then I worked out that all the nervous energy I was using up was leaving me completely drained.

"I sat down and made myself stay calm one day.

"I told myself I was going to lose my chance at Rangers unless I learned to cope."

He did. And in 1972 he was to be the beating heart of the side that made history and lifted the European Cup Winners' Cup with that 3-2 win over Moscow Dynamo in Barcelona.

MacDonald's energy, his passion and his combative style often serve to mask his true talents when you assess his class.

He had this sly stealth that allowed him to steal into the box untracked.

And on that Euro run he plundered the

solitary Ibrox goals that saw off both French side Rennes and Italian giants Torino in nervy Ibrox encounters.

Doddie recalls the air of tension that hung around the side's Spanish base before the Final as minds understandably drifted back to the numbing 1967 loss against Bayern Munich at the same stage.

Willie Waddell and coach Jock Wallace used any motivational trick in the book to psyche up their players as the game beckoned.

And Alex said: "We all had pictures of our families in our rooms and Jock was forever picking them up then thrusting them under our noses and saying: 'Win it for them.'

"It all got a bit heavy and the day before the Final Sandy Jardine, Alfie Conn and I decided on a stroll out of the hotel grounds.

"We found this go-kart track in the little village nearby and they were

whizzing round it at about 60mph, it looked like great fun.

"One taunt led to another and we decided to have a race as long as we took it easy on each other.

"One thing led to another, however, and before you knew it three Rangers stars were crashing through haystacks at 60mph trying to beat each other at go-karts 24 hours before a European Final.

"To be honest, it was bloody terrifying but not half as scary as it could have been if Jock had ever found out."

MacDonald, ever-present in that Euro run, admits memories of the actual game are a little hazy now 27 years on.

But he still finds it painfully difficult to keep a check on his emotions when he recalls the beating Gers exuberant fans took at the hands of baton-wielding Spanish police.

Alex said: "There were a couple of pitch invasions which isn't right and then the fans came on at the end but it was like an explosion of joy, really.

"These fans had waited so long for that, remember, and what happened to them was horrendous.

"It was bang out of order.

"I sat on that bus on the way back after we'd been denied our lap of honour and worried about what was happening to them."

That depth of feeling and his blunt honesty sum up why Doddie remains a massive favourite with the Light Blues legions.

To the fans he is one of them.

He never failed to show his commitment to the cause against Celtic and in 1975 Alex realised the last of his boyhood fantasies when he scored a Cup Final winner against his team's fiercest enemies.

It came with a typical late run into the box and a flicked, diving header. He said: "I remember thinking at the time, please God keep it at 1-0.

""Forget all that stuff about it doesn't matter who scores – I wanted to be the guy who scored the winner against Celtic.

"Towards the end I was kicking balls off the CELTIC line so it could be me!"

His driving desire was made for the Wallace teams of the 70s and when

the batteries needed a charge he welcomed the signings of players like Bobby Russell and Davie Cooper to keep thriving.

He eventually made that switch to Tynecastle where he was appointed manager on his own before later being joined by former Gers team-mate Jardine in an experienced double act.

They took the unfancied Jambos to within a heartbeat of the Double in 1986 only to lose the championship and then the Scottish Cup in a harrowing week.

Four years later Alex was axed and after nine months out of the game he landed the Airdrie job where he stayed until March 1999, masterminding some memorable Cup runs.

Doddie's Diamonds, Scotland's answer to Wimbledon's Crazy Gang in England, reached the Final in 1992 where they lost 2-1 to his beloved Rangers before Celtic also edged the Lanarkshire underdogs 1-0 three years later.

Football still consumes him the way it did when his desire to play for Rangers sent him into fits of nervous exhaustion.

When I called him with the news that he was in *The 100 Greatest Rangers*, his side had lost 2-0 to Morton the night before.

"I'm in? Unbelievable," he croaked, his voice hoarse with screaming at beaten players.

"You have made my day, honest.

"I was just sitting here with the gun and bullets. Now I can put them away again."

MISTER POPULAR... Alex MacDonald got a standing ovation from the Gers fans – when he scored for Hearts!

Bobby McKEAN

THE skills and dreams of a man who cherished Rangers were snatched away in a fume-filled garage when he died at the wheel of his car in a shocking accident.

TRAGIC GER... Bobby McKean died just when his Ibrox career was taking an upsurge

Tragedy is an overused word in a game that shreds the emotions but it's the only one that applies to Bobby McKean.

The death of a gifted midfielder on March 15, 1978, put football into its true perspective.

He had returned home from a midweek night out on a high, recalled to the Gers squad after 18 months of uncertainty on the fringes of Jock Wallace's squad.

Bobby McKean was back in the reckoning for that Saturday's League Cup Final with Celtic. He had everything to live for.

He should have stayed that night at the home of childhood pal Jack Cleland but decided to drive home to be with wife Fiona and daughter Ashleigh as they had to attend a family funeral the next day.

When Bobby arrived home at his Barrhead bungalow he'd locked himself out and couldn't raise anyone in the house.

He opted to sleep in his car and left the engine running – A FATAL DECISION.

A gust of wind blew the garage door shut as he slept and Bobby died of carbon monoxide poisoning. He was just 25.

Glasgow remains a bitterly-divided football city, yet grief unites it.

The scenes of dignity that surrounded the death of McKean would be echoed 17 years later when Light Blues legend Davie Cooper died in the prime of life.

Then, as in 1978, the circumstances again left family, footballers and fans grasping for explanations, there was just one word on their lips. Why?

Almost 1,000 mourners – including Celtic legends Jock Stein, Sean Fallon and Danny McGrain – attended Bobby's funeral at Martyrs' Parish Church in Paisley.

The poignant service was conducted by the Rangers chaplain, the Rev. James Currie.

Gers won that League Cup Final 2-1 with an extra-time clincher from Gordon Smith, yet the result paled into insignificance when they pondered the loss of McKean.

Bobby had grown up dreaming of playing in games like that and his most memorable match as a fan came when he LOST a precious Old Firm ticket.

He recalled: "I didn't get in to Celtic Park until late because I couldn't find the ticket. I was frantic but I got there in time to see Kai Johansen score and give Rangers a 2-2 draw."

Club and Country

STATS

IBROX CAREER 1974-78	
GAMES	
League	91
Scot Cup	8
Lg Cup	15
Europe	5
Total	119
GOALS	
League	12
Scot Cup	4
Lg Cup	1
Europe	0
Total	17
MEDALS	
League	2
Scot Cup	1
SCOTLAND	
1 cap	

Bobby's talents were first spotted when he was just a skinny 15-year-old stand-out on his local playing fields with East Kilbride Burgh United. The club's pride in his achievements would be shown in a match tinged with sadness a decade later. Six months after their most famous player's death, a Burgh Select played a Rangers XI at East Kilbride Thistle's Showpark, with the proceeds going to the heartbroken family Bobby left behind.

Burgh gave McKean his start and he never looked back as he graduated to the Junior ranks with Blantyre Vics, then was quickly snapped up by St Mirren.

Boss Alex Wright brought him through alongside other gifted youngsters such as Gordon McQueen and Iain Munro. They would have fruitful careers as players and manager but McKean's would be so cruelly cut short.

Yet, in these days of £20,000-a-week foreign imports, Bobby's story still inspires starry-eyed Gers-daft kids to dream of Ibrox through all the cold, rain, wind, mud and gravel rashes.

He worked in Templeton's carpet factory and played for St Mirren until his exceptional skills on the park won him the chance of something better.

Bobby cost Gers £40,000 from Saints in September, 1974, the most ever paid then

for a player from the Second Division.

He was to win a championship medal in his first season at the club and become a fans' favourite.

In his first full campaign, a stunning show in a 5-1 mauling of St Johnstone at Muirton sparked calls for Scotland recognition – it arrived the following year.

Bobby was selected in a 1-0 win over Switzerland at Hampden but his cap haul was to stay at just one.

While he'd developed into an excellent asset in midfield, the mazy dribbles of his younger days stayed with him.

His skills were summed up in one jinking run that set up Derek Johnstone's second in the 3-1 Scottish Cup Final win over Hearts in 1976 that clinched the treble.

Inconsistent form blighted his Ibrox career the following season and, at one point, he seemed poised to join an exodus of players heading for the States.

Moves had been underway to land McKean a new life in the USA but then came the hope of his Cup Final recall before tragedy struck.

Jock Wallace had a way with words and what he said in those desperate days after McKean's death still hits home.

He sighed: "I am supposed to be a hard man but when I heard about Bobby... well, I knew I wasn't."

Ron McKINNON

RON McKINNON sat in the stand in the Nou Camp and looked on at the greatest triumph in Rangers' history, knowing that he should have been a part of it.

BIG-HEARTED...
Ron McKinnon was small for a centre-half but his tenacity was immense

As his team-mates lifted the European Cup-Winners' Cup with the 3-2 win over Moscow Dynamo in Barcelona in 1972, choked McKinnon could only curse the broken leg that denied him the medal he so richly deserved.

McKinnon was cheated out of his date with destiny earlier in Gers' glory run to the final on a night of pain and drama in Lisbon.

Gers had won the first leg 3-2 against Sporting and that scoreline was repeated in Portugal to take the tie into extra time.

The match eventually ended 4-3 to the Lisbon side, tied 6-6 on aggregate, and the referee then wrongly ordered a penalty shootout which Gers LOST, before it was pointed out that away goals still counted in extra time.

McKinnon, meanwhile, had fallen awkwardly in a challenge 18 minutes from time and the crack could be heard around the stadium.

His leg was broken in two places.

He was out for the season and the sickening injury was to end his top-flight career as Colin Jackson and Derek Johnstone stepped into the defensive breach.

Ron recalled: "Watching from the stand was murder. I felt myself in there, involved with all the lads – yet I wasn't involved in the action.

"It was hard to bear.

"Ironically, that was the first serious injury I had and I came to appreciate what players like Dave Smith had come through to get back from TWO leg breaks."

McKinnon spent an agonising flight back to Glasgow, despite being drugged with morphine, and when he returned home a plate with 12 screws was inserted in his leg to try to heal the damage.

No anaesthetic, however, could have eased the hurt he felt that balmy night in Barcelona, when football history was made without him.

Yet, in a touching gesture three months after that final, Ron McKinnon DID get his European Cup-Winners' Cup medal.

The club had been given 13 of the treasured prizes and manager Jock Wallace decided to hand one to Ron and another to Colin Jackson who had gone over on his ankle in the build-up to the final and also missed out.

Big Jock said then: "We felt that McKinnon should get one for his great service to the club and to compensate for the disappointments of the season.

"Jackson got the other, because he was involved all the way to the final.

"It was fitting that McKinnon should have that last reward for a career built on his dedication in defence."

Ron was eventually released by Rangers in 1973.

He headed for Durban City in South Africa and loved the country so much he stayed.

He left as a legend. At 5ft 10ins he was not the tallest centre-half but he had pace to burn and worked for hours on his aerial ability.

Ron honed himself into an integral part of the Rangers treble side in 1964 and was capped 28 times for Scotland.

All that from a player who had been FREED by Junior side Benburb before his determination won him a slot at Dunipace and the route to Ibrox.

He actually began his Gers career at wing-half but Scot Symon saw something in McKinnon and axed the towering Doug Baillie, labelling the athletic Ron as the future.

McKinnon, whose brother Donnie was also a professional player with Partick Thistle, fulfilled all Symon's hopes.

Scot was still in charge when Kai Johansen's goal won the 1966 Scottish Cup against Celtic but McKinnon and his mentor couldn't have known then that a five-season famine was about to start.

When it ended in the League Cup Final against the Hoops, thanks to a teenage kid called Derek Johnstone who headed the winner it was Ron – skipper in place of the injured John Greig – who held the trophy aloft.

When he reflects on his career, perhaps moments like that are some consolation for Barcelona – but he confessed: "In the end one tackle, one shattering moment turned my life upside down."

Club and Country

**IBROX CAREER
1960-73**

GAMES
League	301
Scot Cup	44
Lg Cup	83
Europe	45
Total	473

GOALS
League	2
Scot Cup	0
Lg Cup	0
Europe	1
Total	3

MEDALS
League	2
Scot Cup	4
Lg Cup	3

**SCOTLAND
28 caps**

STATS

George McLEAN

DANDY McLEAN was a man with style on and off the pitch but he was brutally jettisoned from Gers in shabby fashion after the humiliating Scottish Cup defeat at Berwick

In the wake of the 1967 Scottish Cup loss to the Wee Gers the club needed scapegoats and chose the strikers.

Jim Forrest and big George were the soccer sacrifice.

Yet Dandy's Scottish record transfer fee when he was bought from St Mirren at the age of just 19 didn't just beat Gers' previous best – it smashed it to pieces.

They inked a cheque for £27,500 to land him and that was £10,000 more than they'd laid out to Raith Rovers for Jim Baxter and Airdrie for Doug Baillie.

George could operate slickly in midfield and attack and the season before his Gers demise he hammered home 41 goals in the three domestic tournaments.

Yet Berwick killed his Ibrox career.

And he admitted: "There are no happy memories of that day. Nobody likes to be beaten by the rabbits in the Cup and nobody likes to be personally blamed for the defeat.

"I still feel that Jim Forrest and myself were unfairly treated after that game. After all the TEAM lost.

"The defence was as much to blame as Jim and I were for missing a couple of chances.

"Still, that's how you're brought up in football at Ibrox. Defeat is a disaster for the club and the fans.

"It could be the worst place in the world when something like Berwick happened."

He was dumped to Dundee as part of the package that brought Andy Penman to Ibrox but George McLean wasn't the type to fade away.

In a colourful career after Ibrox, the star who loved the high life took in Dens, Dunfermline, Ayr United and also enjoyed a spell with Vancouver White Eagles in Canada.

Laughs are never far away when he recalls his playing days, this was a personality player.

He was the type fans loved but he left his managers reaching for the valium.

Here are some classics from the man who, fittingly enough, helped run a pub called The Jester after he quit.

"I always remember when Rangers played Real Madrid in Spain and we were gubbed 6-0. Some of the players complained afterwards about the state of the pitch.

"When the Boss asked me, I said: "Honestly, Mr Symon, the bit I was standing on was brand new!

"The nickname? The fans said it was because all I could read was *The Dandy* but that just wasn't true. I read *The Beano* as well.

"I remember a fitness test at Ibrox one day when we had to lap the track and then simulate a block tackle by hitting the ball against the boundary wall.

"I'd finished lapping the track when the Boss asked if I'd tried a block yet. You should have seen his face when I said: "No, I still fancy the birds!"

Club and Country

IBROX CAREER 1963-67

GAMES

League	69
Scot Cup	14
Lg Cup	28
Europe	6
Total	117

GOALS

League	49
Scot Cup	8
Lg Cup	23
Europe	2
Total	82

MEDALS

League	1
Scot Cup	2

SCOTLAND
1 cap

STATS

GAZ AND CARRY...
Alan McLaren gifts his pal a lift after clinching nine-in-a-row

Alan McLAREN

ALAN McLAREN looked to the skies over Tannadice in exhaustion and relief then almost hugged the life out of closest friend Paul Gascoigne.

Club and Country

STATS

IBROX CAREER
1994-98

GAMES
League	78
Scot Cup	8
Lg Cup	3
Europe	5
Total	94

GOALS
League	5
Scot Cup	0
Lg Cup	0
Europe	0
Total	5

MEDALS
League	2
Scot Cup	1

SCOTLAND
24 caps

It was football heaven for McLaren when he skippered Rangers to the nine-in-a-row win at Tannadice with Brian Laudrup's history-making header sealing the title and a place in the game's folklore for his team.

It was a night of unbridled joy but it was to be the last time Alan played for Gers.

The steely defender signed from Hearts for £1.25million – the man who had shackled German legend Jurgen Klinsmann and Italian superstar Roberto Baggio for Scotland – had been living in shadow of injury for two years.

Already under the knife twice for cartilage trouble, his working week had consisted of swimming from Monday to Thursday, training with his team-mates on a Friday, then playing.

Hardly ideal. But as Rangers hunted that ninth crown, Walter Smith needed men who would go through the pain barrier.

McLaren did it with no questions asked.

He recalled: "I knew I was having an op at the end of the season but I just didn't expect it to be so severe.

"I don't feel playing to the end did me any more harm, the damage was already done.

"I had to keep going anyway, because for spells we had missed players like Richard Gough, Gordan Petric and Craig Moore.

That was the story of Nine, a team down to the bare minimum.

"We'd lost 2-0 to Motherwell 48 hours before Tannadice and I have to admit there was pain in my knee by then – major swelling.

But I wasn't forced to play, I WANTED to play.

"I would have hated to have to play on the final day at Tynecastle as my knee would have been double the size by then but, luckily, I didn't have to."

McLaren, capped 24 times for Scotland, was still dreaming of a place in the World Cup Finals in France back then.

He'd gone to Euro 92 and not played, then starred in every qualifier but one for Euro 96 and missed the Finals in England through injury.

He couldn't know the gut-wrenching epitaph to that United game then, though, as his playing days were ended despite desperate attempts by Dr John Browett – who had saved Gazza's career – to repair the massive knee damage.

Truth is, there was simply no cartilage left on the outside of his right knee.

A hole the size of a two pence piece was drilled in the bone to produce scar tissue which might replace what had been lost.

Alan shuddered: "I saw an X-ray and my knee looked like Swiss cheese, I was just glad I had been under the general anaesthetic when they did that.

"He prayed it had worked, he trained like a

beast trying to make things right but it was in vain.

He'd return for a tear-jerking 20-minute stint in Ian Durrant's benefit match but, at the age of just 27, McLaren's football career was finished.

Stoical by nature, he has borne this heart-breaking development superbly.

He threw himself into an HNC in business at college that Ibrox chairman David Murray encouraged him to take.

Then came the massive bonus of his testimonial match with Gascoigne's Middlesbrough, as this book was being published in March, 1999.

As he faced up to life without football and the prospect of that Boro clash, McLaren was philosophical about what he has lost.

He reflected: "Yes it hurts, of course it does. I had it all and now I must try to build a new life but I have a lovely wife and family beside me and Rangers have treated me superbly.

"Many clubs could have just said: "Your contract was up, thanks for the memories and cheerio" but that's certainly not what this club is about.

They refused to desert me.

"Now I can look to the future, whether it be in business, football or just going round those corporate suites at Ibrox with the head man, Scott Gardiner, schmoozing before matches which I quite like, actually!

"It's an emotional time and, while it's time to look ahead, I'll always have my memories."

Walter Smith's long pursuit of McLaren ended in 1994 when he finally landed the master man-marker and threw him into an Old Firm league debut at Hampden, alongside the powerful but erratic Frenchman, Basile Boli.

Alan marshalled the defence magnificently and watched in delight as Laudrup tore away from his markers to seal a 3-1 win.

He smiled: "I looked up into this little corner of the ground, which had a limited capacity then and there were 3,000 Rangers fans singing: "There's only one Alan McLaren.

"After all the time it had taken me to get to Ibrox, I thought I was halfway to winning them over.

"I loved that day and the 5-1 Scottish Cup final win over my old club, Hearts, in 1996 was up there too.

"The minute the TV mimic Jonathan Watson arrived at our hotel for a show to boost the team, I made a promise to myself that I'd savour it all.

"I did, too, as we played unbelievably.

Brian hit such heights that day that they called it The Laudrup Final and Gordon Durie scored a hat-trick!"

McLaren's stature grew and as titles seven and eight rolled in he was at the heart of it all before the injury began to wear him down in that fateful final season.

There is no bitterness from the man most felt would replace Richard Gough as skipper over the price he has paid for helping Rangers to match Celtic's fabled title run.

He simply shrugs: "I was skipper on the field when we made history and I'll never forget that, although I knew the real man was watching us in the stand – Goughie.

"Still, I wasn't to know it then but that was my last game for Rangers.

"And if you have to go out of the game at the age of just 27, then I suppose that is the only way to do it!"

Tommy McLEAN

THE team bus edged through the heaving streets of Barcelona, heading for the Nou Camp and Rangers' date with destiny.

Those Spanish avenues were a heady cocktail of red, white and blue and Tommy McLean stared out of the window to drink it all in.

These days – 27 years after Gers' European Cup Winners' Cup Final triumph over Moscow Dynamo – McLean has seen both the soaring highs and the searing hurt of football both as a player and a boss.

A fairytale Scottish Cup triumph as Motherwell manager in 1991 was followed by an ill-fated year at Hearts and the failure to recreate brother Jim's glory days at Dundee United.

Back then, though, life was far simpler. Back then Tommy's job was to provide the ammunition for his forwards and few loaded the bullets better.

McLean had been brought to Ibrox by Willie Waddell as the legendary Willie Henderson's replacement.

Yet he could never be pigeon-holed as an out-and-out winger as his craft and cunning made the wide right midfield role his own.

And one day in a footballing life that has taken him through the emotional wringer will always stand out.

Tommy recalled: "I'll never forget the journey into Barcelona. We stayed outside the city and the route in was simply a sea of Rangers' colours. It was a takeover.

"What's often forgotten is that our season had actually ended a MONTH before that Final.

"We were left in a bizarre situation of trying to keep our match fitness up before the biggest match of our lives.

"Jock Wallace tried his best and took us up north to play the likes of Inverness Clach in bounce games but the sharpness dropped a little.

"Sheer adrenalin sent us coursing 3-0 up but it all told in the end and we were hanging on to win 3-2 at the finish."

McLean was the arch provider in the Wallace Treble years of '76 and '78 when the understanding he had with striker Derek Johnstone verged on footballing telepathy.

So often with Gers in the mire a free-kick from McLean would drift perfectly into space for Johnstone to seize on it, one flash of the head and another foe was felled.

McLean isn't inclined to over-analyse what they had, shrugging: "I always could cross a ball, it was my strength.

"Put it together with the fact that Derek came alive inside the box and you had the perfect mix. Teamwork."

A simplistic view perhaps but one that

THE THINKER... Tommy McLean

sustained wee Tam through the domestic challenges that took him back into the arena he craved most.

McLean the player mirrored McLean the manager, a football thinker.

And the battles with the continent's best still excite a man who would so often be painted as a grim, glum-faced villain in Scottish football's pantomime.

He smiled: "Europe always brought me great memories. I just loved all the different challenges it brought.

"From taking the biggest hiding I was ever involved in yet still drawing 1-1 away to Bayern Munich in the '72 Cup Winners' Cup semi to becoming the first team EVER to beat PSV Eindhoven on their own soil six years later."

That 3-2 win in Holland was one of the greatest European displays away from home by a Gers' side and McLean was at the hub of it all.

His curling ball through to Bobby Russell was sensational and the finish as the midfielder glided round the keeper to score the clincher sublime.

All this from a player who'd been offered the chance to join Gers as a kid – and turned them down.

The single-minded, stubborn streak that would characterise Tommy's career was evident even then as he snubbed the opportunity so many dreamed of.

But he explained: "I chose Kilmarnock because I felt I had a better opening at a provincial club.

"I looked at Rangers and with the likes of Alex Scott and Henderson there I knew I was going to struggle."

Footballers depend on gut feelings, live or die by instincts and McLean was proved right.

Killie won the title under Waddell's guidance in 1965 and when Tommy was at his peak his old mentor came calling again.

The Gers supremo refused to let any obstacle bar him from landing his man and jetted out with then Rugby Park manager Walter McCrae to interrupt a Scotland summer tour in Denmark and tie up the deal.

McLean recalled: "It was a strange

Club and Country

STATS

IBROX CAREER 1971-83

GAMES
League	300
Scot Cup	46
Lg Cup	74
Europe	32
Total	452

GOALS
League	35
Scot Cup	10
Lg Cup	8
Europe	4
Total	57

MEDALS
League	3
Scot Cup	4
Lg Cup	3
Europe	1

SCOTLAND
6 caps

situation, I became a quiz question. Which player signed for a team and then made his debut for another side? I signed for Rangers then played for Scotland!

"Willie Waddell had been my boss at Killie and much is made of the link between us.

"I actually only had one season under Willie at Rugby Park but I held him in such a high regard.

"He would influence me as a player and then later when I became a manager too."

McLean the manager was to become an integral part of the modern Scottish game's psyche, portrayed with Dundee United's Jim as the Brothers Grim.

And while Jim famously turned down the chance to boss Rangers, it's often forgotten that Tommy was in charge for three games after his close friend John Greig quit the hotseat in 1983.

Europe beckoned once more after a 2-1 first leg win over Porto and incredibly

Tommy led the side to within touching distance of success over there only to lose a late sickener and go out on away goals.

An Old Firm defeat from Celtic in a match marred by a bomb scare followed but McLean did oversee a 3-0 League Cup win over Clydebank before handing over the reins to second-time-around Wallace.

Yet McLean was made for management and first stop was First Division Morton where he gained promotion – then promptly quit for Motherwell who had just been relegated!

Tommy's trademark intensity, though, saw him work miracles at Fir Park where he reared and sold players like Gary McAllister, Ally Mauchlen, Fraser Wishart, Andy Walker, Tom Boyd and Phil O'Donnell through an incredible decade at the helm.

That Scottish Cup win in 1991 was a tear-stained triumph in the Peoples' Final, a thrilling 4-3 win over brother Jim's United

in the week that saw their father die.

For now the football thinker is restless and ready for the next task. After the experiences at Tynecastle and Tannadice he firmly believes in a managerial set-up where one man coaches the team and another wheels and deals in the precarious market created after the Jean-Marc Bosman ruling. He itches to be involved again as the deal-maker.

But, while he ponders the future, he acknowledges the man who made him his assistant-manager at Ibrox and started him on an illustrious career when his playing days ended.

Tommy stressed: "Management may have hurt John Greig but at the end of this Greatest-Ever Ranger book I hope you are saluting him as the winner, the man who meant the most to the club.

"To me, he epitomises what the club is about. He wore his heart on his sleeve and everyone knew what Rangers meant to him – everything."

Ian McMILLAN

IAN McMILLAN used to spend his Saturday afternoons weaving midfield magic alongside Jim Baxter – then he went back to his day job.

The gifted schemer tagged "The Wee Prime Minister" after Conservative leader Harold, became a Rangers legend despite remaining PART-TIME throughout his entire playing career.

McMillan mixed work as a surveyor with his glamorous life in the Light Blue, a scenario unthinkable to the modern-day fan.

He was 27 when a £10,000 fee brought him from hometown club Airdrie and Ian believes he carried a lack of self-belief to Ibrox with him at first.

He said: "I had little fears nagging away at me. This was such a big club and it was a big leap up from a club like Airdrie.

"That's why I stayed part-time I feel, the thought that I might well need my job to fall back on.

"I suppose I could have been made to feel like an outsider by the other players but, to their eternal credit, that never happened.

"I was treated exactly same as everyone else and my belief in myself grew because of that.

"Looking back, perhaps I should have gone full-time, because there's no doubt it would have made me a much better player."

If that's the case, it's frightening to think just what he could have achieved because, despite the difficulties of his double life, the diminutive McMillan was a mainstay of the Rangers side during a sparkling era.

And he soon found rubbing shoulders with Scotland's footballing elite agreed with him.

He reasoned: "If I was to look through club history, I don't think I could have picked a better Rangers team to play in.

"At Airdrie, I had been used to trying to beat two or three men and then something might open up for you.

"But at Rangers, the minute you got the ball, you would have four players demanding it from you.

"It was a massive difference."

McMillan, the intelligent schemer, was complemented by two very different characters in midfield, the wayward genius and the willing workhorse – Jim Baxter and Harold Davis.

Even now, speaking to McMillan you can sense a frustration that his sidekick Baxter didn't achieve even more in the game.

Ian recalled: "The man was a natural. He had unbelievable ability and a special

trick of just drifting past opponents as if they weren't there.

"I consider that to be a dying art. I still watch a lot of football and I just don't see players commit men the way he did.

"Once he'd taken one out with that move, he then had the passes that could open up any defence and he had Jimmy Millar and Ralph Brand to play to.

"Other players might have to train for hours but Jim just didn't have to think about football. He had a gift."

Davis was the exact opposite, a man who worked on every aspect of his game and a fitness fanatic whose desire and drive helped his part-time partner so much.

Harold's graft and Ian's craft made for a devastating combination.

And McMillan pointed out: "That team worked superbly for one and other and there was no better example of that than Harold Davis.

"He was piling through five sessions a week, while I just had two work-outs with the Ibrox kids.

"Harold was much fitter so we made a pact. I confessed I couldn't tackle and we decided he would do all the work then get it to me to create.

"It seemed to work fine! Seriously, we complemented each other very well and if ever I was slacking, then a shout from Davis or Bobby Shearer soon gave me a kick up the backside."

These days, McMillan is retired but still keeps tabs on his two footballing loves, Airdrie and Rangers.

When he left Gers in 1964 he went back to play for the Diamonds for two years and would go on to coach and then

manage at the club. His house now overlooks Airdrie's sparkling Shyberry Excelsior Stadium and he smiled: "I once lived in a house overlooking the old Broomfield – a place that held a special place in my heart.

"Now my house is situated right next to the new stadium and I still call it Broomfield.

"I refuse to call it the Shyberry Excelsior. I'm afraid, to me it will always be Broomfield."

Fans of both clubs still treasure the McMillan memories and the man himself relished one arena Rangers provided that Airdrie couldn't. Europe!

In season 1959-60 he was part of the side who dumped the likes of Anderlecht, Red Star Bratislava and Sparta Rotterdam to make the last four of the European Cup.

There, the German giants Eintracht Frankfurt beckoned and Ian enthused: "I loved Europe, the whole thing was such an incredible education both on and off the park.

"And one of the ties I enjoyed best was against Eintracht Frankfurt – even though we lost 12-4 on aggregate!

"In the first leg, away, it was 1-1 at half-time and we should probably have shut up shop.

"However, we went out and played that second-half on the attack, as if we were facing Stenhousemuir in the Scottish Cup... We lost 6-1."

The second leg, at Ibrox, brought 70,000 fans – more in hope than in expectation – and they saw McMillan net twice but Gers were still thumped 6-3.

Defeat would not sour Ian's enjoyment

MIDFIELD MAESTRO...
Ian McMillan, nicknamed
"The Wee Prime
Minister", was an
intelligent player whose
brilliant passing set up
goals galore

of a special match, though. He insisted: "I still found it a fabulous experience, in fact, I revelled in it."

The fact that Real Madrid then hammered Eintracht 7-3 in the Final at Hampden just shows you the quality of that particular side.

Six months later, Gers were speeding upwards on a European learning curve and McMillan was one of the creative forces in the side who would eventually make the Cup-Winners' Cup Final and lose to Fiorentina.

Against Borussia Moenchengladbach, in the second round, Ian struck on German soil in a brilliant 3-0 win. Back at Ibrox, things just got better.

In a downpour, McMillan was on fire as his side steamrollered their rivals in an incredible 8-0 triumph.

It was all sealed by one amazing run when Ian bamboozled five defenders before setting up a tap-in for Jimmy Millar. He recalled: "That was an appalling night, the weather was awful and the rain was lashing down.

"I remember that even the fans in the STAND were getting soaked because there was so much water it was leaking through. But they were conditions I relished. I loved a mudlark.

"You could throw the bodyswerve to defenders and if they bought it then the surface meant there was no way they could recover."

The feints and the shimmies, the passes and the class of a part-timer who played for the joy of the game...

No debate, the Wee Prime Minister thoroughly deserves his place in Rangers' Greatest 100.

Dave McPHERSON

DAVE McPHERSON found himself brutally cast out of Ibrox, the victim of one costly mistake, then showed the courage to revive his career and prompt a triumphant £1.3million return.

Slim was a regular under Graeme Souness in the first season of his Rangers Revolution but paid a hefty price for allowing a cross to roll under his foot in a calamitous home Scottish Cup defeat from Hamilton Accies.

Adrian Sprott pounced to score the winner and Dave recalled: "Although I was still in the side after that there was this nagging fear that Graeme had convinced himself that if it could happen against Accies it might happen in a bigger match.

"It was just one error in an otherwise good season for me, yet from then on I was uncomfortable about how he felt about me as a player.

"In retrospect the truth was that he just wanted his own team around him, one he had created and bought. He even tried to get Ally McCoist out of his plans once and that comforted me."

McPherson, who'd made his debut as a raw 17-year-old rookie in 1981 and scored a penalty in a win over Albion Rovers, was allowed to leave for Hearts.

But he revealed one telling moment in the Ibrox inner sanctum that would have a big bearing on his future career.

Slim said: "I was hurt saying my goodbyes but Walter Smith quietly pulled me aside and said he had advised Graeme to keep me but the manager had decided to sell.

"At the time you question if he's telling the truth or just trying to comfort you, but five years later he was as good as his word and brought me back."

In the intervening years the towering McPherson built a reputation to match his physique as he graduated to the Scotland scene.

Eventually capped 27 times, he played at Italia '90 and had a superb championship at Euro '92 to tempt Smith into signing the cheque that sealed a second spell at Ibrox.

And although he was so often shuttled from his favoured centre-half slot to right-back with Gary Stevens injured, Dave was an integral part of the side who won the Treble and went within a hair's breadth of the European Cup Final.

He pointed out: "We actually lost a pre-season friendly that year 2-0 to the eventual winners Marseille and people said we had no hope in the Champions League.

"But that was an experienced squad with a lot of footballing knowledge and we realised we'd played well and weren't far away.

"We went so close in the end after those two draws with Marseille and it was all based on this unbelievable team spirit.

Club and Country

IBROX CAREER
1981-87, 92-94

GAMES

League	232
Scot Cup	24
Lg Cup	37
Europe	29
Total	322

GOALS

League	18
Scot Cup	5
Lg Cup	2
Europe	7
Total	32

MEDALS

League	3
Scot Cup	1
Lg Cup	4

SCOTLAND
27 caps

STATS

"Walter Smith has never been given enough credit for what he nurtured that season."

The game's sages say "Never go back", yet McPherson's second coming at Ibrox was to prove a success until Walter Smith's desire to land Alan McLaren saw the big defender used as a bargaining tool.

He switched back to Hearts and has been a rock at the core of their defence ever since.

Now 35 with three titles, four League Cups and Two Scottish Cup successes behind him, he sees the career crossroads beckoning when his contract ends this summer.

But he will leave with the memory of winning a glittering prize AGAINST Rangers fresh in his mind.

The 1998 Scottish Cup Final with Hearts brought so many tears for close Ibrox friends like Goram, Gough, Durrant, McCall and McCoist as they bade farewell to Rangers.

And Slim admitted: "I had mixed feelings when we won 2-1 because I knew how much Rangers meant to these players, after all I have left the place TWICE.

"But any sympathy had to be outweighed by the joy of finally winning something for Hearts. Everyone of them, yes even Coisty, would have understood that."

■ AUTHOR'S FOOTNOTE: Puzzle your pals with the question: Which Rangers centre-half scored four on his European debut?

The answer is Dave McPherson on September 14, 1983 when he went goal crazy in an 8-0 win over Valetta in Malta. The Gers then racked up a club record aggregate by winning the second leg 10-0 at Ibrox.

He recalled: "You'll never believe this but there was only ONE header. Two were left foot shots and one of those was a chip over the keeper from 25 yards.

"I'm told there is a tape of that game somewhere and this is my personal plea to get a copy. You must know how much it means to me!"

Ted McMINN

ONLY Ted McMinn could score his first goal for Rangers DIRECT from a corner then get his Man of the Match award from racing driver Jackie Stewart – at BOGHEAD!

One bizarre afternoon and a 4-2 win over Dumbarton summed up an enigmatic winger who was constant entertainment in his Ibrox days.

McMinn's first name was actually Kevin. Legend has it that he earned his change by carrying a teddy bear under his arm during childhood kickabouts.

That might have explained the eccentric running style of an unorthodox star who won a 1986 Skol Cup medal before Graeme Souness' patience with him finally snapped.

The player tagged "The Tin Man" – after the Wizard of Oz character – will always remember that first goal.

And he smiled: "The weather was foul, the pitch was a disgrace and the wind was howling up a gale. As I was lining up the kick the flag blew down and as I put it back in I did a wee dance and the fans loved it.

"I couldn't believe it when my corner flew straight into the net!

"I was dancing around so much that I don't think the ref let me get back over the halfway line before starting the game again.

"I got a right rollicking from big Jock for my antics but I did get my Man of the Match award from Jackie Stewart."

Ted's eccentric style on the field was matched by a colourful lifestyle off it – and that was never going to find favour with Souness.

He was caught up in an infamous chip shop brawl in East Kilbride with Ally McCoist and Ian Durrant then sneaked out of the team hotel to a disco, breaking curfew after the team had beaten Celtic.

Souness hit the roof and banned him for two weeks. Ironically, in the first bust-up McMinn and Durrant were to be cleared with McCoist fined £150.

Miserable McMinn was rescued by old boss Jock Wallace who signed a £200,000 cheque to take him to Spain and Seville.

Ted, who also had stints at Birmingham and Burnley and recently returned south after a stint back home coaching junior side Kilwinning Rangers, still can't bear to hear Souness' name.

And he fumed: "He was an ignorant man. He enjoyed trying to humiliate people in front of others and really was a nasty piece of work.

"It was his first job as a manager and he didn't have a clue. Walter Smith was boss in all but name."

When Wallace was sacked at Seville Ted pined for home and Derby County brought him back to Britain. He spent 15 months out with knee trouble and that scuppered his hopes of making the Scotland squad for Italia '90.

Fighting back from that injury, Ted did his rehab work at Lilleshall alongside his old pal Durrant who sums up the McMinn magic best.

Ian grinned: "The best thing about Ted as a player was that no defender ever knew what he would do next. Well, Ted didn't know so what chance did they have?"

Club and Country

STATS

IBROX CAREER 1984-87

GAMES
League	63
Scot Cup	0
Lg Cup	6
Europe	6
Total	75

GOALS
League	3
Scot Cup	0
Lg Cup	2
Europe	0
Total	5

MEDALS
League	1
Lg Cup	1

Bob McPHAIL

BOB McPHAIL won his first Scottish Cup medal with Airdrie and followed the dandy 1924 fashion by hooking it on the waistcoat watch-chain of a timepiece given to the Final heroes by a local jeweller.

If he'd continued that practice he would have ended up looking like Ron Atkinson after a shopping spree and keeled over with the weight.

McPhail, the attacking spearhead of the all-powerful 1930s Rangers side alongside Jimmy Smith, mined an astonishing haul of glinting football prizes.

In a glittering career he won nine titles and six more Cup badges when he left the Diamonds for Rangers.

That 2-0 Airdrie triumph over Hibs was the precursor to untold glory for an inside-left with an incredible eye for goal.

And Bob, whose brother Malcolm had won the Cup with Kilmarnock four years earlier, recalled: "I think that was the best one to be involved in, the first one.

"Remember, I was only 19 at the time and we went back to the town on an open-top bus.

"And our wages were £5 for being in the first 11 and £8 for winning the Cup!"

McPhail made it at Airdrie alongside the great Hughie Gallacher, the man who would lead the Wembley Wizards attack in Scotland's 5-1 hammering of the English in 1928.

Just eight months after their Cup triumph together, though, Gallacher was off to Newcastle United for a British record fee of £6,500.

The disciplined McPhail was no great friend of the man the Toon Army worshipped and called 'Wor Hughie' yet Gallacher would play a key role in shaping him.

Bob played up front beside the genius striker in his debut for the Diamonds in the Cup against Ayr United that year.

But he revealed: "I didn't like him as a person because he was selfish and gave me no advice to help in my first game. Yet as a player he was one of the all-time greats."

McPhail watched Gallacher and learned how to shield the ball and ride tackles and vowed to make the most of his own talents.

Sadly, despite all Hughie's brilliance on the park in a career that brought 541 goals on both sides of the border he killed himself by throwing himself in front of a train in the North East that had hailed him as a God on the pitch.

Gallacher was 54. McPhail – schooled in the trait of self-discipline by his Ibrox manager Bill Struth – mourned.

After he'd won his Gers move a record-breaking run in the Scottish Cup was to follow for the man

SMILING ASSASIN... Bob McPhail will go down in history as one of Rangers' greatest ever goalscorers

the Ibrox fans called Greetin' Boab.

The tag was given to him after he shirracked Torry Gillick and told him to get on with the game as he tried to recover from an injury. It stuck.

McPhail was at the heart of the Rangers side that lifted the famous trophy in 1928 with a 4-0 win over Celtic ended a 25-year wait.

He netted in that one and tasted success once more against Partick Thistle two years later before grabbing a double in the 3-0 1932 Final win over Kilmarnock.

Next up? St Mirren in '34 and another McPhail strike in a 5-0 Final thrashing for the hapless Buddies.

A year later Hamilton Accies were vanquished 2-1 before Bob closed his historic sequence with a goal after just 90 seconds to clinch the 1936 Cup Final against Third Lanark.

His record for the highest number of Cup victories is held with Celtic greats Billy McNeill and Jimmy McMenemy.

McPhail realised his dreams making it at Ibrox. As a Scotland schoolboy international at Hampden he had watched bemused as a little man with a bowler hat and an umbrella went round the dressing-room and patted each boy on the head to wish them well against England.

He didn't recognise the stranger and was chided by his pals – it was the man who would become Rangers' Wee Blue Devil Alan Morton, then with Queen's Park.

Morton's message worked as the Scottish kids won 5-0 and soon enough they were to be team-mates and right away Bob was learning lessons.

McPhail recounts a classic tale when he floated a ball out wide to Morton who made absolutely no attempt to stop it.

The dapper winger had a slick parting in his hair and shot back quickly when McPhail moaned at his lack of effort.

Bob smiled: "He said to me the name of the

102

**Club
and
Country**

**IBROX CAREER
1927-37**

GAMES
League	354
Scot Cup	54
Lg Cup	0
Europe	0
Total	408

GOALS
League	230
Scot Cup	31
Lg Cup	0
Europe	0
Total	261

MEDALS
League	9
Scot Cup	6

SCOTLAND
17 caps

STATS

game is FOOTball and we play it on the ground. Truth is, he didn't want to mess up his hair!"

McPhail, though, developed a taste for the style that manager Struth drummed into the team.

Flick through a Rangers Monthly magazine today and you will see the designer clothes endorsements and the dazzling silk ties of the likes of Giovanni van Bronckhorst.

Struth's men were in a different league.

Gers hero Bob, who still walked straight-backed through his electrical wholesalers well into his 80s, recalled: "For instance, when we played Hearts away we would walk up to Tynecastle from Haymarket Railway Station.

"The team were ordered to wear the bowler hat, white collar, blue suit with a blue nap overcoat and velvet collar, black socks and black shoes."

Bob McPhail, the oldest Ranger alive, will be 94 on October 25 this year.

He is a living legend.

He existed by the code of Struth. McPhail was

picked for the Scotland side at Wembley three times on the trot but never played.

The reason? Gers were in the Cup Final in those seasons and it was played the week AFTER the showpiece against the Auld Enemy. Struth let it be known that an injury would be frowned on and loyal Bob put club before country.

Yet he might never have started his 17-cap Scotland career without a bizarre intervention from his Ibrox manager.

Before his international debut – a 2-1 Hampden defeat from England in 1927 – a Queen's Park official came into the Scotland dressing-room and gave McPhail and the rest of the players a spoonful of a mixture.

He groaned: "It was brandy and port and I had never tasted either. I played so badly in the first-half that Struth came down at half-time and put his finger down my throat.

"It must have been effective because they asked me back!"

Willie MATHIESON

WILLIE MATHIESON may have fit snugly into the footballing cliche of unsung hero but when history was being made this talented left-back was there every step of the way.

When Rangers needed a left-back they could rely on from Rennes to Sporting Lisbon, Torino to Bayern Munich, the quiet Fifer shackled his opponents and played a stalwart role in bringing the Cup-Winners' Cup to Ibrox.

Mathieson was ever-present in the glory run that ended with that 3-2 final victory over Moscow Dynamo in Barcelona's Nou Camp Stadium on May 24, 1972.

In a team full of towering personalities such as John Greig, Alex MacDonald and Colin Stein, Willie was the quiet man.

He'd joined Gers from St Andrew's United and was to enjoy 11 years under four different managers, despite frequent fears about his future at the club.

Mathieson actually asked away in the aftermath of Gers' Cup-Winners' Cup Final defeat by Bayern Munich in 1967 when he was left out of the 16-man squad for the match in Nuremberg.

But five months later, international defender Davie Provan had broken his leg and manager Scot Symon dipped into his reserves.

Mathieson was stunned when he ended his usual 60-mile bus and train journey from his Glenrothes home to arrive at Ibrox and be told he was in the side for a crucial Fairs Cities Cup clash with Dynamo Dresden.

Gers won that one 2-1 to go through and Mathieson was back in favour – yet two years later he was knocking on Willie Waddell's door again looking for a transfer.

The Ibrox supremo talked him round and Willie went on to form a brilliant full-back partnership with Sandy Jardine in that Euro glory season.

Like many Gers stars, Mathieson had to learn to battle through the tough times in one of the most unforgiving arenas of all. Ibrox.

He took his share of stick from the punters who dubbed him Willie Wan Fit.

A nickname which tells you that Willie's right peg wasn't exactly his strongest!

But he overcame all that and hit a two-year purple patch that established his right to be considered amongst the greats.

Wallace had no doubt about Mathieson's qualities.

As Willie continued to frustrate wingers in the wake of that European triumph, Big Jock insisted: "He is the best left-back in Scotland.

"No-one works harder at his game or gives more than Mathieson."

Willie was freed in April 1975 and joined Arbroath before finishing his career on the books of his local team, Raith Rovers.

Ironically, Raith had snubbed him as a kid.

Finally, ligament trouble forced him to hang up his boots.

It's also ironic that the defender who had asked for a move in the days after one heartbreaking European defeat ended up as one of the 11 names that now trip off the lips of every true Rangers fan – the Bravehearts of Barcelona.

Club and Country

STATS

IBROX CAREER 1964-75	
GAMES	
League	174
Scot Cup	36
Lg Cup	38
Europe	28
Total	276
GOALS	
League	2
Scot Cup	0
Lg Cup	0
Europe	1
Total	3
MEDALS	
Scot Cup	1
Europe	1

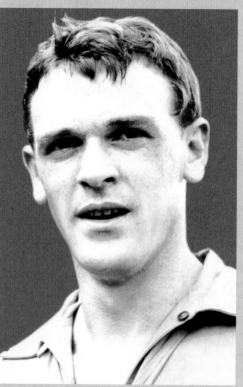

ALL over the pitch, Rangers players turned away frozen with fear, wary of taking the Old Firm penalty that could end the club's 25-year wait to lift the Scottish Cup. Davie Meiklejohn didn't waver – he strode forward and scored.

The sun scorched down on Hampden and he ran forward to rifle the ball home. It was the defining moment of a true Rangers man and the highlight of 18 glory-laden seasons with the club.

Davie Meiklejohn was to be cruelly wrenched from the Scottish game when he collapsed and died at a match while in charge of Partick Thistle. His death was tragic, his life a cause for footballing celebration.

And he never had any doubt about the day that made him, the 1928 Cup Final. He once reflected on his career and said: "I never felt so scared in all my life.

"I realised that failure on my part might lead to yet another defeat. For 10 minutes after that penalty I was in a trance, I have only a hazy recollection of that period.

"If Celtic had realised the state I was in I'd have been putty in their hands. That was the medal that thrilled me the most.

"Not only did we eventually beat Celtic 4-0 but that also put an end to those 25 years of waiting for Rangers to lift that trophy.

"When I scored with that penalty I couldn't even begin to think of the hoodoo. I just ran up and hit it as hard as I could!"

Meiklejohn had joined Gers as a right-half and immediately became a worthy successor to the brilliant Jimmy Gordon. Soon Davie transformed into a superb reader of the game in defence and won the captaincy.

And he didn't believe his duties began and ended with the toss of the coin. He was also master tactician who became Bill Struth's gaffer on the park.

Yet football almost lost Davie before he made his mark. He played for the 103rd Boys' Brigade after starring for Bellahouston Academy but found he couldn't mix the game with his engineering apprenticeship.

He gave up playing but a Govan juvenile team called Greenfield United tempted him back with the promise of trophies. He won four cup medals in five games!

Maryhill Juniors snapped him up and, within two months, the then Gers manager, William Wilton, had made a spying trip to Lochburn Park and made sure the would-be engineer could down tools.

He went on to become the finest skipper in Gers' pre-war history and amassed a haul of 11 championship medals and five Scottish Cup badges.

Davie MEIKLEJOHN

GER GREAT...
Ibrox legend
Davie
Meiklejohn

The late Willie Thornton, himself an Ibrox legend, called this dominating figure: "The greatest player I ever saw."

Meiklejohn won 15 caps in an international career that spanned 12 years and never forgot the lesson of a 2-1 debut defeat from Wales in Wrexham in 1922.

The names Ted Vizard and JT Jones may mean very little to the modern-day fan but they were always etched on Davie's memory banks.

He said: "They ran rings round me that day. If I had a swollen head as a young fellow, then it was knocked out of me in 90 minutes."

His proudest moment, though, came against England. Who else?

Meek's side were given no chance at Hampden in 1931 as England strode arrogantly north, trumpeting the virtues of Everton great Dixie Dean.

They were rated red-hot favourites but Dean was shackled and Scotland triumphed 2-0 under Meiklejohn's captaincy. It was a day he always treasured.

When he retired, Meiklejohn became a star football writer for the Daily Record and he relished the job.

When Hearts and Clyde called he turned down managerial jobs with them to remain behind his typewriter for Scotland's premier daily paper.

But 10 years after he'd retired as a player, the game lured him back in 1947 as boss of Partick Thistle. It was a homecoming for the man who had finally signed for Gers from Maryhill and who would later unearth Celtic star Tommy Burns.

Football was Davie's life yet it claimed him amid the tears and drama of an awful afternoon at Broomfield on August 22, 1959.

Meiklejohn, who was only 58-years-old, had just watched his side tackle Airdrie and was in the directors' box talking over the 90 minutes when he collapsed.

He died in an ambulance on the way to hospital.

Celtic manager Jimmy McGrory said then: "He was as true a Ranger as I was a Celt. When we clashed on the field, we fought it out to the last.

"He was a skipper who did his job without fuss, a big-hearted man who made it clear to the rest of the team what he wanted. And he always got it."

There were 2,000 mourners at Davie Meiklejohn's funeral at the Craigton Cemetery near Ibrox. Most couldn't squeeze in to the crematorium and just stood outside the gates in stunned silence.

Alan Morton, the Wee Blue Devil who starred beside Meiklejohn in his playing days, was a Gers director when he tried to accept the shattering loss of a legend.

His response and the depth of his grief said it all. "No cause was ever lost when Davie was there behind you.

"He will go down in history as one of the greatest Rangers ever to wear the colours."

Club and Country

STATS

IBROX CAREER 1919-36

GAMES
League	480
Scot Cup	72
Lg Cup	0
Europe	0
Total	552

GOALS
League	40
Scot Cup	4
Lg Cup	0
Europe	0
Total	44

MEDALS
League	11
Scot Cup	1

SCOTLAND
15 caps

Alexei MIKHAILITCHENKO

HE languidly caressed the ball with his left foot from 60 yards and his shot landed on top of the net.

That amazing effort, which left the Falkirk keeper scrambling back before he realised the outrageous attempt was inches too high, introduced Rangers fans to football, Alexei Mikhailitchenko-style.

Gers won 2-0 on his debut at Brockville in September, 1991, and in the five years that followed, Miko sparked a thousand pub arguments. Was he a maverick genius or a lazy waster?

He may have been inconsistent but so often he produced flashes of skill worth the punters' admission money alone. And Alexei, now proud coach of his first club, Dynamo Kiev and his nation Ukraine, left Scotland with five championship medals. He was no flop!

His best season was his first campaign in a Light Blue jersey which ended with him being voted *Rangers News* Player of the Year as he helped Walter Smith's side to the Double.

Miko's goals on the run to Hampden helped end an 11-year Scottish Cup hoodoo as Gers edged Airdrie 2-1 in the Final and Smith's faith in an extravagantly gifted player who could boast an Olympic gold medal and a European Championship runners-up badge proved justified.

Gers' owner, David Murray, smashed an historic barrier with Alexei's signing.

The club who went through the £10,000 wall to get Billy Simpson from Linfield and bridged the £100,000 gap to land Colin Stein from Hibs, got their man this time by taking the Scottish transfer record beyond the £2MILLION mark.

The elegant Ukrainian's silken skills won him the transfer journey every player still dreams of – the jet to Serie A.

Sampdoria snapped up Miko and he departed Genoa after a year £540,000 richer with a title medal in his boot-bag.

Yet he left on bitter terms, claiming the jealousy of top name Samp stars Gianluca Vialli and Roberto Mancini had frozen him out.

He would experience nothing of the sort in Glasgow where he was a hugely popular figure with the other players.

Alexei had played in the memorable European Cup clash with Gers in September 1987 when manager Graeme Souness narrowed the pitch to secure a 2-0 win and aggregate victory.

He starred again in a 3-1 pre-season friendly win over the Glasgow giants and Smith never forgot him. Yet the player pondered a move to Scotland long and hard.

Mikhailitchenko found it difficult here at times confessing: "Stop for a fraction of a second and you are robbed of the ball immediately. Yet, although I found the game tough, it was not cruel. There was an

THE £2MILLION MAN... Ukrainian Mikhailitchenko is congratulated by Ian Durrant after a Gers goal

honesty, very few sneak tackles from the back – which I had found so common on the Continent.

"Moving to Rangers meant changing my banners for the third time and, as far as I'm concerned, I played for three of Europe's top clubs in Kiev, Sampdoria and Rangers."

Mikhailitchenko, who was a signing target for Celtic boss Billy McNeill in his Kiev days, will always be remembered as born to frustrate those who live and die by football's work ethic.

It would be amusing now to sit in on a Dynamo Kiev training session and listen to him order someone to get his lazy backside back and defend.

Stuart McCall summed up Alexei best when he smiled: "Miko knew what 'Attack, attack' meant but when you screamed at him: "Defend!" he would completely blank you!"

THEY reckon the phrase "playing for the jersey" could have been coined for Jimmy Millar.

The targetman in the famous M&B Partnership with Ralph Brand was one of the first names on Scot Symon's team-sheet because of that attitude.

Millar had skill to spare but he chose not to constantly chase personal glory.

Instead, the star who had first hit the headlines as a half-back at Dunfermline, developed himself to become the perfect foil for his striking sidekick.

They'd talk for hours about finding new ways to carve up defences but the modest Millar insisted: "Ralph was miles ahead of his time with the things he wanted us to work on.

"He was the brains of the partnership.

"Ralph had electric pace – which I didn't possess – and we constantly worked on ways to use that.

"I'd drop off the centre-half and nod balls through for him to race on to and, after a while, it became like clockwork."

Try to examine the mechanics of a well-oiled goal machine with the likeable Millar and he'll baulk at it at first.

Then, when you draw the comparison with modern-day heroes Mark Hateley and Ally McCoist, he warms to the task.

Jimmy said: "The M&B Partnership was the 60s version of Mark Hateley and Ally McCoist.

"I wouldn't presume to have said that myself but so many others who saw both double acts have.

"Hateley was like me I feel, a team player who always looked to do his best for Rangers."

Most strikers will tell you there is nothing to top the feeling of scoring a goal.

Seeing the rigging bulge on a Saturday is what they work for all week. Millar was different.

And he insisted: "I'm sure that, like me, big Mark sometimes took more pleasure out of setting up a goal with a clever knock-down than he did from scoring a tap-in.

"I reckon that, throughout my career, I laid on more goals for Gers that I actually scored."

For all the assists, all the times he sent Brand haring through, Millar still managed more than a century of Gers goals and some strikes he'll never forget.

Jimmy, who quit playing and had a brief spell in management before running the Duke's Head pub in Edinburgh for 31 years

**IBROX CAREER
1955-67**

GAMES	
League	197
Scot Cup	35
Lg Cup	54
Europe	31
Total	**317**

GOALS	
League	92
Scot Cup	30
Lg Cup	28
Europe	12
Total	**162**

MEDALS	
League	3
Scot Cup	5
Lg Cup	3

**SCOTLAND
2 caps**

STATS

**GOALDEN MILLER...
ace striker Jimmy
battles against the
Partick Thistle defence**

Jimmy
MILLAR

until his retiral in 1995, always remembers the Rangers End raising their hip-flasks to him at Parkhead.

And he smiled: "There were so many magic memories but I think scoring a last minute New Year's Day winner against Celtic at their place must be up there at the top.

"The fans could still drink at the game in those days. I remember looking up and thinking that, with one swing of the boot, I'd sent so many people home happy."

Rangers came to rely on the M&B Partnership when the chips were down, as they were in the 1964 Scottish Cup Final.

In front of an incredible Hampden crowd of 120,982 against Dundee, the treble was on the line. And Dens keeper Bert Slater chose that day to have the game of his life.

Millar, who pocketed a basic wage of £30-a-week through that clean sweep season, recalled: "That came became known as the Bert Slater Final and deservedly so. He was like a man possessed.

"Eventually, I got us ahead but they equalised almost immediately and Slater kept

up the heroics as we tried desperately to get the winner. Finally, Ralph and I scored in the last seven minutes and we got there."

One of the frustrations of tales of that era is the lack of TV coverage.

Rangers fans these days must rely on the misty memories of their dads to describe the class of Baxter, Millar and Brand.

Jimmy still replays the games in his mind sometimes as he braves all weathers to play golf at his local course in Edinburgh and tries to improve his handicap.

He grinned: "It takes my mind off the fact that I'm usually playing crap!

"Seriously, it's a shame there's very little footage of that treble year but when I watch what there is of us in front of all those people in that Cup Final it makes me feel old. I look like bloody Charlie Chaplin.

"Yet I still remember the two goals and that crowd just didn't faze me. I always played the same way, whether it was 2,000 or 120,000."

Jimmy was moved on from Ibrox in 1967 and went to Dundee United but, by then, a

slipped disc in his back was deteriorating and his spell at Tannadice never really worked out for him.

He tried management for 18 months at Raith Rovers but couldn't adapt and said ruefully: "I wanted to be like Jock Stein but I soon discovered that there was only one of him."

Eventually, he bought his public house and made a success of it for more than three decades.

Millar relishes his life and loved the chance to go down Memory Lane and talk about the Rangers.

And he had no doubts about who should scoop the title that Gers fans all around the globe were pondering over.

Jimmy said: "There's no question in my mind who the greatest-ever Ranger would be. John Greig.

"That man has given his life to the club. People said I epitomised what playing for the jersey means and that's flattering.

"But I played beside John and I know his worth – for me, John Greig IS Rangers."

Alan MORTON

WEMBLEY 1928 and a team of tartan terrors write their names into Scottish football history by giving the English the runaround and hammering the Auld Enemy 5-1.

WORSHIPPED DEVIL... Alan Morton, the Wee Blue Devil, was a crowd pleaser

The team who destroyed the pride of England were christened the Wembley Wizards and at the heart of it all was a winger they called the Wee Blue Devil.

Even now – almost 80 years after the day Alan Morton first pulled on a Rangers jersey – that nickname strikes a chord with the Light Blue legions.

Morton was Bill Struth's first signing for Rangers and embodied everything the austere manager felt the club should stand for.

The little winger was dominant and electric on the field, dapper and elegant off it.

He would stroll down Paisley Road West towards Ibrox for training, his 5ft 4ins frame striding ramrod straight as he cut a dash with his bowler hat, leather gloves and trademark umbrella.

Passers-by would glance over and reckon they were looking at a bank manager or a tax collector instead of Rangers' star forward!

And Morton's brolly even became a club mascot with the superstitious Ibrox players insisting they never lost on the days when it hung over his dressing room peg.

In truth, they needed no talismans in Morton's era when this football genius won nine league titles in 12 years before retiring to become a director of the club.

His speed and balance had mesmerised defenders in his playing days and England lived in fear of him throughout his 31-cap international career.

Their Association Football annual once branded him a "holy terror."

Morton had entered the senior game at Queen's Park in 1913, given a start after a recommendation from his big brother, Bob, who was the amateurs' centre-forward.

Ironically, this Airdrie Academy pupil yearned to play for the Diamonds but no-one asked him. That glaring Broomfield blunder was to give Gers one of the most devastating players in their history.

The First World War years didn't hamper Alan's rise and in 1920 Morton switched to Rangers on a bumper £60-a-week contract, which was a fortune back then.

Yet his feet remained firmly on the ground as, all through his football career, he stayed part-time and continued to work as a mining engineer.

To Struth, Morton was worth every penny of the lucrative deal as he mastered the curling shots which provided so many of his goals and became an arch-provider of chances.

He was an instant hit in Old Firm games and terrorised a Celtic rival to score a goal that coined a chorus older Ibrox fans still remember to this day.

"Oh Charlie Shaw, he never saw,
Where Alan Morton put the ba',
"He put the ba' between the sticks,
And left poor Charlie in a fix."

Morton's magic made him an integral part of those Wembley Wizards and 1928 was the greatest year of his footballing life as he shone for both club and country.

The Scottish Cup back then was considered the game's Blue Riband and Gers ended a 25-year wait for the trophy with a 4-0 thumping of the Hoops in the Final.

The Wee Blue Devil hung up his boots in 1933 but remained on the board at the club until June 1971, when illness forced him to relinquish his duties.

Six months later, at the age of 78, the Ibrox legend died in his Airdrie home, within hours of another Gers great, Torry Gillick.

They were buried within a few miles of each other. Morton in New Monkland and Gillick in Old Monkland cemeteries in Lanarkshire.

They will never be forgotten.

Fifteen years after his death, the then Prime Minister, Margaret Thatcher, hosted a Downing Street reception for Gers chairman David Holmes and was presented

Charlie MILLER

SWARTHY Spanish stars Raul and Ivan de la Pena swaggered onto the pitch, brimful of confidence – and staggered off it raving about the skills of a pasty-faced kid from Castlemilk.

Charlie showed the heights he can attain by outshining those two towering Spanish talents, despite a 2-1 defeat for Scotland Under-21s in the last eight of the European Championship.

At the age of 23, midfielder Miller knows he should have the football world at his feet – yet he's standing at a career crossroads.

Under former manager Walter Smith there were times when Miller went off the rails when away from the club.

Amid headlines of one bar-room brawl and other scrapes, he frustrated Smith hugely and, more than once, the errant Charlie was warned he was in danger of throwing it all away.

He said: "I have to learn about life off the park as a Rangers player.

"There have been newspaper reports about me doing stupid things."

But there's one home truth about Charlie Miller – he's worth the trouble. This is a rare talent.

He has dug in and worked feverishly on his fitness under Dick Advocaat, training three times a day and buckling down.

But although that has clinched an extension on his contract until June 2000, Miller has had to watch friend and room-mate Barry Ferguson hog all the headlines for club and country.

Charlie bristles at suggestions that he needs Barry as inspiration, though, and he pointed out: "I don't have to look at him for incentive, because I have already done quite a lot in this game.

"I've got three league medals, I've played in big games and I know my worth.

"The Scotland cap has arrived for Barry and not for me but I know deep inside that I should have been in the team FIVE YEARS ago when I was a Rangers regular."

Miller was a precocious talent, just a 17-year-old kid when he won his Gers debut as a makeshift striker at Aberdeen.

His natural midfield skills can see him burst from midfield, using his vision and attacking verve to devastating effect. He showed that at Dundee earlier this season with two goals in a 4-0 win as he earned a yearned-for start.

Charlie was axed for the next game at

with a specially-commissioned portrait of Alan Morton in his heyday.

A second copy was given to the former FIFA president, Sir Stanley Rous, and he revealed: "I was a linesman when Scotland beat England 5-1 at Wembley in '28 and could never forget Morton. He was outstanding."

The gifts that bamboozled the best of defenders sometimes remained a mystery to Morton himself.

He once smiled: "In my schooldays a football was like a toy to me. The more I played with it, the more I knew of the little tricks it had for puzzling me."

At a club that has spawned the Wee Prime Minister, Slim Jim, Jaws, The Girvan Lighthouse and The Hammer nicknames will always add to the aura. And they'll never forget the Wee Blue Devil.

Club and Country

STATS

IBROX CAREER
1992-present

GAMES
League	82
Scot Cup	7
Lg Cup	11
Europe	17
Total	117

GOALS
League	10
Scot Cup	3
Lg Cup	1
Europe	2
Total	16

MEDALS
League	2
Lg Cup	1

PARTY ANIMAL...
Charlie enjoys the nine-in-a-row celebrations

Aberdeen, however, and he knows he must adapt to life under the demanding Advocaat – or play elsewhere.

Ally McCoist, Ian Durrant and Paul Gascoigne were like brothers to him, always there for advice. But they're gone now and he said: "So many players I knew so well have left and Walter Smith is away too.

"There has been a change here because there aren't so many laughs as we had before. It has become a very serious business now.

"There's a very different atmosphere – this is a European club now.

"Me? The bottom line is I've forgotten what it's like to start a game every Saturday now."

Max MURRAY

MAX MURRAY was Rangers' leading scorer for three years and his scoring prowess meant the Ibrox exit door for players of the stature of Don Kichenbrand and Billy Simpson.

Despite Max's great record, he fought a constant battle to get the Light Blues boo-boys off his back before the superb Jimmy Millar eventually prised his jersey away.

A natural sportsman – he has played off a golf handicap of one – Murray was raised as a player in the Falkirk High School team.

He won schoolboy, youth and amateur international honours before moving from Camelon juniors to Queen's Park, that famous breeding ground for Rangers stars, in 1953.

Ibrox beckoned at the age of just 19 and on October 24, 1956, when Gers played their inaugural European game in the Champions Cup, Murray grabbed the club's first goal on that stage.

It came in a 2-0 win over French side OGC Nice, although Gers were to lose that one in a play-off third match.

Max always fought a soul-searching battle to win over the fans and the naming of the Scottish Cup Final team in 1962 was the beginning of the end at Ibrox for him.

He'd scored twice for Gers in the 3-1 last four win over Motherwell but was axed alongside Scotland star Alex Scott, with Millar taking over once more up front.

It was a sickening blow for Murray.

Seven months earlier, he'd decided to go full-time when he was demobbed from the RAF. That decision didn't pay any immediate dividends, as he suffered through torrents of abuse from the punters and languished as FIFTH CHOICE striker at one time.

But Max bravely battled back and he insisted then: "I couldn't care less for the boo-boys, they can howl until they are dumb.

"I knew full-time training would give me more stamina.

"I was well down the list but I refused to ask for a transfer because I had confidence in my ability."

At the dawn of a new era, all that renewed self-belief ebbed away when he was axed and, to make matters worse for Murray, he had seen that Final as a personal revenge mission.

His last Hampden appearance had been in the League Cup Final against Celtic – and the Hoops won 7-1.

Symon, though, banked on 18-year-old winger Willie Henderson and 21-year-old stopper Ron McKinnon in their first final and Gers dumped St Mirren 2-0.

After he left Gers, Murray switched south to West Bromwich Albion in a £15,000 move but his time at The Hawthorns seemed ill-fated from the off.

He'd been sent off in one of his final Gers reserve games against Aberdeen – his first red card in 10 years of Scottish senior football – and the SFA handed him a two-week ban that disrupted his hopes of a fresh start in England.

Max suffered bouts of homesickness before returning to Scotland for stints at Third Lanark and then Clyde, under his one-time Ibrox team-mate, John Prentice.

Murray has a right now to point to his magnificent goal ratio and question his critics but he refuses to blind with science those who harshly examined his talent.

He smiled: "I'd just shut my eyes and hit hard. If the ball hits the net, you're a hero, if it hits someone on the terraces, you're an idiot. That's life as a striker."

Club and Country

STATS

IBROX CAREER 1955-63

GAMES
League	103
Scot Cup	16
Lg Cup	27
Europe	8
Total	154

GOALS
League	80
Scot Cup	19
Lg Cup	19
Europe	3
Total	121

MEDALS
League	2

STUART MUNRO, rookie footballer, used to pound up Murder Hill with Jock Wallace's voice barking him on and the chill East Lothian winds whipping across the legendary Gullane Sands.

These days, managerial novice Munro walks across the glorious white swathe of 90-Mile Beach, near Melbourne, and ponders how to take new club Gypsland Falcons up the Australian National League.

The former Rangers left-back, now 36, is lapping up life Down Under in his first job as a boss.

And Stuart, a vastly under-rated influence when Souness brought the title back to Ibrox after a nine-year absence in 1987, admits he'll never forget the footballing lessons he had from the ex-Liverpool legend.

Munro stressed: "I've never come across anyone like Graeme, a man who was almost obsessed with winning.

"I hope his attitude rubbed off on me and, while other players who got on his wrong side may take a pop at him, he was the best thing that ever happened to me.

"Also, if you couldn't learn from the likes of Terry Butcher and Ray Wilkins, then there was something wrong with you."

Amidst all the splashing of the cash, a £15,000 Wallace signing from Alloa was to flourish.

And Stuart said: "Winning that first title under Graeme was a rollercoaster of emotions really.

"He was sent off in the first game at Hibs and then went for an early bath again the day we clinched it in the 1-1 draw at Aberdeen.

"I was involved in four championships with Gers but there's no doubt that was the best. Winning it was like a wave of relief."

Munro was the unsung hero of the Souness Revolution. As the Gers manager lashed out millions on rebuilding almost every area of his side, he only ever tinkered with the left-back slot.

Jan Bartram blew it when he slaughtered his manager in the Danish press and Chris Vinnicombe and Tom Cowan were given a chance but Stuart made the job his own.

His form peaked in season 1989-90 when he was voted *Rangers News* Player of the Year by thousands of fans and won a cupboard full of awards from supporters' clubs. The modest

HAPPY DAYS...
a proud Munro
runs out for
another Ibrox
first-team game

Stuart MUNRO

Club and Country

IBROX CAREER 1984-91

GAMES

League	179
Scot Cup	13
Lg Cup	22
Europe	19
Total	233

GOALS

League	3
Scot Cup	0
Lg Cup	0
Europe	0
Total	3

MEDALS

League	3
LgCup	3

STATS

Munro joked: "That was Mo Johnston's first season and the fans were still getting used to the idea.

"I think they just went for me so they didn't have to give it to Mo!

"Seriously, there was always the spectre of other players coming. Tony Dorigo of Leeds was constantly mentioned but that never happened.

"I looked at the likes of Gary Stevens, a £1million right-back, and there was always a fear there but when the cheque book didn't come out big-time for a left-back, I knew I must be doing something right.

"I was delighted eventually when Graeme told me that, as far as he was concerned, the position was mine."

Stuart eventually switched south to Blackburn Rovers in 1991 but saw his progress there hindered by an ankle injury.

By the time he returned, Kenny Dalglish had begun building a £20million side and Munro was squeezed out.

He headed for Bristol City and another meeting with his mentor, Souness, in the FA Cup at Liverpool.

Stuart said: "After all he'd done for me,

I was a part of the team that ended his time as manager at Anfield.

"We shocked them 1-0 and Graeme quit in the wake of that result. I suppose that you can look on that as one of those awful ironies in football."

Munro enjoyed his time in Bristol but returned north for stints at Falkirk and St Mirren – where Tony Fitzpatrick allowed him to cut his teeth coaching the Buddies' youngsters – before Australia beckoned.

Stuart originally went out to play for Sydney United under another ex-Gers player, Davie Mitchell.

Now he's adjusting to a culture shock as a manager with the Falcons and he admits it's all a world away from the days when he starred at Ibrox under Souness.

He stressed: "When Graeme came in at Gers, the level of professionalism there just took off.

"The players were treated superbly and every last detail was looked after.

"Here it's different, our average gates are 2,500 tops and soccer struggles in Australia at times.

"You'll get crowds of 70,000 at games

for Aussie Rules and rugby and cricket pushes you into a corner in the paper. I'm just not used to that!"

He's at work in the state of Victoria, facing the difficulties of four training sessions a week for a part-time team.

Half of the side live in Gypsland's base of Morwell, where Stuart is settled with wife Carolyn, and the rest are 90 minutes away in Melbourne.

The training is split between the two places and Stuart pointed out: "There are only five or six full-time soccer teams in a league of 15 and the rest of us are trying to keep up with them.

"We're lucky the league sponsors give you free flights around this country because the plane trip away to Perth Glory takes FIVE HOURS!"

Still, he's thriving on overcoming the obstacles and proving his worth in Oz.

Yet, when he walks that beach his mind still drifts back to those days when Wallace screamed in his ear at pre-season training.

And he said: "The sands here aren't quite like Gullane was with Jock! Yep, the lifestyle here certainly helps."

George NIVEN

GOALKEEPERS are always caricatured as the game's great eccentrics – and George Niven fits the bill perfectly.

The miner who stood just 5ft 9½ inches tall joined Gers from junior side Coupar Angus in 1947 and he was to eventually replace the fabled Bobby Brown after a patient wait of five years in the reserves.

Niven was always obsessed with his stature between the posts and tried every dodge to cure his weakness.

Platform boots, special stretching exercises, you name it. But in the end they still called him Wee George!

Yet he defied his lack of height and ditched those built-up boots because he couldn't jump in them.

His positioning and athleticism made fans forget his drawbacks.

And the quiet Fifer's modesty and dry humour soon won over the critics too. After one thrashing of Hamilton Accies in 1953 arguments raged in the dressing-room over the score.

Niven cut in and said: "It was eight, I marked them in mud on the post!"

His agility was matched only by his bravery and his injury list reads like an episode of ER.

George fractured his jaw, shoulders, arms, wrists and fingers as he defended his goal. Yet he always played through the pain barrier.

Never more so than in a 1-0 Scottish Cup Final replay win over Aberdeen in his debut season in the first team when he also clinched a title medal.

Bloodied George was carried off for 15 minutes only to return and then boss Bill Struth said: "In all my years I haven't met a more courageous man than Niven.

"He lay on the treatment table and had four stitches inserted inside AND outside his ear. He never said a word."

"He suffered with what must have been excruciating pain and all he asked was that he be allowed back on the field."

Niven knew how to beat the odds, playing in goal in the 7-1 League Cup Final mauling from Celtic would have broken many keepers. George showed the strength of character to recover.

Yet the phrase accident-prone was coined for George Niven. On the eve of his wedding to policewoman Nessie Smith in 1958 he left the Glasgow coffee bar he ran with Gers legend George Young for Dunfermline.

On the way he home he was in a smash and his car somersaulted. The wedding went ahead with the lucky groom sporting five stitches in gashes on his nose and forehead.

Even when George's big chance for Scotland came when he was picked to face England at Hampden in 1960 he was a call-off casualty with a back strain and Frank Haffey deputised in a 1-1 draw.

The emergence of Billy Ritchie put paid to Niven's Rangers career and he played just once in the reserves in his last 10 months at Ibrox.

Still, though, he blasted out of the shadows to be a stand out during seven seasons at Partick Thistle.

Typically, his dedication saw him drop a stone in weight and he played the last YEAR of his career at Firhill with his injured hand strapped up during games.

He finally quit the game at the age of 40 after 22 years at the top. Emergency doctors everywhere breathed a sigh of relief.

Club and Country

IBROX CAREER 1951-62

GAMES

League	221
Scot Cup	32
Lg Cup	59
Europe	15
Total	327

GOALS

League	0
Scot Cup	0
Lg Cup	0
Europe	0
Total	0

MEDALS

League	5
Scot Cup	2
Lg Cup	1

STATS

Jimmy NICHOLL

JIMMY NICHOLL signed for his Rangers idol John Greig then saw The Gaffer quit 14 hours later!

The former Northern Ireland right-back - now boss of First Division Raith Rovers - reckons he must have a record for placing a curse on a Gers manager.

And he still shudders when he thinks back to the bizarre circumstances that surrounded his move. The club were at a low ebb, the team were drowning in mediocrity and an honourable man could only see one way out.

Combative defender Nicholl - who was born in Canada - had been brought in on loan from Toronto Metros to shore up the defence.

After sealing the deal with Greig and his No.2 Tommy McLean the ex-Manchester United player settled own to a Thursday night's kip in the Bellahouston Hotel near the ground. He had no idea of the drama that lay ahead.

On his first morning of training Jimmy's Northern Ireland team-mate John McClelland - who was skipper back then - welcomed him to Gers.

And Nicholl recalled: "I went into the tunnel to do my stretching with Davie Cooper and Bobby Russell. Tommy McLean came in and said: "Right lads, meeting in the dressing-room."

"John Greig came in ashen-faced and said: 'It's been a long time coming lads but I feel now the time is right for me to part company with the club.

"With that he turned on his heels and walked out, he'd been my manager for all of 14 hours."

McLean took the helm for a short spell but the board then decided to give jungle-fighter Jock Wallace the chance to recreate those Treble glory years of '76 and '78. The move didn't come off but Nicholl was left with a lasting impression of a colossus in the club's folklore.

He winced: "Coop would never tire of telling me how the Big Man had mellowed. I still found him helluva intimidating and if that was him calmed down I'd have hated to see the first version.

"But the great thing was that we did manage to win the League Cup for Jock when Ally McCoist scored a hat-trick in the 3-2 win over Celtic."

Steeped in the intense traditions of a troubled Northern Ireland the Old Firm game meant the world to Jimmy Nicholl. His intensity, though, was to spill over in the last game of his first spell before he returned to Toronto.

Nicholl sighed: "Naturally, it was against Celtic and I got SENT OFF. Fortunately, Bobby Williamson scored an overhead kick that proved to be the winner and he got me off the hook.

"If we had lost that game I have no doubts Jock would have kicked my backside the whole 5,000 miles back to Canada."

Nicholl and Williamson would become two of Scotland's brightest young bosses at Raith and Kilmarnock but back then Jimmy reckons he was always in his debt. Fate was to link their Rangers careers - with Nick the constant beneficiary.

Nicholl landed up at West Brom after moving on from Gers and was watching the Souness Revolution with avid interest in 1986 when his chance came to be part of it - right out of the blue.

He smiled: "I was getting ready for a new season and it was the last thing I expected. I'd clashed many times with Graeme in Liverpool-Manchester United matches and that stood me in good stead.

"He'd watched the team lose a friendly 2-0 to Bayern Munich before the opening league match at Hibs and Hugh Burns carried the can.

"Graeme felt he needed an experienced right-back and the next thing I knew the call came - and once more Bobby Williamson got me off the hook.

"This time he was part of the package and if he hadn't wanted to go to The Hawthorns then it was all off. Thankfully, he bit and I was back."

Nicholl was by now a veteran but the advancing years brought clever positional sense to go with his trademark enthusiasm and steely commitment.

He was an integral part of it all as Souness brought the title back to Gers after a nine-year wait.

Many may look upon that time as all too brief but for Nicholl it was a season in the sun he hadn't dared expect.

And he revealed: "That league win was unforgettable and remember it was my first title because I had been a Manchester United player during the glory years of Liverpool and Nottingham Forest.

"I treasured it but the next year it all slipped away when Celtic won the Double and then Graeme hit me with one of the classic lines.

"He came up and said: "Jimmy how do you feel about taking on the job of reserves coach."

"I didn't have to think long. I said: 'Great, I'm yer man.'

"Good," he replied. "Cos, I've just bought Gary Stevens."

"It was the ultimate back-handed compliment. He gave me a job just as he was purchasing my £1million replacement!"

Derek PARLANE

FRANZ BECKENBAUER lost the plot with his team-mates, blew his top at himself then finally chucked it in front of a frenzied crowd at Ibrox – Bayern Munich's Euro dreams were DEAD.

The executioner? A top drawer keeper who defied him? An international striker who embarrassed him? No, an 18-year-old midfielder from the tiny village of Rhu who scored his first goal for Rangers to send them into the Cup Winners' Cup Final.

Derek Parlane had style from the moment he arrived on the big stage at Ibrox on an unforgettable April night in 1972.

The promising teenager had made his first team debut at Falkirk before that but even though skipper John Greig was injured he expected no better than a place on the bench with Alfie Conn waiting in the wings and ready to step in.

Instead coach Jock Wallace walked into a hushed dressing-room 90 minutes from kick-off and Derek recalled: "He read out the team and I did a double-take because I could have sworn I was starting.

"When it was confirmed that I was I almost s**t myself!

"I was handed the No.4 jersey and told the job was to concentrate on marking their playmaker Franz Roth. That was a daunting task."

Rangers had been murdered in the first leg yet somehow emerged with a 1-1 draw thanks to a Zobel own goal.

Now the chips were down and Parlane's jangling nerves were calmed by a quickfire goal from Sandy Jardine. Then dreamland.

Derek smiled: "I'll always remember Sepp Maier coming for a corner and getting a fist to it to clear it to the edge of the 18-yard box.

"It fell to me on the half volley and I caught it sweet to send it ripping in, it was a helluva way to score your first goal for the top team!

"My abiding memory of that game is watching the toys come out the pram for one of the world's greatest players.

"Beckenbauer couldn't handle it and he was screaming at himself and the other Bayern players. He gave up the ghost before the end."

A generation of Rangers fans would be raised on the chorus: 'Parlane, Parlane – Born is the king of Ibrox Park' when Derek was transformed into a striker by Wallace.

But for now this was a rookie midfielder who began his career even further back at centre-half and he was in the limelight for the first time.

Those were halcyon days for the Parlane family in Rhu made all the more special by the fact that Derek's dad Jimmy had been an inside-forward for the club during the war.

Derek reflected: "There we were in front of all the Press pack on the steps on the front of our house getting our pictures taken together.

"Two Rangers players talking about the game, it felt wonderful and I know he was proud of me then.

It was an incredible start to my career."

Greig's gritty return from injury was to keep Parlane on the bench for the 3-2 Final win over Dynamo Moscow in Barcelona.

Any sense of disappointment, though, was quashed by being a part of history and he reasoned: "That was 11 Scottish lads beating some of the best Europe had to offer, it won't happen again.

"There was this camaraderie perhaps only matched by the side who went close to the European Cup Final in 1993, I saw a little of us in that.

"What we had was experienced players like Greigy who would help you so much.

"Any time I was in trouble on the pitch he'd arrive like my guardian angel to get me out of it."

The bench was never going to be Derek's permanent resting place, the following season he was in the team to stay.

There was disquiet amongst the support when Colin Stein was sent to Coventry but the wily Wallace felt he had noticed a strength and a striker's instinct in his rising star.

He was bang on the money.

Within a year Derek was an international striker winning the first of 12 caps in a 2-0 Home Internationals win over Wales in Wrexham.

He became a Gers legend with the top scorer's honour in four of his first five full seasons in the first team and that famous song was coined to herald his exploits.

Smooth and skilful on the park he was slick and stylish off it and Parlane became an idol for hordes of wide-eyed fans.

Ian Durrant won't sing Blue and White Dynamite at his Kinning Park local The District Bar but admits he does belt out the King of Ibrox Park on nostalgic nights.

In a decade of goals there were to be a hundred highlights for Derek, that Bayern strike and another in the 1973 Centenary Scottish Cup Final against Celtic that ended in a 3-2 win for Gers.

Yet his favourite goal remains one he scored in a friendly with Arsenal which Rangers lost 2-1!

He grinned: "It was against Bob Wilson and even now I look at him on telly and think of the best finish of my life. A dream hit."

Derek seemed destined for the path to even greater

Club and Country

IBROX CAREER 1970-80

GAMES
League	202
Scot Cup	25
Lg Cup	51
Europe	22
Total	300

GOALS
League	80
Scot Cup	8
Lg Cup	21
Europe	2
Total	111

MEDALS
League	3
Scot Cup	2
Lg Cup	3

SCOTLAND
12 caps

STATS

stardom when he quit Rangers for Leeds United in a £160,000 deal in 1980.

But it was a case of right club, wrong time. Parlane was to have three managers in just two and a half seasons.

And he said: "Jimmy Adamson signed me but then I got injured for a whole season and we went down under Allan Clarke before Eddie Gray took over.

"It was a club constantly trying to live up to the Don Revie era and not making it. The directors, the fans and even some of the players were living in the past. It was sad that it didn't really work out."

Nowadays it is impossible to think of Rangers as miserly, it is a club where wages have rocketed into the realms of the £30,000-a-week that so divorces star players from the ordinary punter.

Back then, though, there was a feeling from the boardroom that the men who pulled the famous Light Blue jersey over the head should think that reward enough.

Consequently, many of the legends from the 60s and 70s got wanderlust when they left Glasgow and headed for fat pay cheques before they finished.

Parlane was no different.

Derek, who now has a high-flying job as Scotland and Northern Ireland sales manager for sportswear giants Reebok, said: "I went to Hong Kong to play for Bulova and I'm honest enough to say the hard cash attracted me.

"I came back and had a decent stint with Manchester City under Billy McNeill then moved back to Hong Kong to play for South China."

The playing days were winding down now but Derek squeezed in spells with Racing Jet in Belgium, Rochdale in England, back home to Airdrie and then non-league down south with Macclesfield.

When he hung up his boots he settled in Cheshire but recently returned north to live in Ayr. He still looks as if he could play and enjoys the recognition of fans who recognise him to this day.

Derek, also a talented after-dinner speaker, grinned: "They say they miss the days of Parlane and my room-mate for all those years Derek Johnstone up front but I joke and tell them I don't.

"I was sick of doing all the legwork for that big, lazy b*****d!

"Seriously, though, any time I'm a little down I can think back to one of those Saturdays when I heard that song ringing out. 'Parlane, Parlane - Born is the King of Ibrox Park.'"

Andy PENMAN

ANDY PENMAN walked out of Ibrox after six years without a winner's medal to his name – but he left the fans with a sackful of memories.

Penman was a precocious talent. A kid who had the class to be picked in the Everton first team at the age of 15 – a distinction he shared with the legendary Tommy Lawton.

Imagine the hype that would have surrounded a teenager like that today.

Homesickness hit him hard at Goodison, though, and Hearts, Dunfermline and Motherwell all called at Andy's Fife home to try to persuade him to sign. He chose Dundee.

At first he loved the club and they set him up with a job in an engineering firm where he could start his apprenticeship as a motor mechanic.

Andy had all that is required to make it in the game – touch, vision and a hammering shot. He was the perfect creative midfielder.

His ambition was always to go to the top and, as his fame grew, he became convinced he could not realise that dream at Dundee.

A league championship medal had arrived with the famous Dark Blues squad of 1962 and he shone in the side who reached the European Cup semi-final the following season.

Yet, as you pore through the newspaper cuttings of a tempestuous career, they are littered with headlines such as "Andy Asks Away" and "Penman Demands Move."

It began after that title win when the gifted midfielder was fed up with barracking from a section of the Dens' support and demanded a move, only to be swayed by hordes of kids screaming "We want Andy" during a 2-1 derby win over Dundee United.

He fought back to be named the club's Player of the Year that season.

But after eight years there he was to become embroiled in a bitter war with the Dens hierarchy. He even threatened to join a rebel league in America to get away from Dens.

Andy slammed in four more transfer requests in a two-year battle and told the Dens board he had no intention of following his illustrious team-mates Alan Gilzean, Ian Ure and Charlie Cooke south of the border. Penman wanted Rangers.

His appetite for playing alongside the best Ibrox could offer was whetted in 1965 when he starred for the Scottish League, with Gers' Willie Henderson, in a caning of the Irish.

Penman knew Henderson had the intelligence to come short for his passes – and the blistering pace to catch the ball when the Dundee star lofted deft long balls over the opposing defenders.

That game only doubled his determination to

get away from Dens but, on the brink of the deal, he gashed his leg badly in a 1-0 Dundee win at Dunfermline.

It was to be an omen of the illness and injuries that often left a cloud over his sparkling career.

After Rangers lost at Berwick in a catastrophic Cup defeat, the search for Penman's signature was stepped up. He'd won his sole full international cap in a 3-0 defeat by Holland and then on April 4, 1967, Andy finally made it to Ibrox and boss Scot Symon welcomed the most expensive buy Rangers had ever made.

Reserve centre-forward George McLean, who was part of the package, was valued at £25,000 and the £30,000 cheque went to Dens. It was big money back then.

Andy wasn't allowed to play for the first team until the start of the following season because of transfer rules but he settled into life in Glasgow in the Ibrox reserves.

And Penman was part of the biggest spree in Gers' history then, as a further £80,000 had been shelled out to land Alex Smith from Dunfermline and Dave Smith from Aberdeen.

His time at Gers was scarred by those injuries and he was then diagnosed as a diabetic.

But when Penman was 100 per cent fit, there were memories of his class and the clout from his shooting that brought him a superb goal return for a midfielder.

Worries over his health began when Gers rushed him into hospital for 10 days of tests, with the Fairs Cup semi-final against Leeds looming.

There were fears then that his career was over but he returned to health and his ability was never in question.

It was recognised throughout Europe. But there was a storm on a Rangers tour in Sweden when

Penman and team-mate Willie Johnston were tapped by an agent from Portuguese giants Benfica.

Gers boss Davie White clung on to him then but a year later Andy was in dispute with the club because he couldn't get a regular place.

He was to settle his differences under Willie Waddell, though, and the elegant Fifer stayed at the club until 1973.

At the age of 30, he moved to Arbroath on a free transfer and had two good years there before he moved north to become player-manager of Inverness Caley.

Andy was a revelation but still the spectre of illness hovered. A recurring shin injury troubled him and then came the bombshell news that just one more knock there could lead to a serious bone infection.

Andy – now mixing his football with working as a mechanic thanks to the skills he'd learned as a Dens kid – quit the game but the lure was too much. It was the twilight of his career but Penman was still shining and he guided Caley to victory in the Highland League Cup Final to earn his first cup winner's medal in senior football.

The two loser's medals for Gers in Scottish Cup Finals against Celtic had been cold comfort but after all he'd been through, the love of the game kept him playing.

And he helped develop Caley striker Billy Urquhart who was to follow in his mentor's footsteps and join Rangers.

They played a testimonial match for Penman up north in 1979 when an Inverness Select beat a star-studded Dundee XI 4-2. It was a memory he must have cherished. But ill health always plagued Andy and in July 1994 he died at the age of 51.

Craig PATERSON

RANGERS were heading for one of the most shameful results in their European history when Craig Paterson launched the salvage mission for which their stricken fans were praying.

September 1984 brought Jock Wallace's side a powderkeg UEFA Cup draw in the Republic of Ireland with Dublin club Bohemians.

Wallace feared the menacing sectarian undertones and he was proved right as several bouts of terracing violence marred the first leg despite his touchline pleas for calm.

Things didn't go much better for Gers on the field, as they slid to a 3-2 defeat in a torrid match. Football wisdom said that matters would be redressed on Glaswegian soil.

Oh really? Six minutes from time at Ibrox it was goal-less – and the Gers supporters were peeking through their fingers at the action as a nightmare unfolded.

Then centre-half and skipper Paterson popped up to level it on aggregate and Ian Redford headed a winner in the game's dying breath.

A result almost of Berwick Rangers proportions had been avoided but that game is a keynote of the times when Craig was at Rangers. He captained a side forever struggling to live up to the club's former glories.

There was an air of resignation about the next match in the San Siro against an Inter Milan side who included the likes of Walter Zenga and Alessandro Altobelli and the imported skills of Karl-Heinz Rummenigge and Liam Brady.

The match followed script with Inter two up but then Gers rallied and under-pressure Ally McCoist missed a sitter before Rummenigge made it three. It was over.

Or was it? McCoist was axed for the second leg and Paterson's men so nearly pulled off one of the club's best European results of all time with Ally's replacement, Iain Ferguson, scoring twice in a dramatic 3-1 win.

Paterson, a former Scotland Under-21 star, was one of the most highly-rated prospects in the country when John Greig broke Rangers' record and paid £225,000 to bring him to Gers from Hibs in 1982.

Yet he'd broken his ankle on his Hibees' debut and was lucky to even be playing football after a horrific fall down stairs as a kid that saw him spend a year in and out of hospital.

Craig, whose father John was also an Easter Road stopper, said: "I think the fact that my dad always got me a football for Christmas had something to do with my recovery.

"It was always a leather one from Hibs and even though I couldn't kick it three yards it didn't seem to matter."

Paterson was to be part of Greig's new breed at Rangers, alongside the likes of Redford, John MacDonald, Jim Bett and Robert Prytz.

But the transitional team toiled.

Craig did, however, take over from Irishman John McClelland as skipper and led Gers to a second successive League Cup triumph in 1984 when Inter hero Ferguson's solitary goal downed Dundee United.

The arrival of Terry Butcher spelled the end for Craig at Gers and he switched to Motherwell, where he was a huge hit and won a Scottish Cup medal in 1991.

His departure from the club in the wake of that triumph was acrimonious, though, as he feuded with manager Tommy McLean and tried to buy HIMSELF out of Well before joining Kilmarnock.

Craig was part of a Rangers era most would rather forget – but he was a very accomplished defender and it should be remembered that team were, for one fleeting moment, on the verge of being legends!

WHO'S THAT PERSSON..? It's Orjan (left) in action with Alex Ferguson against Hearts

Club and Country

IBROX CAREER 1967-70

GAMES
League	72
Scot Cup	10
Lg Cup	14
Europe	17
Total	113

GOALS
League	22
Scot Cup	3
Lg Cup	4
Europe	2
Total	31

SWEDEN 48 caps

STATS

Orjan PERSSON

JONAS THERN and Jocky Bjorklund have since followed in his wake but Orjan Persson can lay claim to have been the Swedest thing to hit Ibrox.

The dynamic winger with the deft left foot was part of a Scandinavian invasion of Scotland in the 60s and for almost three seasons he was a permanent fixture in the Gers line-up.

Orjan's imaginative signing was the brain-child of Dundee United boss Jerry Kerr who had watched the explosive winger play for Orgryte in a Fairs Cities Cup tie against Dunfermline.

When it came to the return leg, the cheeky Kerr swept into Gothenburg while the Pars were there and opened negotiations for the 22-year-old.

Persson was working as an electrical engineer and the chance to go full-time was a dream come true, the £10,000 cheque was inked and Scotland had a new star.

Orjan was a hugely popular figure at Tannadice and his quicksilver skills inevitably caught the eye of the big guns.

In July 1967 – in a transfer tangle with echoes of the Bosman era of today – Persson declared he was out of contract with United and free to talk to Gers supremo Scot Symon.

After a fraught summer spent wrangling, the shrewd Symon sweetened the deal by allowing Light Blues legend Davie Wilson to go to Tannadice in a swap.

Andy Penman was another who arrived at Gers as Symon reacted to Celtic's

European Cup win in Lisbon by splashing the cash on fresh faces in the wake of his own side's Cup-Winners' Cup Final defeat by Bayern Munich.

It's a measure of inflation in football when you consider that the £250,000 he spent led to Rangers being dubbed the Bank of Scotland side.

Persson scored on his competitive debut in a League Cup tie at Aberdeen and a month later won his place in the fans' hearts with an Old Firm winner.

But with Celtic setting out on their nine-in-a-row title reign, Rangers – who had Alex Ferguson in their forward-line alongside Orjan – needed Euro success.

The signs were promising when Dynamo Dresden and Cologne were disposed of but Gers were vanquished in a Battle of Britain with a Billy Bremner-inspired Leeds United who were to beat Hungarians Ferencvaros in the final.

Persson's second bid to take Europe by storm the following season went one closer, to the last four, before it all ended in tears when the Ibrox fans rioted in defeat at Newcastle United.

There was further misery that season as Celtic humbled a side now bossed by Davie White 4-0 in the Scottish Cup Final and the Swede's Ibrox career was on the wane.

When Willie Waddell became Gers manager later that year, the gifted Orjan fell out of the picture and his trip to Mexico as part of the Swedish World Cup squad effectively put him in the shop window.

After the Finals, he was allowed to move back to Sweden and Orgryte, the club that had

reared him. Orjan never lost his class and made an incredible return to the international arena for the World Cup Finals in West Germany in 1974 – 18 months after he quit the game.

He explained: "A couple of years after I returned home, I decided to stop playing. But I missed football so much that, after six months, I came back.

"I was playing in the Second Division but doing well, despite the switch from winger to midfield as I got older.

"I never expected, though, that my form would be good enough to take me to the World Cup Finals again."

Persson, who eventually hung up his boots after a spell with Swedish Third Division side Kungsbacka, earned 45 caps.

He's still remembered fondly by both his Scottish clubs. After all, he was a Tannadice folk hero who was part of a famous victory in United's first-ever European tie, when they shocked Spanish giants Barcelona with a 2-1 win in the Nou Camp in November 1966.

That scoreline was repeated 21 years later at the same venue by Jim McLean's UEFA Cup stars. And that season Persson – by then a very successful property agent in Gothenburg – saw his former side United arrive in Sweden for the first leg of the UEFA Cup Final against local heroes IFK.

It was a tie the Scots would lose 1-0 on their way to a narrow aggregate defeat. But Orjan proved he has never forgotten his Scottish links.

He supported United that night!

Davie PROVAN

LEG BREAKS. The injury every player dreads and the sickening blow that set Davie Provan on the road to stardom then cost him dear in another cruel twist of football fate.

The harsh nature of football means that a shadow player will prosper from a teammate's agony and that's how it was for Provan after Gers' Eric Caldow was left stricken at Wembley during Scotland's 2-1 win in '63.

With Caldow on the casualty list, rock-solid Davie took over at left-back and he said: "It was a chance through someone else's misfortune and they didn't come along very often in those days.

"There were very few injuries it seemed and teams were never rotated the way they are now. Win, lose or draw – when the manager picked his line-up at the start of the season he would generally persevere."

As Scot Symon's champions swept all before them you needed the patience of a saint when you were stuck in 'the stiffs' at Rangers.

Provan was never one to storm in and ask away, though, and he pointed out: "I spent FIVE YEARS in the Gers reserves and, although demanding a transfer would sometimes cross your mind, you never did it.

"There were few changes and this was a time when Jean-Marc Bosman was just a glint in his old man's eye. Freedom of contract? I was just happy to be called up the stairs at Ibrox to sign another deal."

These days, Davie is a football development officer with Inverclyde District Council and he carries the knowledge of one of Rangers' greatest teams into every training session.

Some of the kids he coaches might never have heard of Jimmy Millar and Ralph Brand but Provan will never forget them.

They were the core of the side who stormed to the treble in '64 and Davie stressed: "Being part of that treble was the highest point for me at Ibrox.

"It was only the second time it had ever been done and there is this feeling that you are peerless. You have, after all, cleaned up and won the lot in one fell swoop. Millar and Brand, Baxter. . . that was a special team."

Three years later, the dependable Davie's continued class in Gers' defence had won him five caps and – despite the upset of Scottish Cup humiliation at Berwick – they reached the European Cup-Winners' Cup Final.

Talking to the players who played in that game has been an education. Over three decades on, there remains a gnawing frustration, a feeling that they faced Bayern Munich in Nuremberg with one hand tied behind their backs.

Manager Symon had been slaughtered for the Cup KO and Provan explained: "Players like George McLean and Jim Forrest had been jettisoned in the wake of the defeat at Berwick. That made it so difficult for us.

"That final will always be remembered for the fact that we went in without a recognised striker. Roger Hynd had a thankless task up front because he was out of position.

"The pressure was on because of the fact Celtic had won the European Cup a week earlier and there was a real feeling of what might have been afterwards. It was a low time."

Four months later, Davie was in the pits of depression, despite Orjan Persson's Old Firm winner, when the curse of the broken leg struck him.

He lay for 35 minutes in numbing pain in the Ibrox treatment room before he was rushed to the Victoria Infirmary.

And he recalled: "It's not a moment you forget. Bertie Auld came over the top of the ball and he knew it.

"These days, you'd be rushed to hospital right away but back then they were telling me 'stamp it off on the park!'

"Ironically, I was driving in Castlemilk one day after we'd both quit playing when Bertie stopped alongside and asked me to be his second team coach at Partick Thistle!"

After Rangers, Davie moved to Crystal Palace, had an enjoyable spell as skipper at Plymouth Argyle, then came back north to be player-coach at St Mirren, where he teamed up with Alex Ferguson.

He quit when Fergie left Love Street before old foe Auld brought him back into the game at Firhill. Then came the Ibrox return in a golden spell as youth team coach and chief scout.

Provan helped bring the likes of Ian Durrant, Robert Fleck and Derek Ferguson through the ranks but Jock Wallace dumped him and managerial spells at Albion Rovers and Dumbarton followed before he moved into SFA coaching circles.

Now here's a quiz question. Which Rangers favourite played against Samba superstar Pele and was on the winning side? Yep, it was Provan.

He smiled: "I was skipper of Plymouth when we played Santos in a friendly and won 3-2.

"We had 37,000 inside Home Park and they wouldn't come out until they got their £10,000 match fee. Our chairman had to rush down the bank to get it!

"Pele scored and, if anyone doubts my story, when I tell it in the house I show them the picture of me and the great man and our wives!"

119

Robert PRYTZ

ROBERT PRYTZ broke a bone in his hand and boss John Greig cleared him to fly back to Sweden for four days of specialist treatment.

PRYTZ STICKS IN SCOTLAND ... Swede Robert won the League Cup with Gers and he still lives in this country

When he returned Jock Wallace was the new manager and he made an immediate impression on the little midfielder.

Robert recalled: "I walked on to the training field and he said: 'Where the **** have you been?'

"I told him about my trip home and the broken bone in my hand.

'Next time,' he growled. 'Have a bloody good excuse for going home – like two broken legs.'

"It took me a very long time to find out Mr Wallace was joking!"

Prytz was just 22 when he arrived in Glasgow from Malmo yet he had already embarked on a Swedish international career that would eventually win him 56 caps.

Back home he had worked in a fashion boutique and a sports shop and mixed that with playing for his club. Now he was in the Old Firm melting pot.

Robert scored on his league debut in a 2-2 draw with Motherwell and then the 5ft 6ins Swede leapt to head the goal that gave Gers their first ever Premier League win at Aberdeen.

Yet Prytz confessed: "It was my first time as a full-time pro and it was a culture shock.

"But although that was generally a bad time for the team it was a side that did have a lot of skill in it.

"I was privileged to play alongside people like Jim Bett, Bobby Russell and Davie Cooper.

"You won't get more creative players to enjoy games beside.

"When Rangers fans conjure up images of that spell in the 80s it sparks visions of an awful pinstripe strip and a team that failed to live up to the Treble sides manager Greig had played in.

Prytz, now 39 and back in Glasgow, still plays for top junior side Pollok as he sits the coaching courses he hopes will help carve out a career in management.

He remains close friends with Ally McCoist and he smiled: "Yep, I played with McCoist but this was the striker who DIDN'T score goals, I played with Coisty before he reinvented himself!

"He did, however, get a hat-trick when I won my only Gers' winner's medal. We beat Celtic 3-2 in the League Cup Final in 1984 and I can always comfort myself with that feeling."

Robert was a clever and thoughtful midfielder and his class in possession was to be recognised in no less than FOUR other top European leagues when he left Gers.

There remains one regret from his Ibrox days, though. He said: "I would have loved to have played in a more successful era and I have watched the Graeme Souness and Dick Advocaat regimes with a lot of interest.

"Their style of play, I feel, would have suited me better but I enjoyed life under both John Greig and Jock Wallace.

"In the end I went because I wanted a pay rise and when Rangers wouldn't give me it I felt I had to go.

"Even then Jock tried to set me up at Queen's Park Rangers and although it fell through that showed the stature of the man.

"He cared about his players and got the respect he deserved because of that."

Prytz returned home to IFK Gothenburg but only briefly before he set off on his travels to Switzerland and Young Boys where he won a championship and a cup.

Next stop was the Bundesliga and Bayer Uerdingen before he won the move every player still prizes – to Italy's Serie A.

Robert reflected: "It's a tremendous place to play but volatile too.

"The first year I was at Atalanta and I enjoyed it and then when I was getting ready to go to pre-season for the next one I discovered I had been traded to Verona for Claudio Cannigia.

"The thing is, nobody told me.

"Still, I had four very happy years there but I was always coming back to Scotland because my wife is from Glasgow and the kids love it here.

"I still enjoy playing and it's fun in the Juniors but my big aim is to qualify as a coach and then hopefully show I can make an impact on a team.

"I'll always remember the impact big Jock made on me on day one!"

Ian REDFORD

IAN REDFORD reckons if he'd signed for Rangers today he would have been a £4million 19-year-old midfielder.

That's the price-tag football inflation would have placed on the head of a player who was a Scottish record buy when John Greig lashed out £210,000 to sign him from Dundee.

Pressure was heaped on the youngster from the off with Rangers in the turmoil of transition as the 1978 Treble team that Greig had captained creaked and grew old together.

The manager needed to find new, young stars and knit a side together but time is the one commodity you do not get at a club like Rangers.

Redford, a strong-running modern midfielder, was in at the deep end. And he knew it.

Ian, now still in the game as a leading FIFA-licensed agent, recalled: "It was mindblowing at the time to be Scotland's most expensive player.

"In real terms now that fee would be somewhere in the region of £4million!"

There can be no better place in football when the goals are raining in and success follows than Ibrox.

But equally, it becomes a painfully unforgiving arena for those who fail in the Light Blues jersey.

Redford had some success but Greig's managerial reign eventually became a time of toil.

And Ian reasoned: "Rangers are a great club but it was a hard era because the side who had won the Treble had aged together and what John really needed was that season of transition.

"Unfortunately, you are just not allowed to have that at Rangers and the pressure kept mounting."

Redford, Jim Bett and Craig Paterson – who broke Ian's Scottish record signing fee at £225,000 – all tried to settle in against a backdrop of fans' unrest.

Ally McCoist joined them and was far from an instant hit as Ian said: "There were dark days when we lost to Dundee in the Cup and all the stands were screaming: 'Ally, Ally get to ****!'

"The thing was I was sent off that day and he took the heat right off me!"

Hampden can be the home of the hero or the venue of the villain. Ian Redford played both roles in Cup Finals for Rangers within the space of six months in 1981.

In the Scottish Cup Final with Dundee United his personal soccer soap opera with Tannadice keeper Hamish McAlpine began when Gers were awarded a spot-kick with the game tied at 0-0 and the game was ebbing away.

Ian pointed out: "We just didn't have a recognised penalty-taker at the time and then we got the shout in the last minute of the Cup Final!

"I remember looking over at Tommy McLean and he looked away – so did

Club and Country

STATS

IBROX CAREER 1980-86

GAMES

League	172
Scot Cup	22
Lg Cup	40
Europe	13
Total	247

GOALS

League	23
Scot Cup	5
Lg Cup	11
Europe	3
Total	42

HONOURS

Scot Cup	1
Lg Cup	2

Bobby Russell. Then the skipper Ally Dawson lobbed the ball to me.

"I thought 'This is it – headlines' and I just concentrated on getting a good contact.

"Sadly, I smashed it down the middle and although Hamish McAlpine dived the wrong way it rattled off his legs."

Gers won the replay 4-1 with a classic performance, though, and Redford's revenge was to be complete in the League Cup Final later that year.

Goals from Davie Cooper and United's Ralph Milne had the game tied at 1-1 when a ball broke to Redford on the left angle of the box.

A deft chip floated high over the stricken McAlpine and into the far corner for the clincher – and sparked a thousand debates over whether he'd meant it!

Even now Ian gets asked the question but he smiled: "That was 18 years ago surely I'd have confessed by now?

"Listen, watch the film. I look up, I see a gap there and the chip goes just where I wanted it. And they can never take a Cup Final winner off you."

Redford's skills and his knack for goals

from midfield – he once scored four for Gers in an 8-1 League Cup win over Raith in 1981 – took him to Dundee United before he switched south to Ipswich.

He returned north to St Johnstone and then moved into management with a spell as player-boss of Brechin City.

Then just when it seemed he might hang up his boots former Gers team-mate Jimmy Nicholl handed Redford the chance of a season at Raith Rovers.

It proved to be a fairytale as Ian was part of the squad who won the First Division title and scored one of the biggest sensations in Scottish football history when they beat Celtic on penalties in the Final of the Coca-Cola Cup.

Ian said: "Perhaps it was fitting the venue for that game was Ibrox where the big time began for me.

"It did take my mind back to my own days there and I do remember there was a lot of pressure on me.

"People these days tend to forget that I was only 19 at the time.

"I have to look back and think that I was in the right place at the wrong time."

Billy RITCHIE

THE QUIET MAN was the fittest keeper ever to haul that famous yellow jersey over his head.

Billy Ritchie worked slavishly at his game and his reward was 12 years at Scotland's most powerful club and a trophy cabinet that boasts five league medals, four Scottish Cup medals and three League Cup prizes.

He saw it all in a career that brought the glamour of the European Cup Winners' Cup Final in 1961 when Gers lost to Fiorentina and the glory of the Treble three years later.

Yet it all began for Ritchie in the humble surroundings of Creamery Park in Bathgate, a venue that many Ibrox stars would grow to dread in the modern era.

Before the advent of the new Scottish Premier League under-21 division the Rangers reserves would play there. A shift at Creamery meant you were out in the cold or on the way back from injury. For Billy, though, it was a field of dreams.

Ritchie started out there with Bathgate Thistle and when he was first signed up at Ibrox the fitness fanatic keeper would dash back for training sessions with his Juniors mates at night.

He'd landed his dream move by accident. Gers wanted Bathgate's No.1 John Neil to play in the third team against Shawfield Juniors but they couldn't get his release because of a cup tie.

Instead Bathgate sent Neil's deputy Ritchie and although John also won a Gers contract it was policeman's son Billy who nicked the chance for stardom.

He was a rock-solid keeper who did the job with the minimum of fuss after winning the right to be called Rangers' No.1 when he took over from George Niven.

Ritchie yearned to win Scotland honours but there were major obstacles. First Spurs' keeper Bill Brown was dominant at the time and then the ARMY wanted him!

Billy was named in the Scotland World Cup 40 for the Finals in Sweden in 1958 but he was stationed with the Royal Scots Fusilliers in Cyprus playing games for his regiment on the sunshine isle. It was Mission Impossible to win the jersey.

Ritchie's international recognition was to be limited to one appearance as a sub in a 3-2 Hampden defeat from Uruguay in 1962.

With Norrie Martin and Erik Sorensen battling for the Gers slot five years later Ritchie left Rangers when Ibrox legend Willie Thornton snapped him up for Partick Thistle. Ironically, he would once again take over from the now veteran Niven.

He later switched to Motherwell where his dedication saw him appointed player-coach until the club was forced to axe him as they slashed their wage bill to survive.

The star who used to rise at 6am to deliver papers from his Livingston shop stayed involved in sport as Games master at Motherwell Technical College.

And he was staring at his 39th birthday when former Old Firm rival John 'Yogi' Hughes gave him a romantic return to football at Stranraer – THREE YEARS after his last competitive match.

Ritchie remains a firm believer in football's work ethic and he reasoned: "I consider goalkeeping an art and when I joined Stranraer the fitness was still there. All I needed to do was concentrate on my ability. I found it surprisingly easy.

"Fitness is the major part of football and I always made sure I didn't fall down on that score. Even if I went to holiday to Majorca that wouldn't stop me training on the beach!"

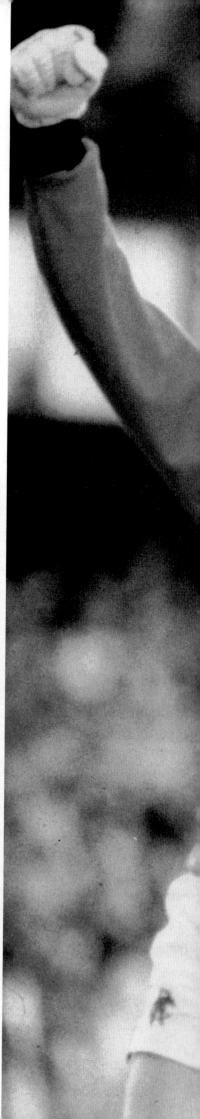

Club and Country

IBROX CAREER 1955-67

GAMES

League	207
Scot Cup	37
Lg Cup	66
Europe	30
Total	340

GOALS

League	0
Scot Cup	0
Lg Cup	0
Europe	0
Total	0

HONOURS

League	2
Scot Cup	4
Lg Cup	3

SCOTLAND
1 cap

STATS

HE'S ON THE BALL ... Billy Ritchie's work-ethic made him a great keeper

Graham ROBERTS

GRAHAM ROBERTS' Rangers career ended in ignominy as he was left a sad outcast on the subs' bench for the reserves in footballing backwaters from Lancaster to Stenhousemuir and Mallaig to Fort William.

It was a punishment exercise, the end game in a plummeting fall from grace for a hero of the fans who had been a driving force in regaining the title in 87 and then taken the captain's armband in the wake of Terry Butcher's leg break.

But it was the price he paid for the ultimate crime in the eyes of Graeme Souness. He questioned the manager's authority as Souness laid into him in the wake of a home defeat from Aberdeen.

Roberts had become a stalwart in a season of discontent that would see Celtic win the Double in their centenary year after Butcher's injury.

Graham's blood and guts bravery had played a major part in taking the club to the last eight of the European Cup where they lost to Steaua Bucharest.

But all that was forgotten in the ill-advised moment when Roberts began to argue back. As the war of words escalated Souness accused Robbo of disrespect.

Fatefully, the former Spurs star said: "If you feel that strongly you should let me go."

Souness replied: "Consider yourself sold." And that was that.

Roberts was ostracised, he trained at different times from the other players and the one-time voice of the dressing-room became so isolated the other players nicknamed him Lord Lucan.

He was eventually sold to Chelsea but only after a public outpouring of grief from the fans who had come to love his clenched fists commitment to the cause.

It came in the final game of the campaign in May 1988, a week after the loss to Aberdeen that had sparked Robbo's feud with his livid boss.

Rangers won 5-0 at Brockville, a result that relegated Falkirk, but all Gers' minds were on the future of the player who had skippered Spurs to UEFA Cup glory a year earlier.

Chants of 'Souness, Souness change your mind' and 'We love you Robbo' rang around the stadium and a poignant banner read: 'We love you Souness, if you love us why are you breaking our hearts?' The manager, though, was not for turning.

Roberts' Rangers career seemed ever fated to end in turmoil, his stay at the club was littered with controversies.

From the red cards against Hamilton Accies in his first season and the Israel B side in a tour friendly to the explosive day when he conducted the Ibrox choir singing The Sash in the 2-2 Old Firm draw that ended up with him in court he was never out of the headlines.

Graham was a central figure in the fracas with Celtic's Frank McAvennie that eventually saw the Hoops striker and Gers keeper Chris Woods sent off.

Terry Butcher later joined them with all four players charged with breach of the peace. His two Gers team-mates were found guilty with Macca cleared and Roberts ruled not proven.

He felt he should have been cleared too and was hurt by that but in reality his actions that day were wrong. He was fanning the flames of a hatred.

Yet he insisted: "It wasn't done out of malice. It was euphoria and I don't regret conducting the choir, it was only a bit of fun.

"The game is crying out for characters who can give the punters a laugh.

"Still that fixture really is something else, it's fought with a passion and a commitment that is quite frightening."

You can't help but dwell on the bust-ups when you consider the Rangers career of Graham Roberts yet that clouds the achievements of a man who came from non-league Weymouth to the glamour of White Hart Lane.

His days there brought him almost 300 league matches, two FA Cup medals and, of course, that European success when his second leg goal against Belgians Anderlecht took the Final to a spot-kick shootout which Spurs won.

The England international was a formidable defender who remains an idol of Ibrox and a fan of the club.

He even had to leave the 1992 Scottish Cup Final win over Airdrie in a POLICE VAN after fans joyously mobbed him outside Hampden.

Roberts, who would later leave Chelsea for West Brom, dealt his Gers days a fatal blow with the Souness row.

And he confessed: "There was an argument, no-one wants to play badly, give away passes or goals.

"Maybe I should have bitten my tongue but I didn't. People ask if I hate Souness but I don't because we were two of a kind – winners."

David ROBERTSON

DAVID ROBERTSON became a soccer symbol of the Game of Hate.

Born and bred in Aberdeen Robertson starred for his hometown team only to become reviled there when he signed for Rangers.

Walter Smith's pursuit of the buccaneering left-back ended at the start of his first season in charge with a transfer tribunal fee set at £970,000. It was a steal.

And whenever Nine-in-a-Row hero Robbo returned north with Gers, he was left in no doubt how he was regarded by the vengeful Dons fans.

David, now in the Premiership with Leeds United, shuddered: "That whole thing between Aberdeen and Rangers was whipped up in the Graeme Souness era and it has just got worse through the years.

"It got so bad towards the end of my days in Scotland that, when I was in the Pittodrie car park, a guy asked me for an autograph and when I stopped to sign it he booted me in the shins.

"Then myself and my wife were walking to the car and a mob began throwing hotdogs at us.

"The final indignity was when they taunted me and said: 'We're going to kill you' then SPAT on me.

"It is a nasty fixture now and I became a scapegoat of it."

Yet despite the menacing undertones he still shone in most of those games against Dons throughout six superb years at the club in a role as attacking left-back that was perfectly crafted for him.

At times Gers would dominate games so much that he was more like a WINGER and he nabbed some stunning goals as his blistering pace took him into the box for clubbing left foot shots.

The service for David in the main came from three sources in his Ibrox days – and they were a trio of very contrasting characters.

Robbo recalled: "I loved playing with Pieter Huistra as he was such an unselfish player. You know, it always puzzled me that he was never a true fans' favourite because if you analyse his play he set up so many goals for the club.

"We clicked straight away on the left and the understanding for him to find me

Club and Country

IBROX CAREER 1991-97

GAMES

League	184
Scot Cup	26
Lg Cup	19
Europe	22
Total	251

GOALS

League	15
Scot Cup	3
Lg Cup	1
Europe	0
Total	19

HONOURS

League	6
Scot Cup	3
Lg Cup	3

SCOTLAND
3 caps

STATS

on my overlaps became almost telepathic."

During Gers' vintage season of 1992-93, Huistra shared the duties with Alexei Mikhailitchenko and like most players Robbo can't help but grin when you mention Miko's name.

Boss Smith once branded Alexei "a master of economy of movement."

Then he sighed: "For the tabloid Press that means he is a lazy bastard."

He was right, and while for the spectator Mikhailitchenko carried all sorts of unpredictable magic, for his team-mates he could be infuriating.

David said: "It was hard to form a partnership with Miko at first because he was asleep half the time.

"Seriously, he was incredibly laid-back but he had wonderful skills and maybe he was a little out of position on the left instead of central midfield.

"But it was funny. I used to hare past him on an overlap and on the way BACK

I'd pass him again as he ambled towards defence!"

After those two enigmatic foreigners Robbo thought he'd seen the lot. Then came a genius.

Brian Laudrup first teamed up with the jet-paced Robertson on a pre-season tour and David confesses he made a slight misjudgement of the Dane's talent at first.

He stressed: "He kept on playing these reverse passes and I wasn't there and I was thinking he was crap. We all did.

"Then you realise the problem is your brain is two steps behind his and YOU are the problem.

"He could just see passes that none of the rest of us could, football-wise he was on a different planet."

Like all those stars who helped win the fabled Nine, Robertson left Ibrox with a trophy cabinet creaking under the weight of his medals.

Yet he has just three Scotland caps, the last of them five years ago after a

124

series of fall-outs with Scotland boss Craig Brown – who insists Robertson tried to dictate that he must be in the team or he wouldn't turn up.

David himself says he simply became fed-up sitting in the stand for his country instead of playing.

Whatever the reason, it is one of the few sadnesses to have blighted his career.

But International woes aside, there remains one game that sticks in his mind – and it would have to be against his former club Aberdeen.

"My favourite game," he enthuses, "was without doubt the 1993 Scottish Cup Final when we beat the Dons 2-1 at Parkhead.

"We'd already beaten them by the same scoreline in the League Cup Final and they were second in the league that year too.

"They were our main rivals in everything, they were my old team and

when we beat them in the Final thanks to Mark Hateley and Neil Murray's goals, I knew we were going down in history as a Treble team."

Yet this player, who took such obvious pride in Rangers' achievements and won his way into the rankings as one of the club's greatest ever left-backs, left in the wake of his side's finest moments.

With the ninth title hardly clinched Robertson was on his way to a new adventure in the Promised Land of the English Premiership with Leeds United.

George Graham saw him as a key part of his new-look Elland Road team but Robbo has been plagued by injuries and the start of 1999 saw him just returning after EIGHT MONTHS out with cruciate ligament damage.

David believes that it is all down to wear and tear, a legacy of that punishing Champions League season for Gers when he hardly missed a game and the

days when he played 40 first-team matches as a 17-year-old for the Dons.

His Leeds stay may have been troubled and now he has to convince new manager David O'Leary of his worth.

But David insisted: "I don't have any regrets about leaving Rangers.

"I felt then it was the right time for me to go and I still do now.

"Something was breaking up and I could see the end of Walter's reign approaching. I just couldn't imagine the place without him.

"There were a lot of senior guys approaching the end and the team had just achieved something so very special.

"I wanted to try the Premiership and I don't look back now – despite all the injury worries – and think I was wrong.

"Besides, the first thing Dick Advocaat did was go out and pay £5million for Arthur Numan. If I'd stayed he'd probably have binned me early doors anyway!"

Bobby RUSSELL

SHETTLESTON JUNIORS to Rangers – in the days of glitzy arrivals from Chile and Italy, it is a bizarre path for an Ibrox star to tread

That was the route taken by one of the most elegant midfielders to grace the Light Blue jersey.

Bobby Russell was a player ahead of his time. If he had been at his peak in the Bosman era of the 90s he would have had continental clubs clamouring to buy his special brand of touch and vision.

These days, the footballing brain that inspired the club to the treble in 1978 helps shape the future of Gers' kids in the Under-15 side. They couldn't have a better teacher.

Russell was 19 when the legendary Jock Wallace watched him in a trial match and asked him to take the massive step from Shettleston to stardom.

And he recalled: "At first I was in awe of the place – in awe of players like John Greig whom I had stood on the terraces and supported.

"As far as I'm concerned, Greigy is Mr Rangers, a figure who commands so much respect, yet here I was playing beside him.

"But I remember scoring the winner on my debut in a pre-season match at Inverness and from there I settled into life at Rangers."

Wallace, the one-time jungle-fighter, is often portrayed as simply an up and at 'em, fire in your bellies motivator.

He was that alright, yet scratch the surface of this rough-hewn manager and there are telling insights to his football make-up.

The Class of '78 who swept all before them in Scottish football had three smooth talents who relied on brains rather than brawn.

Wallace brought together Russell, mercurial wing star Davie Cooper and gifted striker Gordon Smith and Bobby said: "We all arrived at around the same time with exactly the same football philosophy.

"We wanted to play a fast, flowing game and Jock encouraged that.

"He recognised our strengths and there was no way, despite all the clenched fists stuff, that he ruled by fear.

"He was simply a man who made you want to do your very best for him."

Those three signings were to become a massive influence on Rangers as they wrapped up their second domestic clean sweep in three years.

Smith was prolific up front in a lethal partnership with Derek Johnstone, while Russell and Cooper became the stars whose classy signatures were etched on every Rangers glory story, home and abroad.

The European arena was made for the midfield cunning of Russell and on November 1, 1978, in PSV

Eindhoven's Phillips Stadion, the former Shettleston Junior was to give a European Cup command performance.

Gers had drawn 0-0 in the first leg and faced a daunting task on a ground where Eindhoven had previously NEVER lost a Euro match. Then Russell came calling.

His clever run on to a Tommy McLean pass to clip round the PSV keeper and secure an unforgettable 3-2 win was the perfect cameo of a princely midfielder.

Gers were to lose in the quarter-finals to Cologne but, looking back, Bobby smiled: "That night was a high and there were others – like scoring when we won the 1981 Scottish Cup with a 4-1 replay win over Dundee United. Coop was out of this world that night.

"I relished it all and, while many people say if I had been around now I'd be a rich man, I don't grudge the likes of Barry Ferguson a penny.

"I just like watching him!"

Now a whole new generation of Rangers stars in the making are taken under Russell's wing to prepare them for a chance at following in his studmarks.

And the managerial approach? Russell grinned: "I don't go around kicking their a**** up and down the dressing room like Jock did sometimes.

"You can't do that with kids – instead the arm goes round the shoulder and I encourage them to look at the likes of Barry to see what they can achieve."

Those starstruck teenagers could do a whole lot worse than look at their manager to see that.

Russell was to be a victim of the Graeme Souness revolution when – plagued by knee trouble – he was allowed to leave for Motherwell.

Yet, alongside his old pal Coop at Well, he was to come back and haunt the club when he regained his fitness, once scoring the winner against Gers in the league.

If there is one Ibrox regret for Bobby it's that Souness didn't arrive to turn Rangers around earlier.

He pointed out: "You saw the true Davie Cooper when Graeme arrived, he just blossomed again because of the quality of the players being brought in around him.

"But we both enjoyed what was supposed to be the twilight of our careers at Well and I'll always remember those times as well as the Ibrox days. I miss him."

Club and Country

IBROX CAREER 1977-87

GAMES
League	250
Scot Cup	39
Lg Cup	55
Europe	26
Total	370

GOALS
League	31
Scot Cup	8
Lg Cup	6
Europe	1
Total	46

HONOURS
League	1
Scot Cup	3
Lg Cup	4

STATS

AHEAD OF HIS TIME... Bobby Russell was a midfield maestro

Alex SCOTT

ALEX was called up from Junior side Bo'ness United and went straight into the Gers first team to score a hat-trick in a dramatic 4-1 debut win over his hometown side.

He'd hit the headlines and this gifted right-winger never left them throughout a glittering Ibrox career that won him every domestic honour, 16 caps – and a £46,000 move to Everton.

Scott had filled the boots of the legendary Willie Waddell and Alex, himself, was to be at the centre of one of the most furious football debates of his time.

Alex Scott or Willie Henderson – for Rangers or Scotland? That was the question that led to a thousand pub arguments after Ibrox hero Scott was sensationally axed to make way for the 18-year-old boy wonder in the 1962 Scottish Cup Final with St Mirren.

Gers won that one 2-0 and the debates raged on as they battled over the right-wing shirt for club and country, until Alex's FIFTH transfer request was accepted by boss Scot Symon and he chose Everton ahead of Bill Nicholson's Spurs.

It was a titanic tussle between two rare talents and they each had their peaks. Alex was hailed a Scotland hero in the 2-0 Hampden triumph over England in '62 and the following year Willie got the nod in a 2-1 success at Wembley.

By then, Scott was an ex-Rangers player but his Midas touch had seen him win an English title medal with Everton after just three months on Merseyside – and he scored in the clinching 4-1 win over Fulham.

Mo Johnston, Duncan Ferguson, Alex Cleland and, of course, nine-in-a-row manager Walter Smith have all taken the route from Ibrox to troubled Goodison in recent seasons and Light Blues fans could say with justification it was a footballing step down.

When Alex Scott chose Everton, he stood on the road to riches and found himself at England's No.1 club.

Scott had been on £30 basic at Ibrox with £5 appearance money and bonuses. At Everton he was landing £140-a-week.

Yet he insisted that the reason behind the move was one which still haunts Rangers as they face the Millennium in danger of out-growing the Scottish Premier League.

Alex, who won four titles with Gers and would later return north to Hibs, said: "At Ibrox, we had too many games that were too easy. It encourages slackness."

And then there was always the hurt of being deposed by the young Henderson – for a proud and skilled player it was hard to stomach.

Scott admitted: "I never wanted to leave Rangers until it was clearly impressed upon me that they could do without me.

"My dignity was hurt and I felt that I just had to prove myself elsewhere."

He did just that. Alex Scott was a champion on both sides of the border.

Club and Country

IBROX CAREER 1954-63	
GAMES	
League	216
Scot Cup	25
Lg Cup	62
Europe	28
Total	331
GOALS	
League	67
Scot Cup	5
Lg Cup	24
Europe	12
Total	108
HONOURS	
League	4
Scot Cup	1
Lg Cup	2
SCOTLAND	
16 caps	

STATS

Jock SHAW

SCOTLAND'S mining villages saw men like Jock Stein, Sir Matt Busby and Bill Shankly emerge from the grit and grime to rule the football world – and they also produced the great Tiger Shaw.

HIGH AND MIGHTY... Jock Shaw on top of the world after leading Gers to another cup win

Jock was born in Annathill in Lanarkshire but his fierce driving determination on the football pitch ensured that he didn't have to rely on a grim living down the pit.

At 5ft 7ins he was a ball of footballing aggression, the lack of inches more than made up for by supreme courage and snapping tackles.

That's why he earned the nickname Tiger.

Shaw has always treasured the life the game gave him and he loved it so much that his frightening fitness allowed him to cling on to his playing career until he finally retired at the age of 42.

Tiger rose to prominence with Junior side Benburb and his displays there soon saw a future in the paid ranks beckoning.

In 1933, Airdrie snapped him up and for five years the grit and guile of Shaw built him a lofty reputation with the Diamonds.

The big-time move came when Rangers stepped in to sign a cheque for £2,000 and brought him to Ibrox for the season before the outbreak of the Second World War.

Shaw made an immediate impact as part of a title-winning team but then six years would be ripped out of the heart of his career.

There would be Southern League championships, Regional Leagues, Scottish Emergency War Cups and Summer Cups.

And there was even a wonderful Victory

International triumph over England in 1946, when Jock and younger brother David were the full-backs for Scotland in a 1-0 win. But the true currency of Shaw's footballing riches really came when the conflict finally ended and he returned to Ibrox.

Rangers' inspirational captain was a key part of a combination that read: Brown; Young, Shaw, McColl, Woodburn, Cox. The Iron Curtain.

That defence was the foundation of an era of Rangers' success and Shaw would end his career with four title medals, three Scottish Cup and two League Cup badges.

Peacetime international recognition finally arrived in 1947 when Shaw won his haul of four Scotland caps which was only halted there by a family feud. Brother David of Hibs took over the jersey!

Jock returned to play in dark blue in a 1-1 draw with the Auld Enemy at Wembley but suffered defeats by Belgium and Northern Ireland, savouring only the one win against Luxembourg.

With Rangers, though, he remained an uncompromising winner and it is testament to his astonishing fitness levels that he was

38 when he held aloft the 1950 Scottish Cup after a magnificent 3-0 win over East Fife.

Four years later, the man who had come a long way from Annathill enjoyed a lengthy Gers summer tour of Canada and the USA. When they returned, both Jock and Willie Thornton announced that they were hanging up their boots.

Both continued to have a huge influence on the club, with Thornton taking over as assistant-boss to a string of managers and Jock serving the club first as trainer and then as groundsman.

Tiger's legacy still remains at Ibrox in the shape of John Greig who was in awe of this rough-hewn Rangers legend when Shaw was third-team boss.

John, who had a string of wise mentors throughout the years in his rise to the Greatest ever Ranger, admits: "He would gave me runs to the station and I'd look at him and think: "He used to be the captain of Rangers. I wonder if I could ever be like him?"

As ever, Greig picked the right man to look up to and now another generation looks up to him.

Club and Country

IBROX CAREER 1938-53

GAMES
League	169
Scot Cup	27
Lg Cup	42
Europe	0
Total	283

GOALS
League	1
Scot Cup	0
Lg Cup	0
Europe	0
Total	1

HONOURS
League	4
Scot Cup	3
Lg Cup	2

SCOTLAND
4 caps

STATS

Nigel SPACKMAN

NIGEL SPACKMAN reckons his innate knowledge of Ally McCoist's duff left foot brought him his greatest moment in a Rangers jersey.

It came in the Ne'erday Old Firm clash at Parkhead in 1990 as Gers surged forward on a lightning break and Mo Johnston fed Coisty on the left of the box.

Popular English midfielder 'Spacks' takes up the story: "I've heard McCoist say since that it was a cross but if that's the truth, then Ray Wilkins has hair!

"It was an outrageously scuffed shot, if you watch the footage, his eyes and his left boot are pointing towards goal but the ball goes the other way.

"Luckily enough, I was able to wipe away the nosebleed I always got that far forward and score the only goal of the game.

"I knew Ally's left foot and I knew he'd NEVER hit the target."

Boss Graeme Souness had hauled Spackman aside before the game and warned him that, while he had experienced derbies on Merseyside with Liverpool and in London with Queens Park Rangers, they would be nothing like this.

And in a quiet moment after the match, as the champagne bought by delighted fans flowed in his Glasgow hotel, Nigel pondered a match he now admits is like no other.

He said: "I found it hard to describe the experience, the hairs go up on the back of your neck when you walk down the tunnel and what you feel like throughout the ninety minutes.

"The competition of the two clubs for the big prizes, the bitter rivalry, the passion and, sadly, the religious aspect make it an incredible occasion.

"I've given up trying to tell English people what's it's like. I just say 'Go and watch one'."

Spackman came to Scotland in the deal that took fans' favourite Wilkins to QPR but quickly pointed out he was no Razor Mark II.

Instead, Souness had very shrewdly purchased a skilled grafter who would allow the gifted Trevor Steven to shine alongside him. Spacks – ironically these days Wilkins' sparring partner on Sky Sports – was also to develop into a gritty stand-in stopper, a grimly determined on-field leader.

Two games sum him up.

With the title race going to the wire in 1991 skipper Richard Gough was stricken with hepatitis in a hospital bed and Nigel had the armband.

He was to play a critical role in central defence in the final day decider against Aberdeen and he said: "I remember Walter Smith saying to me that Ian Durrant and Coisty were only on the bench in case we went behind and the crowd needed a lift.

"They were nowhere near fit, yet both had to come on and try to last the match for us.

"We had players down all over the place at the end but we won 2-0. Lifting that trophy will live with me forever."

Many players in this book who played in the 1992 Scottish Cup semi-final win over Celtic – when Gers survived with 10 men for 84 minutes to win 1-0 after David Robertson's red card – cite that match as embodying the Rangers ethos.

Spackman, magnificent at the heart of the defence once more, agrees.

Yet he smiled: "I remember peering into the wind and rain at Hampden and seeing Paul McStay hit a screamer that sailed past me but hit the bar and came back out. I thought: "You beauty, it's our night."

Nigel was moved on from Ibrox in 1992 and had a fruitful spell at Chelsea where he reached the Cup-Winners' Cup semi-final only to lose to the eventual winners, Real Zaragoza.

Howard Kendall then took him to Sheffield United as his No.2. He was given the top job when Kendall was sacked but left after a bitter boardroom bust-up at the Blades.

Deposed England coach Glenn Hoddle then earmarked Spackman as an ideal World Cup spy and the first France '98 game on his itinerary evoked memories of his one real footballing regret.

Nigel, who has used his time out of the game to become a fully qualified UEFA coach, smiled: "I was at Scotland-Brazil and all the kilts made me think of my Scottish grandfather and the claim I had to play for them while I was at Rangers.

"Someone back then obviously decided I was too English and I know the FA down here objected.

"But the rules said I could have been capped and I must admit I envy Matt Elliott and Neil Sullivan these days. Nigel Spackman of Rangers and Scotland. ...it had a nice ring to it."

Club and Country

STATS

IBROX CAREER 1989-92	
GAMES	
League	100
Scot Cup	9
Lg Cup	10
Europe	5
Total	124
GOALS	
League	1
Scot Cup	1
Lg Cup	1
Europe	0
Total	3
HONOURS	
League	3
Scot Cup	1
Lg Cup	1

COMPETITIVE...
that sums up the attitude 'Spacks' had to the game in his spell at Ibrox

BOBBY SHEARER watched the ball intently and launched into a scything touchline challenge as it took an awkward bounce.

CAPTAIN CUTLASS... Bobby Shearer's rugged tackling earned him the colourful nickname

Bobby SHEARER

The sickening thud and his swinging right boot took leg and ball to send a clearance careering up the line amid howls of agony during a friendly clash on the sunshine isle of Menorca.

Shearer stood transfixed. This was, after all, only a bounce game and he was the skipper of Rangers.

"Get bloody back into position," hollered the veteran George Young at the heart of the Gers defence.

"But Corky," said a sheepish Shearer. "Ah think ah've broken this winger's leg."

Young was exasperated. "That's not a winger, Bobby, that was the ****ing SUB-STITUTE!" The legend of Captain Cutlass was born.

Shearer, now 67 and battling back bravely from a stroke, still chuckles when he recalls the day he won a famous Ibrox nickname.

That summer tour would never be forgotten because of that incident but Bobby insists there were mitigating circumstances.

He explained: "There were no substitutes then but Scot Symon and the officials of the local side decided we'd have five stripped each.

"They put the benches too close to the park and when I saw the leg coming out beside the ball I just instinctively tackled and won the ball. That was my job.

"I didn't know it was the sub did I? Anyway, from that day on I was Cutlass."

That remains one of THE classic Ibrox stories but there weren't many wingers got a laugh on matchday during the decade that Shearer reigned as Rangers' right-back.

The flame-haired defender made up for a lack of pace with those trademark crunching tackles and very little got past him.

He had been signed from his local club, Hamilton Accies, for £2,000 in 1955 and was to become a model of consistency.

In fact, in one incredible run he chalked up 165 consecutive matches in a halcyon era for his side.

The 1960 European Cup Final when German aces Eintracht Frankfurt lost 7-3 to the peerless Real Madrid at Hampden remains a landmark game for all football followers.

What often slips the memory of many fans is that Gers reached the last four that year, dumping Anderlecht, Red Star Bratislava and Sparta Rotterdam on the way.

They were to be hammered 12-4 on aggregate by Eintracht in the semi-final but

Shearer's side were putting Rangers on the European map.

The following season, they reached the Final of the Cup-Winners' Cup against Fiorentina only to lose the first leg at Ibrox 2-0 after Eric Caldow's penalty miss.

And Shearer shuddered: "I'll never forget after the match that our fans were so upset at the Italians they overturned an ice-cream van.

"It also got a bit nasty over there when we lost 2-1 but I loved those games because you were constantly bettering yourself.

"Mind you, it was hard to think of that in '63 when I was trying to chase Real Madrid's Gento before he squared for Ferenc Puskas to score the only goal. We lost the return 6-0.

"Gento was superb, the only problem was you couldn't get close enough to kick him."

Yet, while that season meant disappoint-

ment on the European stage, on the domestic scene only one word summed it up. Domination.

Under born leader Captain Cutlass, Rangers won the Treble culminating in a magnificent 3-1 Scottish Cup Final victory over Dundee in front of 120,982 fans at Hampden.

Shearer will never forget the day when he became only the second man in Scottish football history to lead his side to the Grand Slam.

And he said: "That game will always be known as The Bert Slater Final after the Dundee keeper who was brilliant in the match.

"I always remember we went one up and then they equalised without us touching the ball again. But that was the ultimate as a

Billy SIMPSON

BILLY SIMPSON stood on the Windsor Park terraces and watched the mighty Rangers lose a glamour benefit game 3-2 to Everton.

It was 1946 and the seeds were sown in the mind of an awestruck Irish teenager. He'd just seen the team he wanted to be a star for.

Simpson – a centre-half – got the break he wanted when he was called to trials at Linfield and then got the shock of his life when he was listed up front! Yet he scored twice in that game and he never looked back.

The tradition that links Linfield and Rangers has brought many Irish stars to Rangers and continues even to this sophisticated day, long after the religious barriers at the club have been smashed down.

When Dick Advocaat signed gifted midfielder Lee Feeney from Linfield this season he wasn't just tying up another glittering prospect.

He was giving hope to a million youngsters in that troubled place who'd love to follow in Feeney's footsteps.

Like Feeney in 1999, Simpson in 1950 couldn't really care less who else was in for him, as long as the Gers topped the list.

He politely told Newcastle United they had no chance.

The courage and grim determination of a player who let NOTHING get in the way of a scoring chance was brought to Ibrox.

Simpson was to become a huge favourite with the fans who yearned to see one of his trademark flying headers hit the net and he made a telling contribution to clinching three titles in the 50s.

Billy's Ibrox exploits earned him hero status in Northern Ireland – and 12 international caps.

And he was a nation's idol in November, 1957, when he became one of the few Ibrox players to have scored at Wembley with the shock winner in his side's 3-2 beating of the English.

The Irish had a useful side then, with Celts such as Bertie Peacock and Charlie Tully in the green, alongside the Rangers' powerhouse.

Sadly, on the biggest stage of all at the World Cup Finals in Sweden in 1958, Simpson pulled a thigh muscle in training and missed every game.

His time at Ibrox, too, was drawing short and after a lengthy meeting of the directors in March, 1959, Simpson was allowed to go to Stirling Albion for £6,000.

Stints at Annfield, Partick Thistle and Oxford United followed and in 1962 he turned down the chance to boss Albion Rovers so he could continue mixing his work as a joiner with a job coaching top Junior side, Pollok.

Belfast-born Billy remains a very popular figure with Gers fans on both sides of the water.

He may have cost what was then a very hefty fee of £11,500 but he paid back every penny – a man who truly was worth his weight in goals.

SIMPSON STRIKES... in familiar fashion, the Rangers No.9 beats a hasty path to goal

Rangers player – and captain – for me.

"Leading the team to the treble couldn't be topped."

Bobby worked in his building business when he quit playing, then he retired a couple of years ago.

He still cherishes the games played beside the likes of George Young.

He has his medals to look back on and four caps for Scotland. But most of all for Cutlass there was the laughs.

And he said: "On international duty once we won 3-0 in Dublin against Eire in a World Cup qualifier and there was pandemonium on the park.

"I stuck the ball up my juke and walked off the pitch with it. It's one of my favourite souvenirs but I still have it upstairs to this day if they're looking for it."

SCOTLAND'S answer to Beckenbauer. Lavish praise but the tag suited the classy, cool sweeper the fans simply called Ice.

Dave Smith was a player ahead of his time, a defender who despised gifting possession to the opposition.

He saw Row Z as a place for a cut-price season ticket rather than a destination for his clearances.

And the comparisons with Bayern Munich legend Kaiser Franz don't faze Smith.

He faced the German in monumental matches for Rangers and he knows his own worth.

There is no false modesty now when Smith asserts: "It's flattering to be likened to him, yes, but I don't baulk at it.

"Any time I played against Beckenbauer I certainly wasn't in awe of him because if you feel like that you're beaten before you even start.

"He played the way the game should be played and he had a lot of attributes I liked.

"His record speaks for itself and if I am mentioned up there with the likes of a World Cup winner then I'm happy.

"One thing is for sure, though, I never went out on a park thinking he was better than me."

Smith had that little streak of arrogance inside him that marked him as special. He wouldn't trumpet his abilities or boast about his worth. Deep down inside he simply KNEW he was a good player.

Dave had the ability to snuff out danger before it truly threatened Rangers then spring forward – all poise and precision – and start the counter-attack with arrowing passes.

He believes that to be a dying art when he watches games now and he stressed: "The way I played came naturally to me, keeping possession and playing out of defence.

"I go to games now and they CHEER defenders when they hoof the ball out of the park. Unbelievable."

Smith, who had a paltry two international appearances for Scotland, was already capped by his country when he

ALL FRANZ ON DECK ... cool-headed Dave Smith was compared to legendary German sweeper Beckenbauer

Dave SMITH

left hometown team Aberdeen for Gers in 1966.

He will always be remembered for his crucial role in securing the European Cup Winners' Cup six years later. And that balmy night in Barcelona was pay-back time for Dave.

Alongside Sandy Jardine, John Greig and Willie Johnston he was a survivor of the side who had suffered Final defeat at the hands of Bayern in Nuremberg in 1967.

He has never forgotten the pain of losing then, a week after arch enemies Celtic had been crowned Kings of Europe following their Champions Cup win over Inter Milan in Lisbon.

Smith sighed: "We were under pressure playing them on their home turf anyway but the heat was turned up in the days leading up to the game.

"Celtic had just won the European Cup and we knew we were expected to make it a Double but Scot Symon chose a side without a recognised striker.

"That led to a lot of negative Press in the build-up to the game and heaped pressure on the likes of Roger Hynd and Alex Smith who were in the starting line-up. It all went wrong and we lost 1-0."

So five years later when a team stepped onto the famous Nou Camp turf intent on making history against Moscow Dynamo there was no player more grimly determined to succeed than Dave Smith.

That was the burning desire inside, on the outside he was once again Ice.

And it was Smith's piercing vision that set up Colin Stein and Johnston for the first two goals before keeper Peter McCloy's colossal kick-out freed Bud to make it 3-0.

Smith pinged passes the best midfield playmakers would envy yet he insists the darting runs being made ahead of him made his job EASY.

He said: "You had Willie Johnston who had blistering pace and Colin Stein who was so quick and strong. They knew the runs to make and I knew how to find them. And don't forget you also

had the perfect timing of Alex MacDonald who would spring from midfield to score so many important goals.

"I shudder to think what Doddie would fetch in the transfer market today."

The closing stages of that milestone match are often remembered as a critical war of nerves.

Yet Smith insisted: "People say we were hanging on that day but I have never thought that. Even at 3-2 I didn't feel shaky, I knew we would cope.

"The saddest thing was that the fans came on when the ref blew for a foul thinking it was time-up.

"That just seemed to prime the Spanish police to wade in when they invaded again at the final whistle.

"It was an awful anti-climax for the boys who had worked so hard for there to be no presentation and no lap of honour.

"For those of us who had been through the nightmare of Nuremberg and that defeat from Bayern Munich this game meant even more yet we had the crowning moment taken away from us."

In the wake of the sickening Spanish violence Gers were to be banned from Europe for two years until a bout of shuttle diplomacy from Ibrox supremo Willie Waddell saw their suspension cut down to 12 months.

It was no consolation to a bereft Dave who rapped: "The ban killed that team, Stein left and so did Bud and it all started to break up.

"That was heartbreaking. The bottom line was that we never got to defend our trophy and that hurt like hell."

When his own Gers days ended Dave had a spell at Arbroath and then looked out the passport to head for South Africa with Arcadia Shepherds and then America where his first stop was Seattle Sounders.

The next airport he touched down in was Los Angeles where he played for the local Aztecs alongside a guy called George Best.

Dave, who can also look back on a

successful spell as player-boss at Berwick Rangers when he won them promotion from the Second Division, reflected: "He was on the wagon then, Bestie, and he was tremendously fit.

"I probably played alongside him during one of the best spells of his later years in the game and he truly was a genius."

Football deals men like George Best and Dave Smith a winning hand in life. They have adulation, money and success and then when the joints start to creak and they stop playing a yawning chasm has to be filled.

For Best the escape route was booze, for Smith it was gambling. From the heights they hit rock bottom.

Best's brief stay in jail for drink driving hit every front page and Smith's demise when he was given a three-year sentence for financing his habit by embezzling from a timber merchant where he worked mirrored George's downfall.

That was 16 years ago now, though, and Dave has bravely rebuilt his life. He sighs philosophically: "Life is about decisions and God knows I made a few wrong ones."

Life outside football once enveloped Dave Smith and left him a sorry victim looking for the easy way out, it would never have happened on the pitch.

There he was peerless, the Scottish Football Writers' Association Player of the Year in that unforgettable season in 1972.

Yet he shrugs: "Sure, I was rated the best that season but was it the best of my life? That's for the journalists and others to decide.

"I simply enjoyed playing every time I went out there and every game for Rangers felt like the best of my life.

"Listen, I'm 55 now but I still play five-a-sides every Friday night and I still have the same feeling of anticipation in my stomach before we start.

"That feeling was there in the Nou Camp that night and it's still there even now."

Club and Country

STATS

IBROX CAREER 1966-74

GAMES
League	195
Scot Cup	30
Lg Cup	42
Europe	36
Total	303

GOALS
League	8
Scot Cup	0
Lg Cup	2
Europe	3
Total	13

HONOURS
Europe	1

SCOTLAND
2 caps

Gordon SMITH

AND SMITH MUST SCORE... For Rangers he usually did.

The phrase that launched a Brighton and Hove Albion fanzine and a thousand after-dinner speeches for Gordon Smith was born from one fleeting moment in an illustrious career.

It came in the last minute of the 1983 FA Cup Final when he was presented with a chance six yards out against Manchester United with the minnows holding the game's big fish 2-2 at Wembley.

Those famous words were howled by the commentator but although the Scot's shot was on target, the ball trapped under the legs of United keeper Gary Bailey. Brighton lost the replay 4-0.

Smith – now a slick media pundit and fully-fledged FIFA players' agent – shrugs off all the wisecracks about THAT miss these days. Even his column in *The Sun* is called *And Smith Must Roar!*

And he said: "People forget that I also scored in the last minute of a Cup Final for Rangers against Celtic.

"I have experienced that rollercoaster of emotions both ways – as a hero and a villain."

Smith's extra-time diving header in the 1977-78 League Cup clinched a 2-1 triumph over the Hoops and it was part of a Treble season as Jock Wallace displayed the managerial craft few gave him credit for.

Wallace is forever cast as the ex-Jungle Fighter, the True Blue motivator.

But there was more to this hard man than the superficial image. Indeed, the iron fist was often clad in a velvet glove.

The steel he wanted in his team was tempered with the silk of players like Smith and the two stars who joined him in a new era – Bobby Russell and Davie Cooper.

Smith was the maverick idol of Kilmarnock and Newcastle United wanted to take him south. Gordon had other ideas but his desire to play for Rangers was to cost two men their jobs.

Wallace landed his man in a £65,000 transfer and Smith revealed: "Big Jock told me it was the end of a FOUR-YEAR chase.

"I had always heard rumours at Killie yet nothing happened. But he explained he'd wanted to sign me since he saw me for the first time when I was 18.

"Killie's boss Willie Fernie stood firm, though, and even when I was allowed to go the board voted 3-2 in favour of the sale and the two who lost RESIGNED.

"This was the stage I wanted, though, it had been my life's ambition to be at a top club like Rangers."

Wallace – who'd lost the opening fixture of that season at Aberdeen – kept Smith on the bench for the second game with Hibs. Gers went down again.

Now the manager needed to regroup and assess matters, everyone knows two defeats on the trot at Ibrox constitutes a crisis.

And Gordon recalled: "He had this fear of me as a part-timer on my first full-time contract, he thought I wasn't fit enough. Out on the track he said: 'This is the hard day.' We ran six 220-metre laps and then stopped.

"I was right up front in the race and afterwards he called me into the office and said: 'Why didn't you tell me you could run like that?' I replied: 'You never asked.'

"But on the way out the office I said over my shoulder: 'By the way your hard day is a WARM-UP at Killie.'

"The laugh was rough and ready and I knew I was in. I scored two in a 4-0 win over Partick Thistle at Firhill and I never looked back under Jock."

Smith gives a telling insight into Wallace and the system he designed ahead of its time.

The role he occupied for Rangers is perfectly summed up by Scotland boss Craig Brown as The Spiv.

It's the man who plays in the hole off the front players in order to damage teams and is allowed to cheat in his defensive duties.

Gordon fitted the bill perfectly and he reasoned: "There's no question there is this common image of Jock Wallace as the fire in the bellies manager and he was that. But he was a football man too.

"He had really studied where I should play – running on from behind as Tommy McLean and Davie Cooper pitched in the service for Derek

Johnstone. Jock had thought that team through, and had pondered all the pieces that made up the jigsaw.

"How could a team that had myself, Bobby Russell, Tommy McLean and Davie Cooper in it be one of a manager who simply loved hammer-throwers? We couldn't tackle a fish supper."

Smith, whose grandfather Mattha had been a Kilmarnock legend, had grown up with his hometown club playing off the cuff. Wallace changed all that.

The solo artist became part of a group that included his own boyhood hero McLean. He'd dreamed of playing alongside Tommy at Killie but feared the chance was gone when the little winger moved to Ibrox.

Now Smith was thriving alongside him and it rained goals in his first year playing in tandem with Johnstone. Yet it all turned sour amidst the rancour behind the scenes between Wallace and the board following that Treble triumph.

Gordon sighed: "At the end of that 1978 season I was lying in bed one morning when my mum rushed up and told me Jock had gone as Rangers manager. I just felt this incredible loss, the man who had signed me was away after just one season.

"It's ironic, 20 years later when it happened to one of my clients, Paul Lambert, at Celtic with the departure of Wim Jansen. After he'd won the title I sympathised totally with his feelings of bewilderment."

Gers skipper John Greig was quickly shuttled from the dressing-room to the manager's office. Gordon didn't know it then but the writing was on the wall.

In 1980 Smith had just signed a five-year deal to keep him at the club but his former team-mate had other ideas.

A £440,000 bid was in from Brighton and the manager wanted it accepted. Smith was left in no doubt about that.

Even now it clearly rankles when he looks back to the dismal day he realised it was over for him at Rangers.

And he groaned: "I didn't want to go and it remains my biggest regret that I did, especially in those circumstances. The way it was handled was wrong.

"We can talk about it these days but John knows when I look back I was so very hurt, it left me gutted that I had to leave Rangers at 25. I was at my peak."

The elegant striker whose goals had dumped the likes of Juventus in a treasured European Cup run was gone.

Yet when Rangers were in dire straits in 1982, Greig ironically turned to Smith on a one-month loan basis to try and pull off a League Cup Final win over Celtic.

Club and Country

IBROX CAREER
1977-80, 82-83

GAMES

League	100
Scot Cup	18
Lg Cup	23
Europe	16
Total	157

GOALS

League	35
Scot Cup	1
Lg Cup	12
Europe	3
Total	51

HONOURS

League	1
Scot Cup	2
Lg Cup	2

STATS

Gordon confessed: "The second spell was a massive mistake. I let my heart rule my head and I should never have done it.

"I was brought back on a month's loan but it was really only to play in that Final which we lost and I was made the scapegoat.

"By then most players felt John had lost the dressing-room and the place had changed – for the worse.

"Bobby, Davie and I – the new breed who came in together – had always remained close. I remember Coop turned and whispered to me in the dressing-room: 'For God's sake, Smithy, why have you come back? It's a different club.' I knew then it was a bad move."

It seemed a lifetime away from the laughs of that Treble year when Smith had to carry a spare suit in his car because he often found his best one floating in the bath.

Another time he had to walk into town with a pair of canvas shoes on that the boys in the dressing-room had written rude messages on.

Those were days he could never really recapture despite staying at Brighton longer than he had been at Gers.

A stint at Manchester City under former Celtic manager Billy McNeill soon followed. Next stop took him to Oldham, where he played alongside a young keeper called Andy Goram.

Then Smith trod one of the most bizarre transfer paths in football history. From Austrian side Admira Wacker to Ayrshire juniors Ardeer Thistle!

He'd relished the continental experience but was ready to hang up his boots and he explained: "It was my dad Bill's ambition to see me play alongside my brother Billy. I couldn't let him down while I could still play."

Smith – who won a league title, two Scottish Cup medals and a League Cup badge in his Rangers days – did have a stint as No.2 at St Mirren.

But he is now settled guiding the careers of top stars like Lambert and displaying his innate knowledge of the game as one of the shrewdest media analysts.

Yet he surely remains one of the best players never capped for Scotland. That must have hurt?

"Jock Wallace constantly pushed my case for Scotland but Ally MacLeod just would not have it," he explained.

"Ally took DJ to Argentina for the 1978 World Cup Finals after our prolific season together. But he left me behind and Derek sitting on the bench and Wallace always condemned that as a major mistake.

"It was an obvious disappointment not to make it but every game for Rangers felt like a cap to me."

135

Graeme SOUNESS

THE studs slashed into George McCluskey's knee then the red card flashed in front of Graeme Souness' eyes as his Rangers debut crashed down around his ears

Mayhem greeted the domineering midfielder who had led Liverpool and Sampdoria to glory when he began his Ibrox Revolution in a 2-1 defeat from Hibs at Easter Road in August 1986.

A 21-man melee scarred that match after player-manager Souness' dismissal and even now, five jobs on from the days when he changed the whole face of Scottish football, the pain remains.

The arrogant strut from the field, he insists, was a mask constructed to hide the anguish inside as his first day at the office turned horribly sour.

Souness, now at the throne of Portuguese giants Benfica, shuddered: "That was the worst day of my entire playing career, no question.

"It was miserable.

"It wasn't just the way it happened but the fact that when I was sent off I looked up at the Directors' box and my dad James was staring back at me.

"He had once broken into Easter Road as a kid to play there on that surface and here he was watching his own boy getting sent off there.

"That hurt me.

"There was only one good thing to come out of that day and that was the togetherness we showed when the going got rough, it was to serve us well that season."

Souness was in the twilight of an incredible playing career when David Holmes charged him with booting a sleeping giant out of its slumbers.

The man who left Middlesbrough to shrug on the aura of greatness at Anfield and then in Italy's star-studded Serie A had retired from international football with 54 Scotland caps after the World Cup Finals in Mexico.

He still felt he had a lot to offer but even now he feels a frustration over his playing days in a Light Blue jersey and his views are typically forthright.

He said: "I was a hunted man when I played in Scotland, I have always felt that.

"It wasn't the case in my own mind but they all saw me as a big-shot coming back home to teach them how to play the game.

"Kicking me was a way to make a name for yourself. Then if I responded I would be given a yellow or a red card.

"Even in the final game of that season at Pittodrie when we drew 1-1 with Aberdeen I was to be sent off.

"That felt desperate to me personally at what was such a high point of my life.

"Yet that first title meant the most to me because it had been such a long wait for Rangers.

"I wanted to make sure the club never again waited nine years for a championship."

A nagging calf injury blighted his hopes of playing more games, yet one virtuoso performance displayed all the swagger and skill he could still muster.

It came in the New Year game against Celtic at Ibrox in January, 1987 when he sprayed piercing passes around and, at one point, sent four Hoops players darting in all directions with a feint and fake.

He never actually touched the ball.

The 2-0 win was hailed not for the scoreline but the level of Rangers' superiority, laced with a bristling brilliance inspired by the boss-in-boots.

Broach the subject with Souness now, though, and he is dismissive, shrugging: "Listen, people still talk to me about that New Year game but I was FINISHED as a player by then.

"I was a shadow of what I had been, mixing playing with managing was almost impossible because you would be travelling to watch players when you should have been resting.

"I under-estimated the difficulty of the job, no question. But still it was all a marvellous experience."

One memory he will always carry with him is having the chance to play in a game of that Old Firm stature with the late Davie Cooper at his best.

Souness had always rated Coop, and sought him out for conversations on the game when they were away with Scotland.

And for a man who thinks of Kenny Dalglish and Gianluca Vialli as his muckers, his regard for the maverick winger is telling.

Graeme, who bowed out as a player as a sub against Dunfermline when the title was clinched in 1990, insisted: "Davie was as skilled as any I have met throughout my career.

"If I do have one little regret from my time at Ibrox it was letting Davie go.

"That was a vital lesson in management.

"I let him go because he asked me to and I allowed him to join Motherwell because he was my friend from Scotland days and I wanted to do right by him.

"It was a mistake because he kept on coming back to haunt me!"

Souness was to pay a massive personal price for dragging Rangers out of the gutter. His first marriage broke up and you have to think the stress he placed himself under was a factor in the major heart surgery he would have to face just a year

SITTING PRETTY...
Souness enjoys one of his more relaxing days during his Ibrox reign

Club and Country

IBROX CAREER 1986-91	
GAMES	
League	50
Scot Cup	5
Lg Cup	9
Europe	9
Total	73
GOALS	
League	3
Scot Cup	0
Lg Cup	2
Europe	0
Total	5
HONOURS	
League	1
SCOTLAND	
54 caps	

STATS

after he controversially quit Ibrox to take over as boss of his beloved Liverpool.

One move he insists didn't cause him nightmares was the courageous decision to break down the sectarian barrier and sign a high-profile Roman Catholic player in Mo Johnston.

He said: "Jock Stein once told me that if there was a good Catholic and a good Protestant player he'd take the Protestant because he knew he could always go back for the other one.

"He knew the other one wouldn't come to Rangers and that's crazy, I hated all that and didn't want anything to do with it.

"No, I didn't have one sleepless night over Mo because I knew in my heart it was right."

These days he is philosophical about the decision to quit that prompted his friend and chairman David Murray to axe him immediately, despite the fact that Gers were embroiled in a title run-in that would go to the final day against Aberdeen.

He remains as single-minded as the kid who once walked away from Spurs at the age of 17 because they wouldn't put him in the first team.

Yet Souness, now happy in Portugal with his second wife, has mellowed. And he pointed out: "Much has been made of

me making a mistake when I left Rangers, but I look back now and know I have never been happier in my personal life than I am now.

"I wouldn't have had that at Rangers and the travels I undertook after that have taught me so much about life and football.

"Mistakes? David Murray would have made a bigger one if he hadn't listened to me and given the job to Walter Smith.

"David originally wanted a big name but I knew he had the perfect successor, the man with the respect of the players, working for him already."

The Kop job became a trauma, he inherited a team that needed rebuilding and in the throes of it all his health failed him.

There's no doubt the surgery that saved his life has changed his outlook and he confessed: "You have to remember this was a club where I'd been skipper and won the European Cup.

"I wanted it so much for Liverpool, I CRAVED making that job a success but it didn't happen.

"I got the FA Cup in two and a half years but the expectation was huge and I accept that I didn't meet it.

"I had to take that job, though, because of all that club meant to me."

Since then the man who guided Gers to

three titles before the lure of Anfield proved too much has travelled Europe amassing more football knowledge and becoming, he firmly believes, a far better manager.

The firebrand who ripped through Rangers has quelled some of his explosive nature and he reasoned: "I've come to know how you can measure success.

"Was it winning a Cup in my year in Turkey with Galatasary or then coming back to learn another side of football by keeping Southampton up in the Premiership? The answer is both, you're operating under constraints and you do the job.

"Going back to Italy with Torino then was my one big mistake. I joined a club that was in the Second Division but I felt with my previous knowledge of Italian football I could make a difference.

"Yet I had come to a club that had signed 17 players on the say-so of agents and journalists and, within six games, they were telling ME that things weren't going right.

"Live and learn. Now at Benfica it's like being at Rangers again. Draw and it's a nightmare, lose and it's a national disaster.

"There are a lot of similarities, but one big difference. I would love to have had £30million to spend last summer like Dick Advocaat!"

Colin STEIN

STAR striker signs for a national record fee then blasts hat-tricks in his first two matches.

INSTANT IDOL ... Colin Stein scored a treble on his debut for Gers

In his third game he's on for another treble until his last minute shot hits one post then runs along the line to bounce off the other and out to safety.

If you spun that line in the *Roy of the Rovers* office the Editor would boot you out the door and tell you to get real. But that's what really happened for Colin Stein at Rangers. Fact is stranger than fiction.

Stein's astonishing start in a Light Blue jersey came after the powerhouse frontman moved to Gers from Hibs for a Scottish best bounty of £100,000 in October 1968. He became an instant idol with the Ibrox support on his debut in a 5-1 win over Arbroath and he said: "I'd actually had a quiet game and then all of a sudden I scored three in eight minutes. It was a dream."

Next up came Hibs, the club who had sold him to Rangers, but there was no mercy from Stein. Even if the rival keeper had been Best Man at his wedding.

Gers won 6-1 and Colin, now a joiner in Edinburgh, still laughs when he recalls the growing frustration of his mate

Thomson Allan as the shots rifled past him that day at Ibrox.

He smiled: "Luck was on my side but who could believe that I'd done it again? Better still they flew past Thomson this time.

"I remember we had a drink afterwards but it was pretty silent. He wasn't really all that pleased for me as it turned out! Still, you couldn't really better a start like that."

Ibrox greats featured elsewhere in these pages – men like Ally McCoist and Mark Hateley – endured months of hell as they tried to win over the Ibrox legions.

Stein clearly didn't fancy the pain of a striker searching his soul for answers to a barren spell. He just kept scoring.

His third game for the club took him to the Republic of Ireland for a Fairs Cup Second round second leg tie against Dundalk.

Gers – with the help of doubles from Willie Henderson and Alex Ferguson – had cruised the first leg 6-1 and November 13 took them to the Emerald Isle.

Big Colin once more found the route to goal but finally his luck deserted him a little. He sighed: "In the last minute I thought I was on for another treble.

"I hit a shot that hit one post, rolled along the line and hit the other upright before bouncing out. All good things come to an end, I suppose!"

Stein, though, was to be a key figure for Rangers in Europe that season as DWS Amsterdam and then Spaniards Athletic Bilbao – when Colin netted in a decisive 4-1 first leg win – were dismissed to set up a Battle of Britain semi-final with Newcastle United.

Gers had been dumped out of the last four of the same tournament by Leeds the previous season and the fans yearned to see new star Stein put the record straight.

Sadly, that raw desire was to turn into disgraceful violence at St James' Park after Geordies' keeper Willie McFaul made an incredible save from Andy Penman's penalty in a 0-0 first leg draw at Ibrox.

Gers were 2-0 down to the Toon and on their way out when a section of the travel-ling support surged onto the pitch in a bid to get the game abandoned.

The players were rushed to the dressing-room as cops waded in to break up skirmishes between rival fans and prevent a full-scale riot.

For 17 sorry minutes the name of Rangers was shamed and after all Stein's exploits, his first Euro adventure ended in tears.

Three years later there would be more pitch invasions in Barcelona – this time in outbursts of joy – as Stein's opener sent his side on the way to a 3-2 European Cup Winner's Cup Final win over Moscow Dynamo.

The batons of the over-zealous Spanish police may have clubbed home that night but Colin stressed: "Despite that souring it, the experience could never be topped.

"That run just built up momentum and we saw off a lot of very good sides like Torino and Bayern Munich on the way."

The victims also included Sporting Lisbon in a tie that became notorious for a referee who didn't know the rules of the tournament and a UEFA observer who saved Rangers.

Gers won the first leg 3-2 with Stein on target twice at Ibrox then tied by the same score in Portugal. The ref ordered extra-time and once more Stein emerged from the game with a double although Gers went down 4-3.

With the aggregate at 6-6, the match official demanded a penalty shoot-out which Rangers LOST but the UEFA man recognised that the Scots' extra-time goal should have counted DOUBLE. Stein and Co. had won a reprieve and the rest is history.

These days Colin looks back and laughs at it all and one Barcelona memory always makes him chuckle when he recounts it at the bowling club where he has turned himself into a player of county standard.

Colin grinned: "I'll never forget Arthur Montford on the bus on the way back to our base after winning the Final.

"There he was with the trademark sports jacket and the big mike and he wanted to interview me live to the nation.

"'Well Colin,' he said, 'which of your goals did you enjoy best?'

Club and Country

IBROX CAREER
1968-72, 1975-77

GAMES	
League	128
Scot Cup	20
Lg Cup	33
Europe	25
Total	206

GOALS	
League	64
Scot Cup	9
Lg Cup	14
Europe	10
Total	97

HONOURS	
Lg Cup	2
Europe	1

SCOTLAND
21 caps

STATS

"'Arthur,' I replied, 'I only scored one!' The look on his face as he began to blush beetroot was priceless."

That same year, after four superb seasons at Ibrox, Stein decided to take the road south to Coventry City.

It was a move he relished and he stressed: "I thoroughly enjoyed myself there. They made me team skipper and it was a very competitive league. It was a good move for me but coming back to Rangers was to work out too."

For the man who had made a comic-book start to his Rangers career there could only be one script when he decided on a second spell with the club – the hero's return.

Stein had come back to sign for Jock Wallace in his hour of need and, as fate would have it, the game that once more carved his niche in Ibrox folklore was on his old stamping ground at Easter Road.

Colin said: "Again it was against the Hibs and I headed the goal that stopped 10-in-a-row for Celtic.

"I suppose I was always going to be remembered for that."

He would stay at Gers until 1977 but, by then, the injuries were taking longer to heal as his marauding style of play finally caught up with him.

Colin Stein was only 30 when he quit playing but he insisted: "I was playing for the Gers' reserves. When you're used to big crowds that can be a downer because you can hear every shout.

"Believe me, I was taking dog's abuse from the punters then and I just didn't fancy it. Going down through the leagues wasn't for me. I didn't want to play unless it was at the top and I hung up my boots."

He walked away with his place in the Gers' history books assured – after that whirlwind start it had to be. And even on the international stage this striker who won 21 caps remains linked to the fabled feat of scoring hat-tricks.

Stein pointed out: "I was the last player to score a hat-trick for Scotland when I got four in an 8-0 win over Cyprus at Hampden.

"I can't believe no-one has matched that yet. For God's sake, it was 30 YEARS ago now and we've played enough Estonias, Faroe Islands and San Marinos for someone to do it!"

CLEVER TREVOR...
A goal against Celtic in the 1993 Ne'erday clash holds a special place in Steven's heart

Trevor STEVEN

TREVOR STEVEN walked out of Old Trafford after talks with Alex Ferguson knowing in his mind that he would become a Manchester United player. And 24 hours later he'd signed – for RANGERS.

That was the pulling power that the charismatic Graeme Souness brought to Ibrox as the driving force behind the revolution that dragged an ailing club out of its death throes.

Steven was hot property, THE midfield commodity of the time after shining in an Everton side that had won the English title and scoring in their 3-1 European Cup Winners' Cup Final triumph over Rapid Vienna in 1985.

Ferguson, of course, controversially axed Souness from the critical World Cup Finals clash with Uruguay in Mexico. There was no love lost between the two explosive Scots.

Now they were at war in the transfer market and Trevor recalled: "On the Monday I had gone to Old Trafford to meet Alex Ferguson and when I came

away I really felt I was going to be a Manchester United player.

"But I told Fergie that I was still going to meet with Graeme Souness the next day because I had promised to do that. And 24 hours later I'd been won over and signed for Rangers."

Chairman David Murray inked the £1.5million cheque with a flourish and Souness had pulled off another coup.

The shrewd Steven – now using his vast knowledge as a commentator for *Eurosport* and a football consultant with top Scottish agent Blair Morgan – analysed the situation the way he does a slow-motion replay these days.

And he reasoned: "What you must remember is that there was no European football for English clubs then. They'd been banned because of the rioting Liverpool fans who'd sparked the Heysel Disaster in the European Cup Final against Juventus.

"Alex Ferguson was NOT a happy man but I was disappointed to read in his book that the deal died because we didn't get on. That just wasn't the case.

"The truth is I just preferred to join Rangers instead of Manchester United. It was as simple as that."

Trev joined an English colony that included the likes of Terry Butcher, Chris

Woods and Gary Stevens and he knew that, with Gers, he would have an almost guaranteed passport to the European arena he loved.

In other seasons Steven might have had pressure heaped on him from the off but he signed alongside a player who grabbed just a few headlines for himself – Mo Johnston.

Amidst the furore that surrounded the club's first major Roman Catholic signing, against the background of Mo's bodyguards and the bigoted fans chained to the past burning their season tickets, Steven settled in quietly.

And when it came to show-time in a sell-out pre-season friendly against a Spurs side that included Paul Gascoigne and Gary Lineker, Trevor got off to a flyer.

He said: "I never regretted choosing Rangers from my first game on, my debut was a day to treasure.

"I got the only goal of the game and that season was to end the way it started, on the same sort of high.

"I scored the header that beat Dundee United at Tannadice and we clinched the title."

Throughout his seven years with the club, debate always raged over Steven's best position.

He was superb for Everton and England wide right yet always privately preferred the role of playmaker.

Souness gave him the chance to be The Guv'nor and he grasped it.

Soon covetous eyes were cast upon him and Trevor and Rangers were about to get an offer they couldn't refuse.

Marseille owner Bernard Tapie is now a disgraced figure in football after he was jailed in the wake of the bribes scandal that enveloped his club.

But back in 1991 he was still at the helm of France's top club and the stench of corruption around the Stade Velodrome had yet to surface. He wanted Steven and he was willing to pay £5.5m.

Trevor, like every Rangers player, had been stunned when Souness quit the club for Liverpool but he pointed out: "I had just signed a five-year contract for Rangers and shown my hand, I knew what I wanted to do.

"But the money was just too much to turn down and I was sold. Within three months of Graeme's departure I too was on my way."

The move was to become a footballing dream and a financial night-mare.

Steven played and trained with a star-studded side that included the likes of Basile Boli, Chris Waddle, Jean-Pierre Papin and Abedi Pele by day and by night he tried to sort out the shortfall in the wage packet he'd been promised.

He stressed: "The move was excellent for me in a footballing sense and I played in midfield beside Didier Deschamps who later lifted the World Cup as France's skipper.

"But they'd budgeted for us to win the European Cup and when we went out early the financial mess they were in really came to light.

"We weren't being paid yet we battled on to win the league before I knew I had to get away. When the chance to return to Rangers arrived I jumped at it."

He was welcomed back to the Rangers' ranks with open arms and walked straight into one of the best seasons in the club's history in 1992-93.

Gers went 44 games unbeaten, won the domestic Treble and were within one goal of the European Cup Final.

Steven was a key part of that Champions League side, lacing games with flashes of brilliance like the precision pass across the Ibrox mud that allowed Ian Durrant to blast in the opener against Bruges.

He'd always relished the Euro stage and those midweek nights under the leaden skies and teeming rain at Ibrox still live with him.

Trev smiled: "That must have been one of the wettest winters in living history!

"The Bruges game –– when we won 2-1 thanks to Scott Nisbet's fluke after Mark Hateley was sent off – was memorable enough.

"But who could ever forget coming back from two down to draw with Marseille?

"We looked dead and buried then and how I savoured that comeback after all I'd been through with them."

Gers were to draw 1-1 in the return in France when a win would have given them a Final slot against AC Milan.

Marseille went on to clinch the trophy then be stripped of it when Tapie's skullduggery was uncovered. Life was never quite the same for the French champions – or Steven – again.

That season was the last when he really peaked with the club as he was pitched into a heartbreaking series of injuries from which he never recovered.

His calf muscle had degenerated so much that no matter how much work he did, he would never cure his problem.

And he sighed: "The harder I tried, the worse it got. That was the ironic thing.

"But it was soul-destroying, especially when I was over 30 and heading towards the end of my playing days.

"Every Saturday should have been precious to me but instead I spent almost all of them in the stand."

He bowed to the inevitable in 1997 and retired but has been in big demand since – both in his business interests guiding players and as an articulate analyst of the game on a variety of TV shows.

So what was his best memory of his Gers' career, what goal will he always cherish? The answer is hardly surprising.

It came on New Year's Day 1993 in the traditional Old Firm clash and Trevor grinned: "Walter Smith had pushed me up front that day because Ally McCoist was injured and when Ian Ferguson's free-kick was headed back by Mark Hateley some sort of instinct took me into the box.

"The header flew into the corner and within 20 minutes of playing up front I'd scored what proved to be winner against Celtic.

"I didn't touch the ball again but it didn't matter!"

HOT PROPERTY...
Trevor Steven

SINGIN' THE BLUES...injury put paid to a career which Stevens feels finished prematurely at Gers

BEDLAM. Gary Stevens couldn't hear himself think on the park and, for the first time in his football life, he felt daunted by the very thought of being involved in a match.

The occasion was his Old Firm debut in August 1988 and the star who won 46 caps for England, two titles and the Cup Winners' Cup with Everton, confirms one long-held conviction north of the border.

It's true, there really is no other game like Rangers-Celtic.

Stevens, a £1million Graeme Souness capture from Goodison, said: "I looked around when we were about to kick off and you honestly can't hear yourself think on the pitch.

"I thought: 'Bloody Hell'.

"Funnily enough, that same thought was going through my head just two minutes in when they scored through Frank McAvennie!"

Gary was to win his war of nerves, though, as Rangers won the game out the park.

They recovered to rattle their biggest rivals 5-1 – and there were still 27 minutes to go when the fifth from Mark Walters was dispatched beyond Ian Andrews.

Souness bought proven quality in Gary and throughout four model years of class and consistency, he was a magnificent asset to Gers.

His pace and stamina at right-back were his trademarks, one minute careering up on the overlap, the next in defence using all the experience he'd gleaned with Everton.

He even scored on his league debut at

Gary STEVENS

Hamilton Accies. Rangers had reversed a trend by bringing big-name English internationals north of the border and the reason for that was easy – Souness.

Gary had cursed the Scotland skipper when his goal for Liverpool dumped Everton in the Milk Cup Final, but he had always held a healthy respect for the hard man who played his football across at Stanley Park.

"Graeme had a charisma and a desire about him that just lured you into his way of thinking," Stevens revealed.

"Sure, he was a tough guy, but he was a truly great player and when you have that in-built respect before you start as a manager then you have a chance."

With Souness at the helm Gary got used to title medals – he won six in all at Gers – and grew to love his adopted homeland.

Even after he left the club for

Tranmere Rovers Stevens kept his house in the picturesque village of Bridge of Allan, an area that has also become home to Terry Butcher and Kevin Drinkell.

Gary grew to respect Rangers' special traditions and feels that was best displayed in the wake of Souness' controversial decision to leave Gers and boss Liverpool.

That, of course, brought the final day title showdown with Aberdeen in 1991 and he said: "It was one of the highlights of my whole career and not just my Rangers days to be honest.

"I have never been involved in a game with so much tension and so much riding on it. We were getting reshuffled all over the place – I actually played four different positions – but still we won it 2-0."

Gary's Gers days were to be numbered after the summer of 1992 when

he broke down in Finland while with the England squad preparing for the European Championships.

An ankle problem worsened dramatically, and he was sickened to be told he could forget the whole of the following season.

Stevens, now training to be a football physio after injury ended his playing days at Tranmere, sighed: "I would play four games in 18 months and for a guy who had hardly missed a match for five years at Rangers, that was very hard to take.

"To make matters worse I missed a great season.

"I wanted so much to be a part of more European nights after winning the Cup Winners' Cup at Everton, but then the one season when we really did ourselves justice was the one I missed.

"To be honest, it hurt like Hell that they could achieve all that without me!"

Scot SYMON

SCOT SYMON will always be remembered as the Rangers manager who was sacked when his team were top of the league – six months after he'd led them to the European Cup Winners' Cup Final. And the Board didn't have the guts to tell him to his face.

LEGEND ... Scot Symon was one of Rangers' greatest bosses

This tale of Symon's days as player and boss at Ibrox should be one of glory yet it is sullied by one of the grubbiest chapters in the club's 126-year history.

James Scotland Symon took over from the legendary Bill Struth as the Light Blues supremo in June 1954. The 13 years in charge that followed were to see him guide Gers to two European finals, six titles, five Scottish Cups and four League Cups.

Yet in November 1967 the manager was on borrowed time as Celtic's might grew. The outrageous decision to axe him was a scandal. The way it was carried out morally bankrupt.

Symon was summoned to a Glasgow house where a businessman with strong Ibrox connections told him his services were no longer required. It was over.

This man who starred at wing-half in the fabled 2-2 Ibrox draw with Moscow Dynamo in 1945 had made the club his life for almost 30 years. He gave them dignity and they treated him like dirt.

Symon – born in Errol, Perthshire – had played for Dundee before heading south to Portsmouth.

Gers brought him back north but much of his playing career was to be scuppered by the Second World War.

A natural sportsman who represented Scotland at cricket as well as earning an international cap, he was content that he could quench his ambition as Rangers manager until the dark days of 1967.

His side were unbelievably beaten 1-0 by the minnows of Berwick Rangers in one of the biggest Scottish Cup upsets of all time.

Symon could have hidden from the Press immediately after the match. Instead he emerged to admit: "This is the worst result in the history of Rangers Football Club."

Jock Wallace like Symon would become an Ibrox managerial legend yet in a twist of irony he was in charge of Berwick on one of boss Scot's darkest days.

That Shielfield shaker when the Wee Gers triumphed 1-0 through Sammy Reid's goal was the making of Wallace. Yet even as his Rangers

reign began to unravel Symon refused to let his core of dignity be eroded by the shame of one humiliating result.

Big Jock recalled: "He came into our dressing-room and congratulated everyone – including the groundsman."

Symon was self-contained to the point that most inside the game saw him as a loner. Single-minded, he simply had a steely belief in his own football formula and he didn't see the need to bounce ideas off anyone.

Study his full managerial record and you can see why. He won two League Cups with East Fife, switched south for a season and took Preston North End to an FA Cup Final. Then came those 13 trophy-laden years at Ibrox.

Yet in '67 he was up against a footballing force that will never be emulated anywhere. Jock Stein's Lisbon Lions.

And Scot would later reflect: "Everything we did was being compared to Celtic.

"They won the European Cup in 1967 but we were termed a FAILURE because we lost in the Final of the Cup Winners' Cup to Bayern Munich the same year.

"The rise of Celtic was the beginning of the end for me. One significant remark I overheard was: 'We just couldn't live with Celtic winning the league title again.'

"They had already won the championship twice in a row and they went on to win it nine-in-a-row but Rangers are still alive."

Symon had styled himself on his own manager Bill Struth and lived by the same iron rules of discipline and integrity. His sacking and the way it was conducted left him bereft.

He was later to say it took him THREE MONTHS to recover from the indignity of his dismissal.

And he sighed: "I didn't want to speak to anyone. I just couldn't have given any more.

"Yet I didn't want to hide because I had no

reason to feel guilty. I had done my job to the best of my ability.

"I didn't realise it in those days but I was ALWAYS under a strain. There were always problems at the back of my mind."

Despite it all there remained the little touches of class that were the measure of the man who discovered John Greig and tamed Jim Baxter amongst other claims to fame.

In the wake of the bombshell news of his departure as Gers manager Scotland's top football writers – men like Alex Cameron and Allan Herron – leapt to his defence.

At times they had sparred with him throughout his reign yet they received letters, in his immaculate copperplate handwriting, expressing thanks for their articles.

Symon recovered to give 18 years of sterling service to Partick Thistle as general manager, director and counsellor at Firhill.

The hurt of his Ibrox exit always lingered, though, and he stayed away from Rangers for 18 long years despite being an honorary member of the club.

It was fitting that he did return for the first time since his sacking just before he died. The occasion? Gers were playing Moscow Dynamo in a rerun of the famous match he had starred in four decades earlier. At last he made his peace with a club he felt had turned its back on him.

Scot Symon died at the age of of 74 in April 1985. The then Scotland boss Jock Stein attended the funeral and Baxter – the errant midfielder he'd made a star – was also there.

Greig – who like his mentor went on to boss the club – had been signed for the club by Symon as a raw 18-year-old and he winced: "I have lost one of the family, that's what it feels like.

"He was like a father to me. Anything I achieved in football was down to him."

Baxter said simply: "He was the finest manager Rangers ever had."

SYMON SAYS ...
Scot's playing
career was cut
short by the war

Willie THORNTON

BILL STRUTH glowered at the fresh-faced teenager sitting in the corner of Rangers' dressing room and asked: "How much do I pay you a week, boy?"

"£1 sir," came the anxious reply. "Well," said the disciplinarian Ibrox manager, "any boy who keeps his boots as clean as yours deserves £2-a-week and that's what you'll get from now on."

Rangers were in Falkirk playing in a benefit match and Willie Thornton was an awestruck kid who had signed for the club four days short of his 16th birthday – not so daft, however, that he didn't know when to keep his mouth shut.

Years later he would still smile at the memory and laugh: "We never dared answer him back so I couldn't tell him that I'd never cleaned my boots in my life. It was my MOTHER who kept them smart!"

Struth's eccentricities in his later years when he walked with the aid of a stick made their mark on his players in more ways than one.

Willie once smiled: "He wasn't slow in whacking any of us on the backside if he thought we were slacking in training!

"Seriously, though, he had a greater effect on my life than even my own father. I never heard him raise his voice but he knew how to deal with players – and they weren't all angels.

"We hardly saw him during the week and before the match the directors would come into the dressing-room. Some of them liked to give the players advice.

"At quarter to three Struth would ask them to leave and tell us to forget everything they'd just said and listen to him."

That £2 wage packet for the stylish centre-forward with the towering leap and the sparkling boots did cause him some unforeseen problems.

Thornton – who was to be capped seven times for Scotland – explained: "At school, I couldn't understand why one of my teachers didn't like me.

"It was only later that I found out the £2-a-week I was getting from Rangers was the same amount she got for teaching me French!"

His league debut came on January 2, 1937, in a win over Partick Thistle and he held a special distinction back then.

Thornton was Rangers' youngest-ever first team player and he recalled: "I was standing in the Enclosure when my name was called out to play.

"I kept my place for eight games and it was a blow when I was dropped for a Scottish Cup tie

DESK JOCKEY... Willie Thornton, a skilful, brave centre-forward, entered football management after hanging up his boots

against Queen of the South at Palmerston.

"In hindsight, it was maybe just as well, because Rangers lost and I always felt guilty if I played in a losing team – no matter what age I was."

Willie had a daunting task when he arrived at Gers, as he tried to edge out the intimidating presence of Jimmy Smith.

The fans loved the battering-ram striker, not least because with keepers left to protect themselves in those days, Smith relished dumping an unprepared goalie into the net!

Thornton won the scrap for the jersey but his footballing dreams were soon to be blown away by life's harsh realities and the Second World War.

The great bravery he displayed on the field of play went with him into the field of battle in places such as Cairo, Tripoli, Anzio and Monte Cassino.

And in the colours of the Scottish Horse

Regiment, he won another type of medal to go alongside the four titles, three Scottish Cups and two League Cups he took as a player.

Wireless operator Willie was the proud owner of the Military Medal for his courage during the Sicily Landings in 1943.

There were still games to be played, though, and he said: "The regiment's matches were played near Anzio and there were no lines round the pitch – only trenches.

"They came in handy, because the Germans had a gun called Anzio Archie that you could hear from miles away. Whenever it popped, we hit the dirt."

When Gunner Thornton returned from the war, football, thankfully, could once more be the centre of his life.

And just as Tommy McLean unerringly found the head of Derek Johnstone, the crosses of Willie Waddell always seemed destined for Thornton.

They terrorised defences in the 40s and when

Gers won their first-ever domestic treble in 1948-49, 22 of Willie's 36 goals were aerial strikes.

Then, when the new decade began, Willie marked the 1949 Scottish Cup semi-final by scoring a HAT-TRICK of headers against East Fife.

His scoring exploits made him the first post-war Ranger to score 100 goals and he was named Scotland's Player of the Year in 1952, just two years before he hung up his boots.

Yet he always believed so much of what was achieved further up the field was built on that Iron Curtain defence Rangers' rivals feared.

Thornton reflected: "The only defence in modern football that was really similar was the Leeds half-back line of Billy Bremner, Jack Charlton and Norman Hunter."

Willie – like another old-time legend, Davie Meiklejohn - also moved in journalistic circles and worked on the racing desk of Glasgow's Evening News. Indeed, he once stopped the presses when he tipped a horse called Peaceful George on the day the old King died!

Football was in his blood, though, and he was boss of Dundee and Partick Thistle before he returned to Ibrox as assistant-manager in 1968.

The depth of this man's contribution to Rangers can be measured by his links with every Gers boss in living memory. He played under Struth, alongside his successor, Scot Symon and was the No 2 to Davie White, Waddell, Jock Wallace and John Greig.

In March, 1985, he retired from his duties as the club's assistant manager and was guest of honour at an emotional Rangers Supporters' Association rally in Glasgow's Kelvin Hall.

Willie Thornton died in August 1991 at the age of 71.

His association with Rangers Football Club stretched through 55 years of a remarkable life. He earned the tag, Ibrox immortal.

Willie WADDELL

MR RANGERS. Willie Waddell detested that lofty tag but he spent a lifetime living up to it.

For 56 years he was an integral part of Ibrox but the man whose beliefs were hewn in the Lanarkshire pit village of Forth never forgot his roots. Or the moment when he made it as a Ranger.

August 29, 1938, found an anxious Waddell staring through the windows of Lanark Grammar School, praying for the bell that would end his studies and send him rushing for Ibrox and Rangers' clash with the mighty Arsenal.

Right-winger Willie was just 16 and when he arrived he looked around the dressing room pensively. His eyes rested on the gleaming brass initials of WW stamped on his prized boots, they were laid out under the bench and that meant just one thing. He had won his debut.

It was to be a fairytale start as, up against the famous Leslie Compton who was capped for England at football and cricket, Waddell scored the game's only goal. Britain's most expensive player Bryn Jones – bought by Arsenal from Wolves for the princely fee of £14,000 – could only watch in wonder.

All this from a kid who had been destined to follow a career as a dental surgeon but had to quit his studies because the outbreak of war cut his earnings from the game and his parents couldn't afford the tuition fees.

It was a day Waddell treasured and 50 years later he walked back onto the pitch with two modern wingers he cherished – the late Davie Cooper and Mark Walters – to relive it.

The man they always called Deedle, the adopted Glasgow rhyming slang for Waddell had become Deedle-Dawdle, recalled: "I didn't know I was to play.

"Bill Struth never told us the team but those initials were stamped in brass on our boots. If yours were laid out you were in."

Waddell, a powerful presence on the flank who was capped 17 times for Scotland, went on to become the source of so many of the goals Willie Thornton scored for the club in the 40s and 50s as his crosses picked out the striker time and again.

And when he hung up his boots, his contribution to Gers OFF the field was to ensure his place in the club's Hall of Fame.

Waddell – like fellow Ibrox legends Davie Meiklejohn and Thornton – originally ventured into journalism and was famed for his searing views on the games. He was embarrassingly frank if what he watched didn't please him.

But in 1957 he was lured back into the game as manager of Kilmarnock and eight years later he was working miracles.

He'd joined Scottish football's other far-sighted young rising manager, Jock Stein of Dunfermline, and jetted to Italy to study the methods of Inter Milan boss Helenio Herrera.

He was a quick learner. On April 24, 1965, Waddell danced a jig of joy across the Tynecastle turf after pulling off one of the most daring heists in Scottish football history.

He recalled: "My Kilmarnock side were two points behind Hearts and we had to go to their place on the final day of the season and win by at least two goals to clinch the title."

They did it in a 2-0 triumph and won the flag by the incredible margin of 0.04 of a goal!

No-one should have been surprised. In 1949 Waddell was in the Gers side who beat Albion Rovers 4-1 as Dundee lost by the same scoreline at Falkirk to hand the Ibrox side the title by a point.

Then four years later he scored the second-half equaliser at Queen of the South to win the championship on goal average from Hibs.

He was the master of the last-day finish and 26 years after Killie's crowning glory he would watch in delight as an injury-ravaged Gers side beat rivals Aberdeen 2-0 in a winner-takes-all Ibrox shoot-out.

Yet, in the wake of the Ayrshire side's victory Waddell – ever single-minded – savoured the realisation of a dream then promptly stuck to a vow made earlier that season and returned to the press box for four more years.

The call to go back to to Ibrox came in December, 1969, when Davie White's ill-fated succession to Scot Symon ended. And for the turbulent decade that was to follow, Willie Waddell WAS Rangers.

Courting popularity was always at the bottom of Waddell's lists of priorities as Ibrox boss – the good name of Rangers came first.

Players like Willie Henderson would storm out and claim he'd wrecked their Ibrox careers but racking up enemies never seemed to trouble a man of stark contrasts.

This is a book about heroes but to make it there often requires the sort of

stubborn self-belief that leaves bitterness in its wake.

There's no question Waddell could be intransigent – no doubt that he could be difficult.

But those who knew him closely will tell you that, while he could be difficult and domineering, he would also be kind and caring to those who had earned his respect.

His was the stern voice of a footballing visionary. The splendour which surrounds the supporters at Ibrox may have been embellished by David Murray's millions but it was Waddell's revolutionary blueprint.

He had borne the brunt of the Ibrox Disaster that took 66 lives on Stairway 13 as fans were crushed to death after a last-gasp goal in an Old Firm clash. The pain of that fateful day never left him.

Three years later, he travelled to the World Cup in Germany and saw the Westfalen Stadion. The home of Borussia Dortmund became the model for the new Ibrox and Waddell put together a £12million package to turn his dream into reality.

If ever a fan sought a momument to The Deedle, all they need do is look around them on matchday.

He had, of course, inspired his side to glory in that 3-2 Cup-Winner's Cup Final success over Moscow Dynamo and fought to quash their Euro ban after the pitch invasions that marred a glory night.

Euro overlords wanted Rangers kicked out for two years but Waddell had the suspension cut to one.

Yet he was to see his club bedevilled by the disease of hooliganism and came close to the end of his tether after yet another riot in Birmingham forced a "friendly" with Aston Villa in 1976 to be abandoned.

He waged war on the louts then famously vowed that the days when Rangers refused to sign Roman Catholics were over. For once, he wasn't as good as his word and it would be 13 years before Murray's courage and Graeme Souness's conviction brought Mo Johnston to Ibrox to bury a tainted tradition once and for all.

Waddell was one of the architects of the switch to a Top 10 Premier League in 1975 and four years later Scottish football was rocked to the core when he quit his post as Gers' supremo – at the age of 57 he was a victim of burn-out.

He reflected: "When I came to Glasgow, I was a hick from the sticks, Rangers moulded me.

"I was from a wee Lanarkshire mining village and coming to Ibrox was like moving in off the reservation.

"The first time I was in Glasgow was when I was 15 and I played a trial for the Gers at Firhill. That was it for me. There was a pride about it all and a tradition that went deep inside me."

He had given so much, worked 14

hours a day seven days a week and overseen massive changes at the club.

And he admitted: "My batteries are completely run down, I've worked long enough and hard enough for Rangers. It has been my life.

"I'm so intense about Rangers and I know people describe me as abrasive. My opinions have not always suited many others and I have not agreed with everybody."

Yet for such a forthright man he was reticent when it came to listing the achievements of his Rangers reign.

Waddell shrugged: "Some people talk about the Cup-Winners' Cup, some people talk about the new stadium.

"But so many people had a hand in all these – Jock Wallace, the players and the directors. I was just a part of it.

"Maybe, though, I helped bring back the pride. I wanted people to have pride in the club and themselves.

"I wanted people to feel the same way I did when I came in from Forth as a teenager."

Willie Waddell died at the age of 71 after a heart attack in October 1992.

More than 1,000 mourners, led by a Who's Who of Scottish football, were there to pay tribute to a man who had been player, manager, general manager, managing director, vice chairman and honorary director at Ibrox.

Yep, he may have hated the tag Mr Rangers but that's what he was.

Mark WALTERS

GRAEME SOUNESS signed a lavishly gifted footballer for Rangers and forced a nation to look deep into its soul.

Mark Walters, a £500,000 buy from Aston Villa, had a dazzling double shuffle that became one of the trademark moves the fans loved to see and bewildered defenders grew to hate. He was a winger born to be a crowd-pleaser.

Yet he suffered some of the most sickening abuse ever dished out to a player in Scotland. His sin? He was BLACK.

Walters had to endure the animal noises, bananas thrown at him – even one of his own fans was banned from Ibrox for screaming racist filth.

He'd made his debut in a 2-0 Old Firm New Year defeat in 1988 but the shameful taunts were to reach a height in a draw with Hearts at Tynecastle when darts, golfballs and even a pig's leg were hurled at the Englishman.

And Mark, still an idol of the fans today at Swindon Town, confessed: "Graeme had said to me before I signed that because of the lack of black players I might take some stick but I never imagined how bad it would be.

"There were times at the start when I thought, can I take any more of this? But the fans rallied behind me and that instant rapport made me stay."

He paid those supporters back in style. Naturally two-footed, the shuffle he'd perfected since he was a 10-year-old kid watching Johan Cruyff on TV became a yearned-for moment on a Saturday.

Walters was a sensation both creating and scoring in Gers' 5-1 mauling of Celtic in his first full season.

And when the title was on the line on the final day of the campaign in 1991 against Aberdeen, it was his cross that found Mark Hateley to head home one of the milestone goals in the club's recent history.

Yet, in the wake of that triumph and after winning his only England cap in an era dominated by the likes of Chris Waddle and John Barnes, Walters chose to leave Gers.

The man whose middle name is EVERTON followed Souness to Liverpool but the move – like his subsequent switch to Southampton – didn't quite pay off.

Both manager Walter Smith and chairman David Murray tried to make him stay but Mark said: "I was faced with the dilemma of staying at Ibrox or trying to make a name for myself at Liverpool.

"No matter how well I performed for Rangers there was always the belief amongst clubs and fans down south that the standard in Scotland wasn't a patch on their own.

"When the Liverpool deal came up there was very little left for me to win in Scotland and Rangers weren't making a big impression in Europe.

"In the end I felt that if I played well for Liverpool it would be impossible for England to ignore me. In the end Souness gave me 24 hours to give him an answer and I thought "yes" was the right one at the time.

"Now that I have had time to reflect on the move I have to say that I made a BIG mistake leaving Ibrox when I did."

CROWD PLEASER ... Mark Walters

Club and Country

IBROX CAREER 1988-91

GAMES

League	106
Scot Cup	14
Lg Cup	13
Europe	10
Total	143

GOALS

League	32
Scot Cup	6
Lg Cup	12
Europe	2
Total	52

HONOURS

League	3
Lg Cup	2

ENGLAND
1 cap

STATS

CLOAK AND DAGGER Graeme Souness arranged to jet Ray Wilkins into Glasgow in the dead of night, signed his contract in-flight over the Channel then bundled his new playmaker into a disguise to keep the signing quiet.

Hours later Razor had left a miserable spell at French giants Paris Saint Germain behind and he was in the midfield maelstrom of a 3-2 Premier League debut win over Hearts at Ibrox.

He insists he had a howler.

Disguise or not in that bizarre transfer caper, once the former England skipper settled at Gers there was simply no hiding his class.

His passing brilliance and sweet touches as his side's playmaker were only matched by the professionalism and dignity the former Chelsea, Manchester United and AC Milan midfielder brought to the Light Blue jersey.

These days, Wilkins is one of television's most insightful analysts after his latest management job at Mohammed Al-Fayed's cash-rich Fulham turned sour.

His respect for Souness the player and the man remains and he smiled: "I think Graeme bought me as his own replacement and I have always considered that a huge compliment.

"His calf injury wasn't too clever and he knew he was toiling to keep going.

"He needed another holding midfield player and I'll always be delighted he chose me.

"It's true that we signed the contract over the Channel at 3am. He'd picked me up in the private jet in typical Souness style and, along with Walter Smith, we agreed the deal in mid-air.

"Then when I got to Glasgow Airport I was handed a hat and scarf and bundled up in disguise so the signing stayed under wraps until the match the next day.

"The preparation was far from ideal and even though we won 3-2 I always remember that I was pathetic.

"I'm just glad I improved a little after that."

Ray WILKINS

RAZOR SHARP... Ray Wilkins

For Rangers fans, there will always be one defining moment of Ray's time with the club and it offered a stark contrast to the deft skills he became famed for.

It wasn't a cute chip or a measured pass but a thumping volley that tore past Ian Andrews in the 5-1 hammering of Celtic in 1988 and won its place as one of the best goals in Gers' history.

Ray revealed: "I hit it right on the sweet spot and it tore in. You know you have struck those ones right because it's so true you hardly feel it leave your foot.

"I actually believe the goal I scored for England against Belgium in the 1980 European Championships was a better one but I know the one I'll always be remembered for in Scotland!"

Wilkins' farewell to Gers in November 1989 remains a touchstone moment.

In the fog at Ibrox against Dunfermline he was given a standing ovation as he trooped off the pitch for the last time in tears after a 3-0 win.

Typically, he marked his departure with a sublime ball to Mo Johnston to open the scoring.

Yet deep inside, Ray felt a complex mix of conflicting emotions.

He admitted: "The farewell was a momentous day. Part of me inside was saying that I was going too early.

"But the other feeling was one that I could see Ian Durrant, Derek Ferguson, Trevor Steven and Ian Ferguson developing and I might end up in the reserves.

"I just didn't want that as it would have marred the experience for me so I left."

Ray would go on to play for QPR, Crystal Palace, back to Loftus Road as player-boss and Wycombe Wanderers before a spell at Hibs that brought him another of those famous welcomes from the Gers faithful.

Leyton Orient was the last place he laced his boots before Fulham but for all the ports of call in his magnificent career Ibrox provided his favourite souvenir.

Ray went not only with the gratitude of those supporters but a touching private acknowledgement of his worth from the players he left behind.

They commissioned a portrait of Wilkins in Light Blue from artist Senga Murray and Ray said: "I have a lot of nice memories in my study but none more precious than that picture the guys got for me.

"All the autographs are there in gold script down the side and it means the world to me."

Master of the under-statement but the truth is Wilkins' influence on Rangers was felt long after he'd left the club to return to his native London and Queen's Park Rangers.

Souness had hammered the Italian discipline of his own days at Sampdoria into the Ibrox players – now, in Ray, he had the perfect dressing-room lieutenant to keep enforcing his regime.

Even now players such as Ian Durrant and Ian Ferguson will tell you of the massive influence rubbing shoulders with Wilkins had on their careers.

Wilkins, the star who earned 84 caps for England and saw it all in the game, was constantly on a voyage of footballing discovery.

Paris hadn't worked out as he planned but Rangers were to revive him.

And he said: "It had been four and a half months of awful difficulties at PSG but there is no way your whole career can be plain sailing.

"I learned a lot about myself as a person rather than a player in France.

"I learned to cope and I got a move I'll always be grateful for."

WING KING...
Davie Wilson
prepares to
cross the ball
against Third
Lanark

Davie
WILSON

JOCK STEIN, Bill Shankly, Sir Matt Busby – the icons of Scottish football shared their pit village upbringing. Davie Wilson was hewn from the same seam.

From coal dust to goal dust. The blond winger reared in the gritty surroundings of Newton, near Cambuslang, became one of the most feared wingers in Rangers' history.

Players such as Alan Morton, Willie Henderson, Davie Cooper and Brian Laudrup tormented full-backs – but none was as lethal as Wilson.

These days Davie is a welcome figure around Ibrox as he shares memories of his feats with corporate guests in the opulent suites overlooking the pitch this dyed-in-the-wool Ranger always yearned to play on.

Scottish football's Boys from the Black Stuff have often been painted as men who grabbed football as their only escape route from the harsh reality of life down the pits.

That notion certainly carries a degree of truth, yet there is no sense of deprivation from Wilson when he recalls his roots.

He is proud of where he came from, thankful that the tough mining community gave him a sense of belonging.

And he was to help inject a spirit of togetherness into a lavishly gifted forward line that also included Willie Henderson, Ralph Brand and Jimmy Millar.

Davie reflected: "So many greats of my era came from a mining background, there were no silver spoon upbringings then.

"Those villages were places where you didn't have to lock your door and everyone knew each other."

The success of one of their own then was something to be treasured, not scarred by petty jealousy – even if the local boy made good was an Old Firm rival.

Davie's debut makes for a remarkable tale and he smiled: "It came in a midweek game when we won 5-2 at Motherwell and the CELTIC Supporters' club in the village ran a bus to see me.

"I scored twice and it was an unforgettable night.

"Mind you, they'd always liked me, ever since I'd played for the Catholic Boys' Guild as a ringer called Davie Murphy!"

Scoring a double on his debut set the tone for a career of goals from Wilson at Rangers as he became an integral part of the dominant Gers side of the early 60s.

That team – who reached the European

Cup Winners' Cup Final in '61 only to lose 4-1 on aggregate to Italian giants Fiorentina – played with a swagger and Wilson would often lay bets with the M&B partnership of Millar and Brand over who would score first. Davie won his fair share of wagers.

And on March 17, 1962, he was filling his pockets with his winnings after he became the only post-war Rangers player to score SIX in a competitive match in a 7-1 crushing of Falkirk at Brockville.

Davie lapped up moody Italian Marco Negri's haul when he scored the lot in a 5-1 humbling of Dundee United but admits he walked away with a sly smile when the sulking assassin came up one short of the double hat-trick.

And the star who won five Scottish Cup medals in a glittering career said: "That Falkirk match made me chairman of the Six-Goal Club in Scotland.

"I was glad to welcome in Celtic's Dixie Deans, because I was getting lonely. Membership, though, is hard to earn."

An average of almost one goal every two games is phenomenal for a winger and it didn't happen by accident.

Wilson was a dedicated trainer, constantly practising cutting in from his left-wing beat and shooting into the far corner.

He was a naturally right-sided player who MADE himself left-sided and became the perfect foil for Willie Henderson on the other flank.

Celtic fans of that era watched those two through their fingers. Wilson and Henderson were the bare hands that would gradually close in from either side and throttle their rivals.

Davie explained: "Willie was class at going down his wing at pace then beating people and while I would do that now and

Club and Country

IBROX CAREER
1956-67

GAMES
League	227
Scot Cup	38
Lg Cup	71
Europe	37
Total	373

GOALS
League	98
Scot Cup	21
Lg Cup	28
Europe	10
Total	157

HONOURS
League	2
Scot Cup	5
Lg Cup	2

SCOTLAND
22 caps

STATS

FOILED...
Wilson is thwarted by a brave save from the Dunfermline goalkeeper

again, really I was mostly about goals.

"Any time I see Ally McCoist I remind him that I had a better scoring average than him as a Rangers player.

"He has been my favourite since I became a fan once again, although you could never hide the class of Davie Cooper."

Yet, while there will always be a grudging admiration for Wilson from Hoops followers, there will always be a charge levelled at him too. They label him "The Greatest Diver of All Time".

Gers fans in the 80s may have reckoned John MacDonald – who was to earn the nickname Polaris for his antics – was the prince of the penalty box theatrics.

But three decades on, Wilson is prepared to confess: "Let's just say that I was well-known for winning penalty-kicks in extreme situations.

"I was quick and when people tackled me I had a habit of falling. The Celtic fans didn't just worry when I was in the penalty box, they started getting scared when I crossed the halfway line!"

Behind the humour lies the story of a whole-hearted player who also netted nine times in just 22 games for Scotland.

Yet perhaps his finest hour in Dark Blue came as a DEFENDER at Wembley in 1963, when he shuttled to left-back after team-mate Eric Caldow had broken his leg.

Wilson's impudence was to play a key role in ticking down the clock to glory and he grinned: "We were 2-1 up with a minute left when the keeper, Bill Brown, gave me the ball.

"Our bench were screaming at me to get up the wing and hit their byeline.

"I did just that but then I turned back and came all the way back to give the ball to Brown again."

MILESTONE...
Davie before making his 500th league appearance

Willie WOODBURN

SINE DIE. Banned for life. Words that you feel have no place in professional football now.

They are the words that will haunt Ibrox legend Willie Woodburn to his dying day.

The daunting centre-half with the short-fuse temper they called Big Ben was given the most controversial punishment in SFA history when he went before the beaks on September 14, 1954.

His crime had been to lose it after an awkward tackle in a League Cup tie against Stirling Albion at Ibrox.

The game was in the last minute and Gers were cruising two up when Woodburn crashed into a no-holds barred tackle with Stirling's Paterson.

Willie's leg twisted badly in the impact and Woodburn lashed out, head-butting his opponent.

And he recalled: "Right away I knew I was in big trouble, it was the fifth red card of my career.

"I shouldn't have done it and I deserved to get punished but never did I think that I would get that verdict from the SFA.

"I was coming towards the end of my playing days anyway and a six-month ban would have finished me.

"But life? Rangers were my life and they took that – and my dignity – away from me."

It seemed that 17 seasons at the top and 24 caps for his country were forgotten because of one moment of madness.

When Rangers striker Duncan Ferguson nutted Raith Rovers right-back Jock McStay at Ibrox in 1994 and ended up with 44 days in Barlinnie Prison comparisons were drawn with the Woodburn Affair. That was simplistic and wrong.

Ferguson paid for a string of scrapes with the law before the McStay flare-up and is now an £8million player earning fortunes at Newcastle United.

Woodburn had his means of making a living snatched from him and even in times that seem archaic 45 years on the Players' Union were ready to intervene.

Willie, though, didn't want that and

Club and Country

STATS

IBROX CAREER 1936-55

GAMES
League	216
Scot Cup	38
Lg Cup	71
Europe	0
Total	325

GOALS
League	1
Scot Cup	0
Lg Cup	0
Europe	0
Total	1

HONOURS
League	4
Scot Cup	4
Lg Cup	2

SCOTLAND 24 caps

said simply: "The decision had been made and although people say to me I would have a right to feel bitter about football how could I?

"For 17 years Rangers had given me so much of life and I experienced a lot and met some marvellous people.

"So I don't feel bad about football today and I still watch Rangers on TV and try to get to Ibrox whenever I can manage.

"I don't particularly like talking about that incident although I know folk want to sometimes. I prefer to think of the days when I played under my manager Bill Struth who always checked with my landlady at my digs to see if I was in bed by 10pm!"

Woodburn had been reared a Hearts fan and snubbed rugby at Heriot's School in Edinburgh to play football. It was a good call.

The apprentice plasterer was used to staring at walls in his day job but when he was training at Ibrox he was once more glaring at the brickwork.

Trainer Arthur Dixon set Willie a routine where he had to smack a ball against a wall with both feet. He used to wear a trainer on his right and a boot on his left so he worked better on the weak side and he became two-footed.

Woodburn's rise was startling and by the start of season 1938-39 he was a first team pick at centre-half and lapping up the wages of £4-a-week.

But just 24 hours after a 2-1 win over Third Lanark at Cathkin on September 2, 1939 the evil regime of German dictator Adolf Hitler threw his life into turmoil.

Even wartime couldn't kill the Scottish passion for football and there would be Southern League games with visiting star names guesting for the teams.

Woodburn – ever the fierce competitor – was never an ardent fan of these "friendlies".

And he grew to hate them even more in September 1942 when he suffered severe knee damage as Hibs crushed Gers 8-1. For the boyhood Hearts fan living in Edinburgh this was torture.

Willie's spirits nosedived even further when big George Young took over his berth at the core of the club's defence and it was only a year after the war finished that he was able to reclaim the jersey he cherished.

He recalled: "Even now I remember him moving across to right-back and there being a feeling of accomplishment that such a magnificent player was being shifted for me.

"People often ask which player I admired most and there were so many in my era, I was very lucky.

"If you think of the list there was Young, Willie Thornton, Willie Waddell. These men were Rangers giants and are still thought of as that

THE ORIGINAL HARDMAN ... Willie Woodburn was banned for life and his livelihood was ripped away

today. But if there had to be one then it would be Sammy Cox.

"He was such a gifted defender and would always look to pass when in trouble.

"He was ahead of his time."

Rangers were to pick up where they left off before the war and win the championship with the man they called Big Ben outstanding.

When told of the legend of Woodburn I had always assumed he'd been given that nickname because he was built like the famous clock at the Houses of Parliament.

Turns out the roots are far more humble. Woodburn belted such a medley on the microphone at a celebration after his side had spanked Benfica 3-0 in a friendly in Portugal that he was named after the venue and re-christened Ben!

That trip was also notable, Woodburn remembered, for Gers travelling by plane and dodging the leisurely cruise to away destinations.

Another milestone was approaching ON the pitch – The Iron Curtain was about to drop.

That was the name given to an almost impregnable defence that lined up: Bobby Brown; George Young; Jock Shaw Ian McColl; Willie Woodburn and Sammy Cox.

The fact that over 50 years on every one of those players features in this book tells you all you need to know.

There were memorable matches, especially against arch rivals Hibs, and Woodburn relished the clashes with centre forwards like the Easter Road side's Lawrie Reilly.

Willie, who owned a car business with his brother and was a football writer for the News of the World before he retired, said: "There were so many good players to face then but I feel he was the best. He was once in dispute at Hibs and we all wanted him to sign for Rangers!"

Willie Woodburn was to play in four title teams and win four Scottish Cup badges and two League Cup medals in his Rangers career. He played in three Wembley games against the Auld Enemy, winning two and drawing one.

These days there's pain in ageing legs in his Edinburgh home to remind him of Gers but he can cherish the memories of the days when he deserved his place alongside the greats.

Journalistic nature meant one of the first questions I asked was about that life ban and I suppose that will always be the case, it's human nature.

Yet one mad moment and one crazy SFA sentence shouldn't be the sum of a career. Willie Woodburn adds up to far more than that.

SHUT-OUT KING... Chris Woods shows why he holds the Premier record for consecutive clean sheets

Chris WOODS

CHRIS WOODS left Rangers with two very different records – one was for clean sheets, the other was a criminal rap sheet.

To this day, Woods bristles at the breach of the peace guilty verdict handed down to him when the long arm of the law drew football into its clutches after a powderkeg Old Firm clash at Ibrox in October, 1987.

Celtic's striker, Frank McAvennie, barrelled into Woods after he had held a cross and that sparked a skirmish between the players which saw the goalkeeper's English team-mates Terry Butcher and Graham Roberts rush in to get involved.

As ref Jim Duncan toiled to keep the lid on a simmering match, he sent off Woods and McAvennie with Roberts – who had raised his hands in the fracas and looked the guilty party – escaping Scot-free.

Gers skipper Butcher was also ordered off later and Roberts, who had taken over from the banished Chris between the sticks, was taken to task after the match for controversially conducting the Ibrox fans through their battle hymns.

In an astonishing showdown, Graeme Souness's side were 2-0 down before storming back to clinch a remarkable draw with goals from Ally McCoist and Richard Gough.

The drama dominated the back pages then but it was soon shifted to the front of the newspapers with the bombshell news that the Procurator Fiscal would be taking action against the shamed stars.

Woods, Roberts, Butcher and McAvennie were all to be hauled up in court.

Football was in the dock.

Chris groaned: "It was LUDICROUS and the police didn't help any of us after we'd been given the red cards.

"Once McAvennie got his sending off, I knew I was going as well to even it up.

"The thing is, just before that Frank barged into me and I tipped the ball over the bar. I maintain to this day that, if a free-kick had been given, then he'd have been wary of trying it again and none of the trouble would have started.

"I was up in the directors' box watching an Old Firm game of 10 v 9, it was bizarre.

"There was Graham Roberts conducting the choir, then I was leaping all over the place when Richard Gough equalised in the dying minutes.

"After all that had happened to me, it was the sweetest feeling.

"Woods and Butcher were found guilty, McAvennie was cleared and Roberts was given the uniquely Scottish – and wholly unsatisfactory – verdict of not proven in one of Scottish football's

most explosive episodes. Chris paid another price, too. He was banned from the Skol Cup Final and could only look on once more as deputy Nicky Walker played his part in a 3-3 draw with Aberdeen before Gers edged a classic 5-3 on penalties.

Woods, though, affords himself a wry smile when he thinks back to the helter-skelter early days of the Souness Revolution.

After striker Colin West, Chris was the second Englishman lured north to reverse football's normal trend as Gers' new boss went about reshaping the club.

When he made his debut at Hibs in 1986, there were more fireworks as his manager was sent off and 21 PLAYERS were booked in the melee that followed.

Chris recalled: "There was massive hype surrounding us in that first game, because it was the debuts for myself and Terry.

"I remember the melee breaking out after Graeme clashed with George McCluskey. The one that sparked it all might have been ugly but the rest was handbags at dawn and 21 of us were booked.

"Only Alan Rough didn't get booked and I remember saying to Roughie later that at least I'd shown I was quick off my line!

"McCluskey had walloped an elbow into my face at a corner before that and there was a lot of that flying about that day as we lost 2-1.

"Welcome to Scotland! We lost the second game 3-2 at home to Dundee United and looked in real trouble but we went on a run from Christmas that simply burned up everyone else."

The championship was to be sealed in style at Pittodrie with a 1-1 draw as a 10-man Gers team showed true grit to survive another red card for boss Souness.

A nine-year wait for the title was over and there was an outpouring of joy as Rangers fans invaded the pitch.

It was the climax of the biggest footballing adventure of Woods' life.

And he said: "The punters were trying to lift any possible souvenir from us.

"This guy was trying to yank my gloves off and I'm screaming at him to let me undo the Velcro because he was breaking my fingers!

"There was a massive traffic jam on the way home but no-one cared.

"There were fans running along by

the side of our bus and we'd pick them up and give them a drink. The feeling that day proved to me that I had done the right thing.

"I know people raised their eyebrows down south when I came to Rangers but once Graeme spoke to me he gave me a tour of Ibrox and all I wanted to do was see the place full."

Chris came to revel in those packed houses throughout five years as the club's undisputed No 1. And before the three foreigners rule cut his Gers days short and prompted the arrival of Andy Goram, there was a landmark record to celebrate.

Woods set a British shut-out best of 1,196 minutes without losing a goal – a run that began against Borussia Moenchengladbach on November 26, 1986 and wasn't ended until January 31 the following year.

Ironically, when he did lose one it sparked the worst result of his Rangers career and a Scottish Cup defeat that evoked memories of the Berwick Rangers humbling 20 years earlier.

Chris said: "I always remember that I was about seven games in to the run and I asked Walter Smith what the record was. He knew but he wouldn't tell me.

"It became a matter of pride to me.

"Not only was there the normal desire to keep the ball out and have a clean sheet, there was now an added incentive.

"Then came a Cup clash with Hamilton Accies and I beat it. Sadly, it was the only cheer we got all day. Adrian Sprott scored and I still shudder when I hear his name.

"That went from a personal high to one of the lowest days I had at Rangers and I always remember their keeper, Dave McKellar, was magnificent.

"He saved everything we hit at him and I couldn't believe it afterwards when I was told he was a Rangers man. He didn't show it."

Chris's Rangers career was only ever interrupted by injury, the worst coming when he displaced his shoulder.

Woods secretly took injections to play through NINE MONTHS of pain after that. But that was nothing to the agony he endured when he was told he was being replaced.

He was heartbroken. Chris left for Sheffield Wednesday and had a stint in America with Colorado Rapids before returning to Southampton and Burnley then concentrating on coaching.

But he confessed: "I didn't want to go."

Y George **YOUNG**

GEORGE YOUNG was 6ft 2ins and he weighed 15st. He was the Rangers and Scotland captain, this was a BIG man in every footballing sense of the word.

Yet for all his ability and all his strength he relied hugely on the good luck charm of a champagne cork he carried in his pocket.

He was, of course, christened Corky and he'd pop open the bubbly on six occasions as a championship winner at Ibrox.

Young was a dominant force at Gers and a centre-half of true international quality. When caps were harder to come by his record of 53 was to stand for a long time.

And he never had any doubt who he owed for helping him towards the heights.

The names of Bill Struth and Scot Symon will always live large in Ibrox history and they were the hub of Rangers for George Young.

As skipper he was the bridge between the dressing-room and the imposing figure of Struth and he recalled: "He always had a chat with me before talking to the players and I made sure we were a team on and off the field.

"It was a family affair and we were proud of that. We were never out of each other's houses away from the club."

Rangers back then were seen much as Dunfermline in the Scottish Premier League or Wimbledon in the FA Carling Premiership are these days.

They were firmly tagged as the Route One specialists.

It annoyed Young and while he was no great lover of complex tactics he insisted there was thought in it if they did employ the long ball.

George explained: "We were always accused of being a defensive side who would hit long balls upfield in the hope of scoring. Nonsense!

"It was more coincidence that Willie Thornton scored goals with his head from my clearances from the back.

"In fact, we used to practise this so that when the long lob was on Willie knew exactly where to go."

Yet while he yearned for a football life without jargon and to see the game kept simple

GLORY DAZE ...
George Young
was to win many
more honours
with Rangers

CORKY CAPS IT ALL OFF ... George Young, capped 53 times for Scotland,
with testimonial committee members Don Revie and Bobby Shearer in 1985

he did listen to football thinkers he respected – like Symon.

In the bath after matches Scot would talk big George through what he thought were the good and bad points.

And Young reasoned: "Everything he did on a park meant something. He was a traditional half-back who liked to go forward.

"He passed magnificently, he fought hard for possession and he directed everyone. Playing with Scot stretched my career because he saved me two years of learning.

"I learned more from him than any other player. It was obvious to me that he would become a good manager – and he did."

George bowed out of football in 1957 at the age of 34 after earning the last of his 53 Scotland caps in a 2-1 win over Switzerland in Basle.

He was manager of Third Lanark for a spell in the early 60s and was as uncompromising in his views on coaching as he had been as a player.

George groaned: "Too much coaching and tactics stifles skilful players.

"At Third Lanark I had a forward line of Goodfellow, Hilley, Harley, Gray and McInnes. They scored 100 First Division goals in one season. And I didn't have to tell them how to play – they were entertainers.

"I often wonder what would have happened to the Hibs Famous Five of Smith, Johnstone, Turnbull, Reilly and Ormond if they'd been told how to play by a coach determined to show he knew more about the game than they did. Would we have had a Famous Five?"

Many felt Young's experience should have been better used in Scotland when he quit playing but his fame still held true right across the Pond.

In 1981 George sold his famous Tillietudlem Hotel in Crossford, Lanarkshire to emigrate to Canada with his footballing knowledge in

demand both in coaching and TV roles. The dream turned sour, though, and he was soon back home.

There was bitter controversy four years later when Rangers refused to allow a testimonial match for Young to be played at Ibrox.

The chairman John Paton was sympathetic to the idea but the club felt allowing the game to go ahead would mean a spate of requests from former players.

A feud ensued and Gers stars were banned from playing in the glamour match for one of the club's greatest captains.

George's game was switched to Brockville with his old pal Don Revie bossing an Anglo Select that included the likes of Kevin Keegan and Joe Jordan.

Big Jaws was none too pleased at wearing an England shirt, though, and vowed to get it dirty as quickly as possible.

His side took a 4-0 hiding as Brian McClair and Stevie Cowan both grabbed doubles for a George's Premier League XI.

While Revie was raging, Young himself had at first appeared philosophical about that testimonial decision and joked: "I've had a few kicks in the teeth in my time but you can always get a new set of dentures."

Yet deep down it clearly rankled and the air wasn't to be cleared on his feud with Rangers until present club chief David Murray healed a seven-year rift by inviting Corky to be his guest at a 1992 win over Hibs.

George watched with interest – and still he hankered for a return to the days when the game was less defensive and fans saw more thrills.

It's true that nostalgia can often cloud your vision, send mists swirling over your footballing perception.

But ask yourself a question. When George Young died, Aberdeen 'fans' sang, booed and chanted through a minute's silence in his honour. Which era would you rate best?

Club and Country

IBROX CAREER
1941-57

GAMES
League   293
Scot Cup   50
Lg Cup   83
Europe   2
Total   428

GOALS
League   22
Scot Cup   5
Lg Cup   4
Europe   0
Total   31

HONOURS
League   6
Scot Cup   4
Lg Cup   2

SCOTLAND
53 caps

STATS

159

PLAYERS' LIST

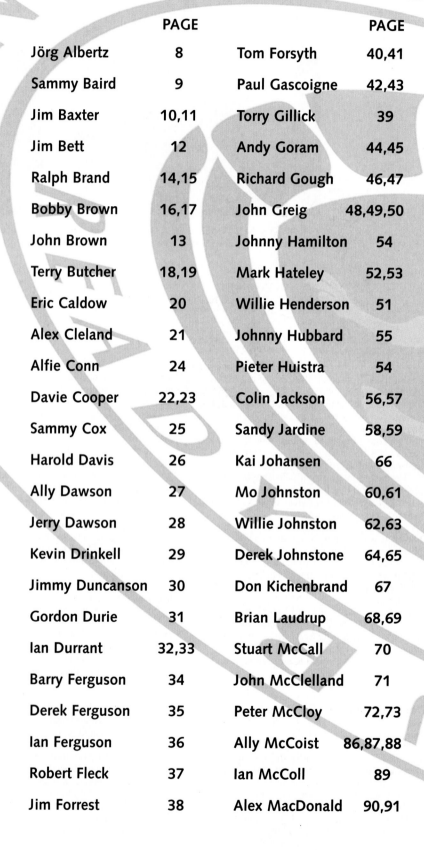

GREATEST Rangers

DEDICATION

THIS book is for Flora and Neil Frazer. If ever I needed encouragement I've always known where to turn.

AUTHOR'S ACKNOWLEDGEMENTS

WRITING a book when you're a real author, I'm told, is hard enough. Writing one while you are trying to hold down a day job at Scotland's biggest paper takes a toll on your family.

I was committed to "Rangers: The 100 Greatest" before a very difficult and emotional time for my wife Lorna yet she continued to offer the same unswerving support and sound advice that has been there for 13 years now.

And to my kids Caitlin and Bruce, as always, thanks for the smiles.

I'm also in debt big-time to William Walker whose statistical knowledge of all things Rangers never fails to astound me. He was a true professional, invaluable.

Others too numerous to mention have played a big part but Brian McSweeney at First Press, Rangers News Editor Euan McLean and King of the Contacts Book Gavin Berry deserve much respect.

Finally, to Hugh Keevins - the Sunday Mail's Old Soldier - thanks for keeping me sane.